What is a city—a place for people to live, to work and to play—where homes and work places, shops and schools, theatres and parks are linked to each other by good communications and where people can lead a full life—or an overbuilt, polluted, traffic plagued environmental hell where life is full of frustrations and dangers ?

Walter Bor describes the problems imposed on the urban environment by modern life, explains the techniques by which the planner may combat these problems and shows how the techniques have been and are being applied in a variety of situations. He shows the effects of growth and development on large and small urban areas, and how both obsolescence and affluence contribute to the complexities of planning a human environment.

He looks at the place of planning within the changing political framework and examines the movement towards a greater flexibility in plan making and a greater degree of public participation in the planning process.

He turns then to transportation in towns —how can people move about to make the fullest use of available jobs, shops, schools and leisure places by public and private transport. Housing—how to build homes without putting families at the top of high rise, often socially disastrous, blocks of flats. These are some of the problems which must be solved if urban life is to be acceptable. He takes these problems and shows not only ways for solving them, but also what happens if they are not solved.

The aesthetic quality of urban design in response to social and economic needs is an integral part of a satisfactory urban environment and he discusses examples from past, present and future, of preservation, redevelopment and of the creation of new towns. He is particularly concerned with the introduction of the vast new scale of high buildings and urban motorways into our cities.

Having looked at the physical, political and social aspects of urban planning Walter Bor re-emphasises the need for a comprehensive urban planning approach as the only means to achieving the best possible life and environment for the people in towns and cities.

Walter Bor, well known for his contributions to town planning both in Britain and the United States, studied architecture at Prague University before he qualified as an architect and town planner in England. He was in private practice in London until joining the London County Council as an architect planner in 1947. His work with the LCC was primarily concerned with the comprehensive redevelopment of London's East End and he took charge of this project in 1958. In 1960 he was appointed Deputy Planning Officer to the LCC, with special responsibility for civic design.

Two years later he left London to become the first City Planning Officer for Liverpool. Here he set up a new multi-disciplinary City Planning Department and in 1965 he and his team published a planning policy report for the whole city, in the form of a draft urban structure plan followed a year later by the Liverpool City Centre Plan, and in this book there are references to this work.

In 1966 Walter Bor returned to private practice, becoming a partner in the firm of Llewelyn-Davies Weeks Forestier-Walker & Bor. He is responsible for directing his firm's planning and housing work and in his book he draws upon examples from some of the projects in which he has been involved, including housing in Washington New Town, the Plan for the new city of Milton Keynes, redevelopment plans for Glasgow and Cambridge and urban renewal schemes in the USA, in Toledo, Ohio, and Elmwood II, Detroit.

He combines his practice work with teaching at the School of Environmental Studies, University College, London. He is a Past President of the Royal Town Planning Institute and one London.

THE MAKING OF CITIES

"The City, the City, my dear Brutus—stick to that and live in its full light! Residence elsewhere—as I made up my mind in early life—is mere eclipse and obscurity to those whose energy is capable of shining in Rome."

Marcus Tullius Cicero

THE MAKING OF CITIES

Walter Bor

LEONARD HILL
LONDON 1972

An Intertext Publisher

First published in 1972 by
Leonard Hill Books,
A division of
International Textbook Co. Ltd,
158 Buckingham Palace Road,
London SW1

ISBN 0 249 44071 7

Printed in Great Britain by
Butler & Tanner Ltd, Frome and London

*To our children who will
inherit the cities we make*

Foreword

Until recently planning was a technical subject understood only by professionals and specialists. But nowadays planning problems in general, and urban problems in particular, are invading every aspect of life. More and more people of all kinds want to be able to understand the issues and to participate in debate and action. It is of course impossible to participate effectively without understanding the subject. And the subject of planning is extraordinarily complex and hard to grasp.

It is not a homogeneous body of knowledge and skill, but a thoroughly heterogeneous mixture of science, practical experience, judgement and idealism.

After 25 years of business experience—much of it abroad—I was thrown in to the deep end of the world of planning: first in 1965 as Chairman of the Economic Development Committees for Building and Civil Engineering, and then again in 1967 as Chairman of a New Town Development Corporation. I discovered the hard way how little I knew and how much I had to learn before I could apply experience and skills learnt in other fields: simply because I did not know enough about the maze of planning.

Walter Bor, in writing this book, has taken on a vitally needed but daunting task. He has set out to make the nature of planning comprehensible to a layman while maintaining the rigour of discussion and presentation appropriate to a professional subject. From my point of view, I only wish he had written it five years ago!

It should be invaluable to the very many people who will—and ought to—read it.

1972

Campbell of Eskan

Preface

Urban planning has undergone radical changes in recent years and is now using a highly sophisticated methodology with its own language which is virtually incomprehensible to the uninitiated. As the planning process diversifies, so the range of disciplines which come together in the planning team expands—physical planners, architects and engineers are joined by, amongst others, economists, sociologists and management scientists. Within this context, a vast new literature has been produced in recent years by professional planners and specialists for their professional colleagues in an effort to advance the frontiers of knowledge in various fields of planning.

At the same time, there is a growing need for the intelligent layman to be better informed, to understand more fully the nature of planning and the courses of action open to us in the re-shaping of our environment. These non-planners, vitally interested in planning, range from the decision-makers in the role of elected representatives and public and private investors to the public at large whose participation in the planning process is growing in importance. Yet few books, to date, are concerned with providing them with a synoptic view of inter-related planning problems and opportunities in our towns and cities. The main purpose I had in mind in writing this book was to do just that.

I have tried to give the reader a deeper insight into our urban planning problems and an understanding of what makes our cities the places they are: full of contradictions, of great convenience and utmost inconvenience, of innumerable opportunities and as many frustrations, of great beauty and desperate ugliness.

I have also attempted to show the forces which affect and shape our urban environment, how this environment operates as a whole and in its several parts, and how the planner's philosophies, policies and techniques function within this ever-changing framework.

While this book is mainly about urban planning in Britain and the United States, reference is made to examples in many other countries. I have illustrated salient points not only with accompanying photographs, plans and sketches, but also with short case histories appearing in appendices to the appropriate section.

I have, throughout the book, referred to examples with which I am familiar and in several instances I have selected work in which I have been involved, both in public and private practice, so that I could speak from personal experience.

Contents

Part 1

Growth and Change

1 The City and the Region

"Cities have an infinite capacity for adaptation to new conditions of life."

Lewis Mumford

The world population is rapidly increasing, though the rate of increase varies considerably from country to country. For instance, by the year 2000 the population of the United Kingdom is expected to increase from over 55 million to 66 million, i.e. by about 350 000 per year whereas in China the present 800 million population may increase to 1400 million by about 20 million a year. A fast growing proportion of this world population lives in urban areas. Already there exist 1382 cities of 100 000 and more, 92 of which have populations of over 1 million. New York and Tokyo have already surpassed the 10 million mark, with Greater Paris developing in that direction. There are many reasons why the urban population will continue to grow: with greater efficiency in agriculture, fewer people will be needed to work on the land, while big cities will continue to offer maximum choice in jobs, homes, education, culture and recreation. Within the cities, existing populations grow in size due to the very opportunities which city living offers.

Within this context of a rapidly growing urban population, our towns and cities are constantly undergoing change, although they differ in the rate with which this change occurs. While some have been growing at a steady rate, others have expanded very rapidly. The buildings which make up the towns and cities change even more rapidly. For instance, the average life of a building in England is 47 years and considerably less in the USA. It is true, of course, that at the same time some towns whose economy is no longer viable are declining, like mining towns in Wales, or have died, like the ghost towns in New Mexico, USA.

However, while a small percentage of towns are declining, the overwhelming majority of our towns and cities are growing rapidly and will continue to do so to an increasing degree. So pressing is this problem of finding room for a rapidly growing urban population that the French are thinking of a future Paris stretching in linear form from the present city to the coast, to accommodate a growth to 12 million by the year 2000.

3

Madrid. Ghost town in New Mexico, USA. A former small mining town, now deserted.
Photo: Walter Bor

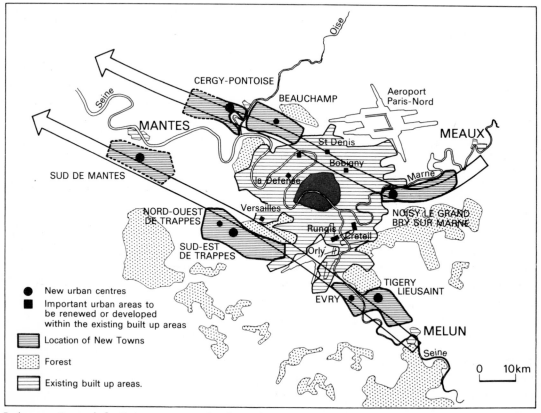

Paris, 2000. Proposals for Paris to grow to a city of 12 million people stretching in linear form along two main growth corridors

One of the major problems in urban planning is how to reconcile healthy urban growth with viable living and working conditions which could be negated by excessive pressures, traffic congestion, noise and air pollution. At the present time, this rapid growth is taking place in cities within and around an urban fabric built for much smaller populations with less space demands and lower vehicle ownership. Something has to give—either the urban fabric must be radically adapted to accommodate the new growth—and this will involve very costly investments and is likely to take decades to be fully implemented—or the growth must be attracted elsewhere, for instance to new and expanding towns.

As a rule, a combination of both approaches is found necessary, though the degree to which one should be emphasized over the other may be of vital importance and calls for strategic planning decisions at national and regional level. Although I shall be primarily concerned here with the planning of urban areas, such planning can only be really effective if it is conceived within the wider sub-regional and regional context of which our urban areas are integral parts. Many fundamental urban planning issues can no longer be solved within the administrative boundaries of individual planning authorities. Amongst these are: residential overspill (that is the rehousing of people for whom there is no room within existing cities), locations of employment areas, transport and recreation, or indeed the decision which town should grow and to what extent, and from which town should growth be deflected (e.g. an historic city). Some form of regional and sub-regional planning is therefore essential to deal with such problems in a rational and effective way.

I was made acutely aware of this lack of regional and sub-regional planning when as City Planning Officer for Liverpool my team and I attempted to produce a plan for the city. Whereas officially our planning responsibilities were confined to the area within the administrative boundaries of the County Borough of Liverpool, many of the most pressing social and economic problems of the city could not possibly be resolved within these boundaries. However, even during the four years of my term of office, important steps were taken towards a better understanding of the sub-regional and regional problems.

The sub-region of Liverpool covers broadly the whole of Merseyside and working parties of planning officers from all the constituent authorities joined in a massive joint study, the Merseyside Land Use Transport Study—MALTS (see Appendix 6), and in doing so gained an insight into the problems of this sub-region. At the regional level, the North-West Economic Council produced a study for the North-West Region (North-West Economic Planning Study, 1965) which was a useful first step towards an appraisal of the region's needs and opportunities.

There is at present no effective regional planning machinery in operation in Britain. The 1947 Town and Country Planning Act, an otherwise most enlightened piece of planning legislation, firmly established the post-war planning organization on the basis of the then existing local government structure of county councils, county boroughs, urban and rural district councils; in doing so it froze planning thought within the individual planning authorities whose interests more often than not conflict and frustrate effective regional planning. However, events have long ago overtaken the 1947 Act pattern of fragmented planning which often cut across several county council boundaries and engulfed many county boroughs, and city regions have by now emerged as an established fact.

The British Government has to some extent in recent years recognized the need for regional planning by establishing twelve Economic Planning Councils, but their function is limited to economic planning and is in any case only an advisory one. The need is in fact for executive regional and/or sub-regional authorities which would be responsible for social, economic and physical planning to produce the strategic framework within which the urban and rural areas would be planned in detail. Such a pattern has in fact already been established in other countries such as Holland where the recently established 'Rijnmond' (Rhine Estuary) authority is an example.

In 1965 the Dutch Government established Rijnmond as a new special authority covering 23 municipalities in the Rhine estuary, Rotterdam being the largest and covering almost 525 km² of land and 75 km² of water, with a population of over 1 million. The administration will consist of a Rhine Estuary Council with 81 members, elected directly by inhabitants of the 23 municipalities. The members of the Council are elected for a period of four years by and from the persons listed in the polling registers of the municipalities in the area. The Rhine Estuary Council will be responsible for the layout of harbours and industrial sites and the location of industry on those sites, housing and the allocation of housing accommodation, cross-river communications and the construction and improvement of roads and waterways, open-air recreational facilities and the control of water and air pollution.

Within the regional/sub-regional context, many different patterns of growth of towns and cities are possible. The most traditional form for major cities is peripheral growth, but this is least satisfactory since an increasing number of people are housed further away from city-centre facilities with the main radial communications becoming increasingly overloaded and the city centre increasingly congested. It was in response to these difficulties that the satellite town principle was developed in Britain, according to which basically self-sufficient new towns were developed within the orbit of existing major cities.

This approach, while relatively successful in the first 20 post-war years, is now proving inadequate and is giving way to a new concept, the city region with groups of semi-independent urban areas each with their own centres but linked to the main centre and with each other by fast public transport facilities and motorways, and facilitating a fair amount of commuting as well as trips for shopping, entertainment and recreation within the region. The city region is emerging as a reality which provides for a great variety of jobs, homes, shopping, cultural and entertainment facilities. The Merseyside Finger Plan, for instance, suggested in Liverpool's Interim Plan, is based on this concept.

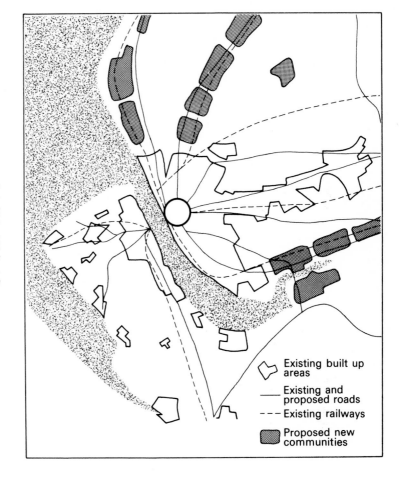

Merseyside Finger Plan. A diagram illustrating a possible sub-regional growth of Liverpool along main lines of communications with semi-independent communities, each with their own shopping and employment facilities but linked by rapid transport to Liverpool. *From Liverpool Interim Planning Policy Report*

Existing built up areas

Existing and proposed roads

Existing railways

Proposed new communities

2 Growth and Decay

Problems of obsolescence

"The real 'slum' is any environment which denies people the freedom to fulfil themselves."

D. H. Lawrence

Much of the environment created during the last 100 years and dating back to the 1870s is still with us. Twenty-seven per cent of our housing stock was built before 1881; we have inherited endless rows of mean little houses, with no trees in the streets, dank and gloomy factories, the coal tips and the industrial dereliction generated during this period of the first industrial revolution. Millions of people still have to live and work in these conditions today. In Liverpool, for instance, in 1965 nearly one-third of the total population of the city lived in houses which the Medical Officer of Health regarded as slums and in some of the smaller northern towns this proportion is even higher. In these slum areas children have nowhere to play but in the streets.

In Great Britain 3 million families live either in slums or in greatly overcrowded conditions. The report 'Our Older Homes—a Call for Action', produced by the Ministry of Housing and Local Government, emphasizes that overcrowding and multiple occupation are an equally important factor in creating slum conditions. In spite of large-scale slum clearance and of the tremendous increase in new house production and in the building of new schools and the creation of new open spaces, our society has so far failed to eradicate effectively the sores which were created a century ago. Even in such modern cities as Caracas well over 25 per cent of the people live in makeshift shelters—the ranchos—without proper sanitation or drainage, while the plight of the slum dwellers in some of the largest US cities has reached an explosive situation. The market-orientated supply of housing does not in fact cater for a substantial sector of the US population who are too poor to compete in the housing market. As Dean Stone, Dean of the Graduate School of Public and International Affairs, University of Pittsburgh, put it: "the immediate challenge in most cities is to eliminate the impoverished and disadvantageous conditions of a sizeable proportion of urban inhabitants".

Typical obsolete environment in Middlesbrough.
Photo by courtesy of the Borough Engineer's Department, Middlesbrough

Children in Liverpool slums play in the streets.
Photo by courtesy of Liverpool City Planning Department

One might well wonder whether we have determined our priorities correctly and whether we are spending enough on creating a better physical environment for our people. Vast sums of money are being poured into quickly obsolescent armaments and tremendously costly space exploration, while we fail to create a decent environment for millions of our people. As Mayor John V. Lindsay said: "I would not want the United States during coming years to be described by future generations as a society that stood amidst the filth, the oppression and the violence of the slums . . . and shot rockets to the moon."

In our cities we are still facing a difficult problem of vast areas of slums and obsolete housing which have to be rebuilt to contemporary standards. At present rates this process will take many more decades and will probably have to continue well beyond the year 2000. In the meanwhile millions of people will have to continue to live in sub-standard conditions with associated problems regarding physical and mental health. But even if this process of wholesale clearance of slum and twilight areas could be speeded up considerably, are we sure we are tackling this job in the right way?

Salford, Lancashire. Sub-standard terrace houses due for demolition in the foreground with one of the new residential tower blocks rising in the background. *Photo: Walter Bor*

Let us first look at what we have to destroy in order to redevelop. It is true that most of the houses and little workshops are sub-standard compared with contemporary methods of construction. Few have damp-proof courses, the sanitary arrangements are poor, as a rule only a few of the houses have bathrooms, lavatories are often shared or provided in the form of outside privies. However, the structural conditions are not uniformly bad and the internal space standards are often quite reasonable. What dissatisfies people often more than their inadequate houses is the low standard of the immediate outdoor environment. The study of Deeplish, an area in Rochdale, given in 'Our Older Homes—a Call for Action', after concluding that approximately two-thirds of 400 houses without standard amenities could have them installed, has this to say about the external environment: "An important contribution could be made by the local authority to the environment by making up and repairing streets, improving lighting, removing eyesores, creating playgrounds, amenity areas and spaces for car parking and closing certain streets as throughways." These are modest contributions which could make an obvious impact and encourage owners to improve their properties.

There are also other important social considerations to be borne in mind. The young and able may welcome the opportunities presented by the redevelopment of such older areas. But these areas often exhibit a long-established working-class culture heavily dependent on family and kinship ties, and an intricate and stable network of relationships between homes, local shops, clubs and pubs, as is shown in Wilmot and Young's book *Family and Kinship in East London*. These relationships are inevitably disrupted when the bulldozers move in. Even the most sensitive social development planning cannot entirely avoid the distress caused by the sudden loss of support and security given by these social patterns, particularly in the case of old people who have lived all their lives in one such neighbourhood.

Thus we have this contradiction between physical obsolescence and social cohesion, and the problem is how not to destroy the best of the latter while dealing with the former. Clearly, some changes will be necessary when the worst houses are pulled down. But must all the houses be pulled down and must this operation be done in so ruthless a manner as has hitherto so often been the case? The desire for a clean sweep is of course understandable, since it simplifies matters administratively and may make possible a radical wholesale renewal and the building up of a total new environment. But it is this very over-simplification of the problem, this brushing aside of inconvenient but highly relevant issues, which has led to many mistakes in urban planning generally and urban renewal in particular.

We have been renewing the slum and twilight areas with inadequate thought to social aspects and we have cleared too large areas, thoughtlessly destroying existing social patterns in the process. In any case we do not possess the resources to apply this technique to the remaining growing areas of obsolescence.

From this one can conclude that a reassessment is urgently needed in two ways: those areas which have to be cleared may well have to be renewed in a more gradual and thoughtful manner, and those areas containing old but structurally still sound housing may have to be renewed, not by wholesale demolition and rebuilding, but by selective demolition to permit the insertion of such facilities as local open space and garages, and by rehabilitation and modernization of the remaining housing stock. Thus the basic aim would be the raising of the quality of the environment while retaining much of the existing and desirable physical and social fabric. Successful examples of such a thoughtful policy can be seen in the Brandon Estate, South London, where terraces of early Victorian houses were rehabilitated as part of a comprehensive revitalization and redevelopment scheme, and in Society Hill, Philadelphia, where amongst others a historic square was rehabilitated and transformed into a pedestrian precinct.

Apart from these problems of growth and change which are so difficult to resolve in old centres in relation to the contemporary city, the changes which have occurred within these centres have also seriously aggravated the situation. With the growing trend towards more office jobs, coupled with the steadily rising central-area land values, housing was gradually pushed out of town centres to make room for offices. The commuter problem and the traffic loading on the already totally inadequate street network increased while the social life of the centres was simultaneously impoverished, as housing, small shops and theatres were being replaced by a multitude of offices, empty after 6 pm.

Brandon Estate, Southwark, London—where rehabilitation of Victorian houses (middle and top of model) has been combined with new residential development (in the foreground). *Photo by courtesy of the Greater London Council*

Brandon Estate, Southwark, London. Terrace of rehabilitated Victorian houses. *Photo by courtesy of the Greater London Council*

Philadelphia, USA. Delancey Park in Society Hill District which has been rehabilitated and turned into a pedestrian precinct. *Photo: Walter Bor*

The reintroduction of residential uses has still so far largely remained a pious hope frustrated by the astronomically high land values. However, there are some recent examples of new housing in Central London, such as a new block of flats in Berwick Street in the middle of London's Soho and on a more massive scale in the Barbican (City of London). However, such housing has to be either heavily subsidised or the rents will be so high that they are within the reach of only a small minority who can afford them.

Right Berwick Street Market, Soho, London—with a new residential tower block in the background. *Photo: Tony Brooks*

Below High-density city-centre housing in the Barbican, City of London. The 400-ft tower block accommodates 111 flats. Architects: Chamberlin, Powell & Bon. *Photo John Laing & Son Ltd*

The planning problems of town centres and central areas are thus made up not only of the difficulties of adaptation to new functions but also of the impotence of planners to apply effectively rational planning controls in the face of inflated land values and political and economic pressures. But this is still not the whole story. These centres, being or at least containing the oldest parts of the towns and cities, include as a rule most of the historic areas and buildings. But since by their very nature these areas and buildings have in some cases outlived their original functions and require a good deal of adaptation and maintenance, owners of such buildings and indeed whole areas have over the years found it more profitable or expedient to pull them down rather than to retain and rehabilitate them.

American cities have their problems of obsolescence too, but they are of a somewhat different nature. There are of course the vast areas of overcrowded tenement blocks like New York's Harlem or Bedford-Stuyvesant which are as disgraceful as the slums of European cities such as Naples or the Gorbals in Glasgow. But in recent years the rapid increase in abandoned tenement blocks has greatly aggravated the housing situation which in cities like New York is rapidly approaching a crisis. One hundred thousand apartments were lost by abandonment in the period 1965–68. One of the reasons for this is that the owners of many buildings have not been receiving enough rent to run their buildings properly and, faced with enormous costs for repairs and maintenance, they have simply abandoned their buildings. This means eventually that the people living in them are forced to leave, since the building services deteriorate and the structure itself becomes unsafe and uninhabitable, Jason Nathan, the former head of the City's Housing and Development Administration, calls the emergency 'a disaster more real than ten hurricanes'.

This situation has been caused in part by the movement into new quarters of people who could in fact afford to improve their present housing. Many people migrate to the suburbs and their apartments are taken over by Negro and Puerto Rican families, many of whom can barely afford to pay the controlled rents in the building. Gradually the buildings deteriorate and an area that was once a decent neighbourhood becomes an unsafe and insanitary slum. The process ends with the building owner simply shrugging his shoulders and leaving the property to fend for itself. The problem is compounded by rising costs in the building industry, by union demands and by general lack of sufficient government funds adequate to replenish the housing stock.

Apart from these obvious slums there are also many parts of inner suburbs in US cities which consist of what at first sight looks like housing of a reasonable standard, often in the form of individual houses with gardens and trees and apparently at reasonable densities. However, on closer inspection one finds that most of these houses are in multiple occupation, have been poorly built and are badly equipped. Compared with the very high standards of a typical middle-class suburban housing area, these too are slums and the people living there know it only too well.

The usual method of dealing with these areas in US cities was to bulldoze them and for either the municipality to redevelop with high-rise, high-density public housing of little distinction or more often for private developers to redevelop with town houses and high-rise flats for middle and upper-middle income groups. The poor, with a high proportion of coloured people, are forced to crowd into the adjoining areas which, because of overcrowding, in turn become the new slums, or they leave for the outskirts. In their eyes, the urban renewal plans become 'Negro removal plans'.

The growing dissatisfaction of the poor population with this kind of urban renewal policy, finding its expression in violent riots, has persuaded the Federal Authorities of the need to rethink the whole process of urban renewal. Having been involved through my firm in Detroit and Watts in the new approach to the revitalization of slum areas which is now emerging, one cannot but be impressed by the genuine desire to work out more equitable solutions for the benefit of the urban poor (see Appendix 1). Communities in other towns, like Racine, Milwaukee, have decided not to wait until large areas become obsolete. The Johnson Wax Company has commissioned a study for the revitalization of the southside area of Racine (Appendix 2), while Nassau County, one of the richest counties in the USA, has initiated a study of the pockets of poverty within the county (Appendix 3).

Obsolescence is, no doubt, one of the major problems in our towns and cities. While a good deal more has been and is being done to meet this problem in Britain than in the USA, the methods employed have been found wanting and are under reconsideration in both countries. Much of our historic heritage and older areas has been lost through neglect, thoughtlessness and greed. But given a carefully worked-out policy of preservation, conservation and rehabilitation it is not beyond us to resolve this problem of old buildings and areas in a sensible, civilized and socially acceptable way.

Appendix 1

Elmwood II, Detroit
Planners: Llewelyn-Davies, Weeks, Forestier-Walker & Bor

In Detroit, an area known as Elmwood II, about one mile from the downtown area, was originally scheduled to be redeveloped for middle and upper-middle income groups. The Metropolitan Detroit Citizens Development Authority (a private concern with the backing of the Union of Automotive Workers) in conjunction with the Ralph Bunche Community Council (representing the Negro residents of Elmwood II) decided to depart from the original policy. Instead, low-cost housing within the reach of the resident population was to be provided at a cost of approximately $12/sq. ft (instead of the $18 originally envisaged). My firm was called in to prepare plans and layouts in association with a US firm of architects and in close collaboration with the clients (the MDCDA and the RBCC); these have been approved by the City Council and the Federal Authorities, and work on this housing is now in progress.

The plan is based on a circulation system, which allows free and safe pedestrian access throughout the scheme to link homes, play areas, parks, community units, shopping, etc.

Figure 1. Elmwood II, Detroit. Typical cluster of houses grouped round sunken car court (bottom right) and a pedestrian play and sitting area (top left). In between these two groups is a single-storey building containing four old people's flats

Figure 2. Elmwood II, Detroit. Houses grouped round a parking court. *Photo by courtesy of Detroit Eddison*

The cluster pattern which we proposed grouped dwellings between sunken car courts and around pedestrian play and sitting areas (Figures 1 and 2). Each house has its own private garden on one side while on the other there is access to a common meeting-cum-play space within direct supervision by neighbours.

This example illustrates an approach to urban renewal and obsolescence which was worked out in full collaboration with the local community, an approach which is now emerging strongly in the USA. If successful and applied quickly to large slum areas in US cities there may yet be hope of tackling this vast and explosive problem of the urban poor before it is too late.

16

Appendix 2

Racine Revitalization Study
Planners: Llewelyn-Davies Associates, New York

The Johnson Wax Company have initiated a planning study to revitalize a neighbourhood of Racine, Milwaukee, USA, involving an area of 104 city blocks. This neighbourhood houses 8000 people, comprising families of varying ethnic and economic backgrounds. For example, one-third of the population is black and approximately 300 families are Spanish American. Housing in the area varies from deteriorated low-income property to expensive residential areas fronting Lake Michigan.

An important aspect of this study is the fact that planning proposals were being prepared at a time when only 10 per cent of the properties are in need of major repairs, and this will mean that clearance of buildings will be minimal. However, present trends indicate that severe physical and social problems will arise if remedial action is not taken in the very near future.

The principal objective of the programme is the preservation and restoration of the neighbourhood without large-scale clearance. Thus the proposals for the area (Figure 1)

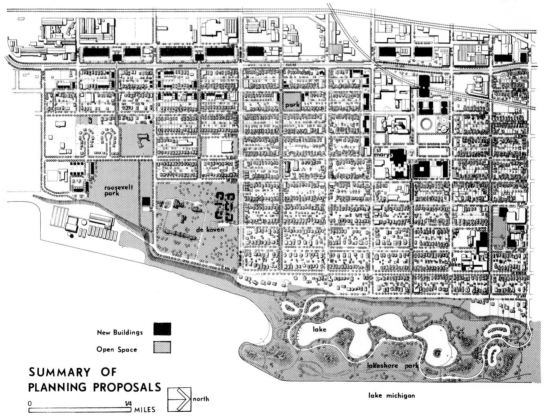

Figure 1. Racine, Milwaukee. Plans for revitalization

Figure 2. Racine, Milwaukee. The local planning office of the consultants in a shop is open to local visitors. *Photo: Paul Buckhurst*

place emphasis on the rehabilitation of existing structures, combined with proposals for new social and commercial facilities which are presently lacking in the area. The major recommendations involve the improvement of the traffic circulation in the neighbourhood, the development of a network of neighbourhood parks and the provision of new shopping, health and social facilities for local residents.

Considerable efforts have been made to involve the local residents in the planning study. A large number of meetings were held with resident groups in which the future needs of the neighbourhood were identified and discussed. In addition, a number of residents worked with the planning staff in carrying out a series of household interviews during the initial stages of the study. The planning consultants opened an office in a disused store front in the study area and invited local residents to comment on the planning work carried out during the course of the study (Figure 2).

A specially constituted Citizens Advisory Committee has been formed to advise the planning consultants and to direct the policy of the programme. The Committee is made up of residents from the local community, members of local government and representatives from important businesses and institutions in the area.

Following the publication of the recommendations, the planning staff will assist in the initial implementation of the planning proposals. Implementation will involve the active cooperation between the community, private enterprise and City, State and Federal governments.

Appendix 3

A Study of Constraints on the Poor in Nassau County, Long Island, USA
Planners: Llewelyn-Davies Associates, New York

This study was prepared for the Nassau County Planning Commission and was funded by the US Office of Economic Opportunity.

Within the past ten years Nassau County has expanded into what is, in effect, a vast suburban area forming part of the metropolitan area surrounding New York City. Although it is one of the most wealthy counties in America, with a population of 1·3 million, it contains at least 200 000 residents who live in considerable poverty.

The hypothesis of the study is based on the fact that the poor are greatly disadvantaged because they are isolated within communities which are remote from public services and ineffectively served by public transportation. Furthermore, their mobility is limited since few poor families own automobiles. For those dependent on public transit it is both costly, especially on a meagre income, and inconvenient to satisfy minimal daily needs. A series of interviews with low-income residents, together with questionnaire surveys, were conducted during the course of the study in order to identify the problems facing the poor due to lack of mobility. Half of the families interviewed were without cars and these families faced severe difficulties in reaching the health, social and shopping centres that are dispersed throughout the county.

For example, many families who are without cars must walk considerable distances—over a mile in some cases—to reach the nearest bus route. Families living in outlying areas of Nassau County who rely on bus services face journeys averaging approximately 75 minutes in order to reach the County Hospital. Equivalent journeys by car would take between 20 and 25 minutes.

An analysis of the rail, bus and taxi operations in the county showed that the existing deficiences were due primarily to the lack of coordination within and between the various transport services. County bus services, for example, are provided by 17 separate companies, with each company operating within its own territory. It is therefore difficult for passengers to transfer or make connections from one route to another.

The study proposed a reorganization of the public transport network that would better serve the 'captive' riders, i.e. those unable to afford or unable to use private cars. A recommended mass-transit loop to serve the major employment and service centres of the county would connect to high-speed feeder routes—such as express bus services—which would in turn provide direct links to those communities where large numbers of the poor presently live. In addition, the study outlined the need for local health and social service centres which should be located within easy reach of the poor communities.

Problems of affluence

"The quality of life in urban America does not match the affluence of our society."

President Lyndon Johnson

Affluence and poverty

There is mounting evidence that fully developed countries are moving into an era of increasing affluence. In Great Britain, for instance, although the growth of the Gross National Product has been relatively slow and is likely to continue to grow at a modest rate which could range from between $2\frac{1}{2}$ per cent to $3\frac{1}{2}$ per cent per annum, this increase would mean that real incomes (allowing for inflation) would double (at a $2\frac{1}{2}$ per cent growth) or nearly treble (at a $3\frac{1}{2}$ per cent growth) by the year 2000. This in turn will have some profound effects on people's life styles, not only in terms of almost universal car ownerships and spacious housing, but of shorter working hours which will leave more time for further education and vastly increased leisure activities.

Yet, within this broad pattern of growing affluence, pockets of real poverty are likely to increase. It has been a feature in fully developed countries such as the United States for the gap between the affluent and the poor, particularly the poor black, to widen with increasing general prosperity. As Martin Luther King said of the American Negro: "He lives isolated on a lonely island of poverty in an ocean of material prosperity." This does not mean that the poor are likely to become poorer in absolute terms, but rather that they will appear to be poorer relative to the growing affluence of their more fortunate fellow citizens by whom they are being left behind.

There are serious problems of poverty in Britain too, albeit on a relatively much smaller scale than in the USA. For instance, in spite of the fact that the UK has been a Welfare State for several decades now, there are some half a million families, involving well over a million children, who live below the poverty line. One of the most urgent social and economic problems of developed societies will be to close this widening gap.

The mixed blessing of the motor car

It is indeed ironical that some of the results of greater material well-being and a higher standard of living should have a much more damaging effect on our urban environment than all the old age, obsolescence and dereliction of the whole urban areas we considered earlier in the chapter. Yet this is so. The impact of the private motor car—this symbol of a higher material standard—on the quality of the environment of our urban areas has been more damaging and all-pervading in a shorter space of time than the whole depressing but geographically confined process of dereliction. And while there is some hope that, given the will and resources, we may one day resolve the problems of dereliction, a solution or even partial solution of the problems caused by the increasing ownership and use of private cars is not yet within sight. This is not only so because the sheer quantity of vehicles, which is exerting an inexorable pressure on our urban areas, is still rapidly increasing, but also because effective restrictions on the use of the private motor car and to some extent of goods vehicles—however rational—are politically inexpedient.

Growing space demands

The problem caused by greater affluence is not, however, confined to that of the increasing numbers of vehicles in urban areas. An equally difficult situation arises from the demand for more space of all kinds: more space for living and working, for education, recreation and cultural facilities. Since there is already a fierce competition for urban land amongst the various users, this conflict will increase in intensity as space demands escalate. As was said in the Ministry of Housing and Local Government Housing Advisory Group report 'Homes for Today and Tomorrow' published in 1961: "Domestic axioms of the sixties are the increasing independence of the teenager, the increasing homework of the student, the increasing storage of the family's leisure wear and leisure gear."

The office boom

But the inevitable increase in vehicle ownership and space standards resulting from greater affluence are only part of the story. Drastic changes in employment and in the retailing pattern which are also due to the requirements of a more fully developed society must be added to the kind of pressures which a more affluent society exerts on its urban environment. Growing automation and a general shift from manual to office work and service employment has in recent years resulted in many more office jobs being generated per square foot than industrial jobs, particularly in the centres of our towns.

Many planners, including the visionary Sir Patrick Abercrombie, in his County of London Plan 1943, grossly underestimated this trend and concentrated almost entirely on the problem of decentralizing manufacturing industries. The Government was slow to appreciate the growth in office employment and until 1964, when the Office Development Certificate was brought in, only industry was controlled by means of industrial development certificates. For instance, since the war, in Central London alone 60–70 million sq. ft of offices have been built which resulted in between 300 000 and 350 000 new office jobs.

This unprecedented growth of offices in our town centres, while clearly meeting a real demand, has had in many respects a most damaging effect upon the urban environment. Because of the great concentration of employment within city centres which were not designed to accommodate it effectively, congestion has been greatly aggravated and the commuter problem in particular has assumed unmanageable proportions; neither public transport as it exists nor the private car have been able to cope with the peak loads in a civilized way. Since the rents obtainable from offices were many times those which residential accommodation could yield, many central residential areas have practically disappeared to make room for offices, either in adapted houses or in new office blocks erected after the demolition of residential accommodation.

In place of this central area housing, which provided accommodation at reasonable rents for a variety of people often in need of a central location, vast office complexes have been built to be occupied only during the working hours of a five-day week. With the tendency towards shorter working hours, it is likely that these office blocks will be used even fewer hours and days in the not too distant future.

The City of London after the war in 1945. Cannon Street Station in the foreground, the Barbican area in the background. Most buildings do not exceed 6 storeys, the spires of the Wren churches stand out as landmarks. *Photo: Aerofilms Ltd*

Two or three centuries ago the centres and central areas of our cities of today constituted the whole town with open country beyond; today the same centres and central areas are the focus of commerce and shopping, administration, cultural and entertainment activities for much larger urban areas surrounding them. While all this increased activity and pressure has built up in town centres, their road structure remains largely unchanged.

In the City of London, for example, the mediaeval road pattern was basically retained after the Great Fire in 1666 and the wartime bombing, and apart from a few new streets built during the Victorian era and a short stretch of the new London Wall and Blackfriars Bridge underpass, which were built since the war, the street network was largely frozen by rebuilding after the Second World War blitz. Before the war Wren's dome of St Paul's Cathedral and church spires still dominated the skyline. After the war, however, a substantial number of buildings doubled and trebled in size. Thus we now have 20- and 30-storey blocks superimposed upon the essentially mediaeval street network.

This example illustrates our failure to arrive at clear concepts for the growth of our city centres—in the case of the City of London one had the choice after the blitz of either

The City of London, 1969. A view of the same area as the previous photograph shows how the scale of the buildings has increased dramatically. The spires of the Wren churches have been dwarfed but the basic mediaeval road pattern has been retained. *Photo: Aerofilms Ltd*

retaining and rebuilding its essentially mediaeval street pattern and scale of buildings or making a fresh start with a modern street pattern and a 20th-century scale of buildings. In the event the compromise of high buildings within a mediaeval core has destroyed much of the City of London's old charm without transforming it into an efficient 20th-century business centre.

Growth and change in shopping

Next let us look at the changes in retail patterns. The unprecedented variety and quantity of goods of all kinds, the increasing ownership of refrigerators and cars have had a profound effect on shopping. As a consequence, shopping as a daily activity of the housewife is declining and the need for good parking facilities near shops is increasing. Gone are the days when the High Street traders relied a good deal on passing vehicular traffic, when one would pull up one's car in front of a shop. Most shopping streets are heavily congested and parking, even stopping, has had to be prohibited. Many of the little shops strung out along the main roads are leading a marginal existence and are being pushed against the wall

23

Notting Hill Gate. London. A rebuilt shopping street after a road widening is typical of the bland anonymity of many new post-war shopping centres. In this case, no attempt was made to create a pedestrian shopping precinct and the heavy A40 traffic pours through this new shopping street and effectively severs the shops on either side from each other. *Photo by courtesy of the Greater London Council*

by the more powerful, efficient and cheaper multiples and supermarkets, even without the intervention of road widenings or comprehensive renewal schemes.

There is ample evidence that upon redevelopment only a proportion, rarely exceeding half of the displaced shopkeepers, take up new premises, mainly because they cannot afford the new economic rent. It is true, some local authorities insist on the reinstatement of the largest possible number of these smaller shops in renewal schemes, mainly for social reasons, but the economic difficulties often defeat these good intentions and we are running into the danger of town after town having very similar if not identical shopping centres wished upon them by developers whose main interest is to let their shops to as few but as powerful shopping concerns as possible. And shopping centres, one of the most important elements in the life and individuality of a town, are becoming increasingly indistinguishable by their bland uniformity and absence of individual character.

A great deal of capital has been and is being invested into the modernization and even complete rebuilding of major and minor shopping centres up and down the country. In many instances adjoining authorities are in competition with each other, and in the absence of objective regional and sub-regional assessments of shopping needs, there is a distinct danger of multiplication and over-provision. Indeed, there are doubts whether some of this investment will not be overtaken by yet further changes in the shopping pattern, particularly by the pressure for out-of-town shopping centres on US lines.

That the prosperity of town-centre shops, and indeed their very existence, can be very seriously affected by such sub-regional out-of-town shopping centres is by now well known

Out-of-town shopping centre at Oakbrook, West Chicago. *Photo: Wyckoff Studio*

from numerous examples in the USA. It is true, there are many reasons why this American pattern need not repeat itself in Britain, where town centres have stronger historic associations, urban development is more compact than the low-density sprawl of American cities and the public transport system—inadequate as it may be—is still far more efficient and popular than that of most US cities. Nevertheless, there is no room for complacency. The role of out-of-town shopping centres will have to be squarely faced on a sub-regional, regional and national level and the approach will have to be an open-minded one.

It is true, of course, that the counter-attraction of out-of-town shopping centres could very seriously undermine the viability of central-area shopping facilities in some towns. For instance, a proposed shopping centre at Haydock on the M6 motorway midway between Liverpool and Manchester, while it would have had some detrimental effect on shopping in these two cities, would have made impossible central-area renewal in the smaller Lancashire towns in the vicinity, such as Warrington and Widnes, because it would have deprived them of the main revenue-producing use, namely shopping, which helps considerably to finance their town-centre renewal. On the other hand, for small historic towns under pressure, a well sited and designed out-of-town shopping centre might relieve them of some of these pressures and could thus help considerably to preserve their priceless heritage. It may well be, however, that a happy compromise can be evolved in new cities where the shoppers' demand for good accessibility by private car and unrestricted parking facilities can be met within an urban context.

Increasing leisure demands

Finally, let us consider the increasing demands of leisure as they affect the urban environment. These demands are both of a sophisticated and unsophisticated kind, their space demands range from a playground or small swimming pool to special centres, vast sports stadia and regional parks. As far as the urban environment is concerned more people will have more time on their hands and be able to use it as they please. Failure to provide for this situation has already resulted in much boredom, and frustration is closely related to vandalism and juvenile delinquency. Once again we are up against competing demands for space and financial resources. Much ingenuity and imagination will be needed to meet these rising leisure demands with the limited spatial and financial resources at our disposal. The multi-use of buildings, play spaces and parking facilities will have to be employed. Swimming pools, assembly halls and playgrounds of comprehensive schools sited near district centres could, for example, be shared by the pupils in daytime with the public in the evenings, week-ends and during school holidays. These and similar approaches would not only make better use of our resources but would also help to retain life and activity in buildings and spaces which at present are used only during limited periods.

All these demands of an increasingly affluent society taken together lead one to conclude that one of the most important features of such a society will be increased mobility. Travel by public and private transport will grow as people will wish to avail themselves of an increasing variety of opportunities in education, shopping and leisure. The provision of good accessibility throughout the city for everybody will therefore be a prime objective in the planning of our cities, and the respective roles of public and private transport will therefore be discussed in some detail in Part 2.

A well-designed playground in Churchill Gardens, Pimlico, a high-density housing development in London. Architects: Powell & Moya. *Photo: M. Murray*

Small swimming pool in Tapiola New Town, Finland, shared by a group of residents. *Photo by courtesy of the Managing Director. Tapiola*

3 The Changing Planning Ideas and Techniques

"It is an instinct with me to attack every idea which has been full grown for 10 years, especially if it claims to be the foundation of all society."

G. B. Shaw

Old and new planning concepts

We have inherited such a mixed-up jumble of conflicting land and road uses that most of the first attempts at modern town planning were concerned with bringing some sense and order into this confusion. Most efforts went into the separating out of what were considered to be incompatible land uses. For instance, as a reaction to housing being all mixed up with factories, offices and warehouses, separate zones were advocated for each use. Such an approach is still valid for such types of uses as heavy and noxious industries and massive warehousing causing smell, noise and traffic of an order which is incompatible with good living conditions.

However, this approach became a dogma and planners went to extremes in its application. Sight was lost of the fact that some science-based concerns or small and clean service industries and professional offices are by no means incompatible with housing if thoughtfully planned. As a result of this rigid interpretation of a basically sensible concept, vast purely dormitory housing areas have been created and industries concentrated into large compact areas often far away from residential areas. The life in the housing areas was deprived of local employment possibilities, particularly for married women, and the commuter problem was aggravated. Town centres were filled almost exclusively with shops and offices, and the uncomfortable congestion during working hours gave way to desertion after closing time, again aggravating the traffic problems in day-time and creating a social desert in the evenings and at week-ends. And so the original good intentions of strict single-use zoning to improve living and working conditions have produced unforeseen detrimental side effects, both of a physical and social kind.

The horizontal segregation of different land uses is also largely ignoring the fact that in existing towns two or even more uses like shops, offices, residential and small service industries often occur in the same building without serious disadvantages. In fact it is this admittedly haphazard and unplanned but nevertheless often workable intermixture of uses which makes some urban areas such lively and interesting places, and it is the almost total segregation which tends to make the single-use areas dull and lifeless. It is true, of course, that there is a limit to the amount of intermixture which is acceptable and which can function well, and that much depends not only on the degree to which this is done but also the way it is organized. No doubt certain conflicts are inevitable in such an arrangement, but I believe that planning should not even try to eliminate all the conflicts but should confine itself to eliminating the worst excesses and to allowing for some of the minor conflicts and contradictions to work themselves out. After all, life itself is full of such conflicts, the partial solution of which makes it interesting and forever changing as it develops from one situation to another.

If it is accepted that there is much to be said for some form of judicious intermixture of uses and activities, the question then arises as to how this may be achieved successfully. Let us begin with existing situations where in fact different uses occur in the same area or even the same building. Instead of taking a rigid work-to-rule attitude of 'this area is zoned for residential, therefore such and such a use is not permitted', it may be necessary to study each problem in some detail to see whether in fact the proposed use is one which can be permitted and which indeed may be an asset to the area, even if it does not look so tidy on the zoning map. The vertical sub-division of buildings can provide cheap small-scale accommodation which is often difficult to find and yet essential in any city.

There is a distinct danger that the small traders, artisans and business men could be eliminated, together with the cheap central-area flats for small households who want to live near their centrally located employment. It may well be that, upon close examination, certain objectionable uses may still have to be refused, but this would be quite a different matter compared with the present tendency to out-of-hand rejection of what according to the book is a 'non-conforming use'.

It is likely, however, that the intermixture of uses in existing buildings will mean in most cases the acceptance of some makeshift arrangement since the buildings and roads serving them were not originally designed for it and must be adapted as best they can. In new urban development, where old properties are demolished and replaced, particularly in town and local centres, new and interesting possibilities are opened up to design multipurpose structures which could meet the needs for such buildings in a more effective form than converted old buildings. An example of such a new multipurpose building is Place Bonaventure in Montreal, consisting of three floors of hotel over one floor trade centre, over five floors of merchandise mart over two floors of exhibition hall, over two floors of covered shopping, and the whole thing over the Canadian National Railway lines. This is described in detail in *Architectural Design,* August 1967.

A corresponding effort has been made to separate road users in the same systematic way. While there remains clearly the need for physical separation of pedestrians from the fast-moving traffic on major distributors and even local distributors, it is neither essential nor

Place Bonaventure, Montreal, Quebec. A good example of a multi-use building in which shopping, an exhibition hall, merchandise mart, trade centre and hotel all function well under one roof and on top of a railway. Architects: Affleck, Desbarats, Dimakopoulos, Lebensold, Sise. *Photo by courtesy of 'Official Architecture and Planning'*

Garage court at Fredericksburg, Denmark, where slow-moving vehicles and pedestrians mix without detriment. Architect: Utson. *Photo: Alan Turner*

really practicable to keep pedestrians rigidly apart from the slow-moving vehicles in the garage courts (which in any case provide attractive if unofficial playgrounds for children), particularly as the demand for a high provision of garages in or adjoining houses increases. A study of this problem in a housing area in Washington New Town carried out by my firm has led us to the conclusion that such a rigid separation is not necessary or indeed desirable (see Appendix 4). A civilized example of integrating car access and parking in this way comes from Fredericksburg in Denmark.

After all, however successful we may, and one hopes we will, be in creating many traffic-free precincts in our urban areas, we shall not succeed in re-organizing all or even the majority of them so that pedestrians and vehicles are physically separated and the older children must sooner or later learn to live with the motor car.

There is an unmistakable tendency in modern town planning to go for formulae which appear to solve obvious and detrimental conflicts and then apply them universally and indiscriminately to any situation. It is a convenient over-simplification which often ignores the complexity of a particular problem and the need to adapt theories to particular situations. This sort of over-simplification applies even more to the social structure than to physical aspects. The theoretically attractive idea of the neighbourhood organized around two primary schools and one secondary school with its own shopping facilities has in many instances failed to correspond to the actual social pattern which exists or evolves. As car-ownership increases and people become more mobile they will often prefer to drive a few miles to meet the people they really want to see and patronize the shop of their choice rather than conform to a planned, pre-conceived pattern of inward-looking 'neighbourliness'. In any case, no neighbourhood, however well planned, can cater for the vast variety and multiplicity of social occasions which are a daily occurrence in town life.

We are still insufficiently aware of the complexity, particularly in social terms, for which we must plan to provide the physical conditions which would optimize freedom of choice and the richness of life. It means we must abandon attempts, however well meaning, to prescribe everything that is plannable and adopt instead an approach to planning which provides positively for the fullest scope of foreseeable and unforeseeable opportunities which will not fall into the neat pattern devised by over-orderly and somewhat clinical minds. Indeed all one can and perhaps should reasonably plan for is to provide as rich a choice as possible for people to use facilities of all kinds over wide urban areas while providing for essential local services.

Jane Jacobs conveyed some of this thinking in her book *The Life and Death of Great American Cities*. Christopher Alexander in his essay 'A City is not a Tree' (*Design*, February 1966) develops the Jane Jacobs approach systematically and argues cogently against the hierarchical structure which planners almost inevitably give to new towns. Alexander uses the example of the tree with its trunk, main and subsidiary branches, twigs and leaves, as an illustration of a hierarchical system in which the only relationship between its component parts is through the hierarchy. He advocates the adoption of a more complex structure such as prevails in existing towns, a semi-lattice, which allows for a variety of relationships and overlaps between individual elements and functions. Such a structure, he claims, corresponds in fact to social realities.

An attempt is being made in the planning of the new city of Milton Keynes in Buckinghamshire to provide a framework for such a freer social interaction. Instead of structuring the new city in the form of inward-looking neighbourhoods with their centres in the middle, residential areas will be developed within a grid of main roads with local activity centres at the safe midway crossing point of these roads where safe under or overpasses for pedestrians will be provided. Up to four such centres would serve not only any particular residential area bounded by the main roads but also four adjoining ones, all within walking distance of the homes in these areas. In this way, it is hoped, will the options which people can exercise be greatly increased (see Appendix 5).

Another development which falls into the category of questionable segregation is the tendency in urban renewal of slum or obsolescent areas to replace them by one-class communities. This phenomena is particularly marked in British cities, since this kind of renewal has been almost exclusively the responsibility of local housing authorities who accommodate families from their long housing lists in these renewal areas. And since the housing lists are made up almost entirely from the economically weaker section of the community, almost all the new accommodation in rebuilt renewal areas is allocated to them. As the *Architectural Review* put it so trenchantly in its November 1967 issue:

"Through wholesale clearances, the living tissues of still valid community life have been thoughtlessly destroyed, and have been replaced by a sterile segregated pattern of living to which people may take generations to adapt. Housing ghettoes have been built in cities and on the edge of towns with inadequate transport and footpath systems to link and lock them into the existing pattern of communication, and to allow towns to cater for the gregariousness of people—which is their proper function. Monuments or architectural images have been created as irrelevant to the needs of the people as to the visual structure of the town or city."

Urban renewal in US cities has been suffering from opposite defects, in the sense that the poorer population who lived in the slum area was removed and the new development let at high rents to middle and upper income groups which ironically enough are also single-class communities but of a different kind. This is yet another aspect which tends to create situations in towns upon rebuilding which in some ways are less satisfactory than those which they replace.

It is true, of course, that most towns have distinct 'working-class', 'middle-class' and 'upper-class' areas, but it is also a fact that apart from these, there are still many areas, particularly in the inner parts of our towns, where boundaries are indistinct between different classes of the community, where porters, waiters and draughtsmen share houses or live in the same block of flats as journalists, professional and business men. The fact that this mixture of classes and professions tends to disappear upon redevelopment is not, however, part of a planned social development but simply a not fully appreciated by-product of an otherwise often very enlightened housing policy. This new problem would be mitigated if, for instance, more cooperative housing on Scandinavian lines, which caters for a wider range of classes, were also introduced. This would incidentally also help to solve by owner-occupation such problems as maintenance of buildings and spaces between them, which is often a major problem in subsidized local authority housing. But to date the amount of housing of this type which has been provided by Housing Societies and Associations is still very small indeed in Britain.

31

Appendix 4

Barmston village housing, Washington New Town, Co. Durham
Architects: Llewelyn-Davies, Weeks, Forestier-Walker & Bor

The main objectives in the design of 300 houses and village centre are the provision of a high degree of car penetration which would allow for most cars to be parked close to the home, coupled with safe and sheltered pedestrian movements between groups of houses and through the village centre to the old town of Washington. Houses were to be grouped around communal greens to form places with their own identity and mutual interest.

The concept therefore consists of three basic elements: the garage court, the garden court and the pedestrian streets (Figure 1).

Figure 1. Barmston Village Housing, Washington New Town, Co. Durham. The model shows the layout consisting of garage courts, garden courts and a pedestrian village street leading to the village centre on the left. Cars and pedestrians mingle in the garage courts

The garage courts are designed to combine convenient vehicular access to dwellings with an acceptable environment by limiting the number of dwellings and cars per court to 24, by designing for low car speeds within the courts and by generous tree planting to break up views of parked cars. The garden courts consist of the private gardens of the houses surrounding the courts, which give access on to communal greens with toddlers' play spaces, which with their different landscaping help to give different identities to different housing groups.

The pedestrian links consist of a principal pedestrian spine route in the form of an 18 ft wide street with L-shaped houses designed to safeguard privacy and to give protection from wind. This route collects, along its length, pedestrian ways, some of which are in the form of diagonal short cuts, and leads through the village centre to the local bus stop (Figure 2). The centre consists of a primary and a junior school, five shops, a working man's club and a meeting hall for the use of the 4500 residents of the village.

Figure 2. Sketch showing pedestrian street leading to village centre in the background

Old and new ways of plan making

"Essentially, the problem of planning demands the solution of an equation with many variables representing different ways of expanding human efforts so as to give the maximum human opportunity for action and the best biological and sociological environment for humanity."

Professor J. D. Bernal

Britain's 1947 Town and Country Planning Act (operational since 1948) which has broadly governed all planning activity in Britain until the passing of the 1968 Town and Country Planning Act was probably one of the most enlightened and comprehensive planning legislations in the world. However, 20 years is a long span in a fast changing society and inevitably major changes in the approach and its detailed application have become necessary to bring this legislation up to date and project it into the future. Some of the original intentions of the Act, such as the clear definition of planning principles and policy, as opposed to its detailed application have been lost sight of and too rigid an interpretation has tended to inhibit the forward-looking planning of existing urban communities. By tying the planning legislation to the existing local government structure of County Councils, County Boroughs, non-County Boroughs, Urban and Rural Districts, effective regional planning, as was mentioned earlier, has been frustrated by the conflicting vested interests of these individual planning authorities.

A remarkable amount of development in Britain during the first two decades after the war proceeded in an orderly and planned way which has earned the respect, and even the

33

admiration, of the civilized world. In particular, the 28 New Towns which have been or are being planned to date represent a creditable achievement. However, much of the planning during this period was largely action-orientated 'hunch planning' based on subjective guesses and a set of well-intentioned but often quite subjective 'do's' and 'don'ts' rather than on scientific methods and objective criteria. For instance, no real attempt was made during this period to assess traffic requirements realistically or to any degree of accuracy, and to plan for transport and land use in a fully integrated way.

Many of the planning ideas which were implemented after the war had been conceived several decades previously and had already been overtaken by events. But the basic shortcoming in planning during this period lay in the great over-simplification of planning issues which were in reality much more complex and therefore required a more sophisticated methodology to meet them. Typical of this tendency to over-simplify was the practice of producing, after survey and analysis of the planning problems, the plan—the one and only plan—and no serious attempt was made to investigate and discuss alternatives in order to arrive at the best possible solution. There has also been an inadequate appreciation of the essentially continuous nature of the planning process. This was reflected in the statutory development plans which, though in theory subject to quinquennial review, took many years to prepare and approve, were difficult to alter, and were therefore in practice reviewed only every ten years or so.

The growing realization that reform was urgently needed, both of the actual planning methodology and of the implementing machinery, led to the setting up, by the Minister of Housing and Local Government, of the Planning Advisory Group (PAG) in 1965, of the Royal Commission on Local Government in England under the chairmanship of Lord Redcliffe-Maud in 1966, whose report was published in 1969, and publication of the Conservative Government White Paper 'Local Government in England: Government Proposals for Reorganisation' in 1971. The proposals for local government reorganization will be discussed in Part 2 (Politics and Urban Planning). The Planning Advisory Group's Report 'The Future of Development Plans' was published in 1966 and its main recommendations have been enacted by Parliament and are now embodied in the 1968 Town and Country Planning Act.

The basic criticism of existing planning procedure voiced by the PAG report was that the existing development plans were too definite for towns and country as a whole over too long a period ahead (20 years), yet insufficiently detailed in areas where action of some kind or another (renewal, rehabilitation or conservation) was contemplated in the foreseeable future (up to ten years). It was also thought that the whole planning process was too cumbersome, that the Ministry was involved unnecessarily in too much detail rather than giving guidance to planning policies and that there has been an inadequate participation by the public in the planning process.

The report therefore recommended a new approach which would consist of preparing a Planning Strategy Report and a simplified type of development plan in the form of urban and county structure maps which would illustrate the main long-term land-use and transportation policies but would not attempt to show any details. Those areas where action was likely to take place within the next ten years or so were to be defined as action areas and three-dimensional plans would indicate the detailed proposals for these areas. One or several such action areas could form an integral part of district plans which should be prepared to ensure that individual action areas were planned as part of the overall planning of their districts. The district plans and action area plans would be drawn on ordnance sheets showing each property and would thus illustrate firm planning/transport proposals which would also form the basis of development control in these areas.

While the urban and county structure plans would be submitted to the Minister to ensure overall consistency in planning policies, the district and action area plans would be local plans which would only in exceptional cases require the Minister's approval. The public would be brought more effectively into the planning process by participation in discussions and hearings of all types of proposals, ranging from broad principles to detailed building plans.

The Planning Advisory Group's report recommendations have already been largely implemented in the planning of Liverpool (as described in 'Liverpool Interim Planning Policy Statement and Maps', 1965) where, as a member of the PAG, I was in a position to apply them as City Planning Officer for that city, and since then other planning authorities have followed or are following suit. While the basic PAG recommendations were found sound and workable in Liverpool and were of enormous help in defining the main planning objectives quickly and effectively, the implementation of the suggestion for greater citizen participation was found to be a more complex and lengthy process than had been anticipated. The Government, recognizing the importance and complexity of public participation, set up a special committee, the Skeffington Committee, whose recommendations will be discussed in Part 2.

The PAG's fresh approach to planning as now embodied in the new planning legislation of the Town and Country Planning Act will provide the framework for planning in Britain during the next decade or two. It implies the use of a much more sophisticated planning methodology than has been the case during the past 20 years. Many of these new planning techniques were evolved in the United States where planning theory has in many ways advanced more rapidly than in Britain. One suspects that one of the reasons for this is that American planners, frustrated in the practical application in the field, due to lack of effective planning powers, poured their considerable energy and ability to think logically and make full use of modern technology into perfecting planning techniques, whereas the action-orientated and basically pragmatic British planners were too busy implementing planning on the ground to develop significant planning theory. However, these differences in emphasis have by now become less distinct as British planners, benefiting from new American planning thought and techniques, are now developing their own sophisticated methodology while US planners are becoming increasingly involved in action-orientated planning.

Amongst the new techniques which are becoming available to planners are those which have been already developed in operational research. In general terms operational research involves the identification of the subsidiary parts of a complex human activity and of the relationship between these parts in terms of performance required to make the whole activity work effectively. In the application of operational research to planning situations, mathematical techniques of evaluation are used and mathematical models are produced to simulate the real situation.

Critical path analysis can also be applied with advantage to planning, for instance to the redevelopment or town-building process, or to assist the planning of scarce resources such as local authority expenditure or capital works and staff time. Above all it can help to clarify the planning process. A critical path analysis consists of producing a graphical plot of a sequence of activities of known duration leading towards a specified end in the most effective way and in the shortest possible time. The identification and reorganization of activities around a critical path can only be drawn up after a complete evaluation of the needs, product, manpower and time necessary for the completion of each component.

Foremost amongst the new planning methods which have been evolved in recent years are the land-use/transport studies which, for the first time in the history of planning, are attempting to bring together simultaneously planning of land use and transport as an integrated concept. Based on surveys by questionnaires and home interviews (rather than by just counting existing traffic) overall requirements of the population are assessed and projected into the future. Various alternative strategies are then explored, varying for instance in the degree of decentralization and dispersal of major employment centres, together with resulting traffic patterns. From these, the best alternative is selected and developed in order to produce the best possible urban and country planning policies. Such an approach was adopted, for instance, in the Merseyside Land-Use/Transport Study (MALTS) which is outlined in Appendix 6.

As the public is encouraged to become more involved in the planning process, it is increasingly necessary for planners to be able to demonstrate clearly to the public the evolutionary processes whereby they have reached their decisions and why certain proposals have been recommended as the preferred or 'best' solution to the problem. This is particularly the case where planning issues are complex or involve a number of strategic alternative choices. By being able to set out the arguments for and against each alternative clearly and objectively, the reasoning behind the recommendation can be understood and discussed, and if necessary questioned.

This method of examining a number of alternative opportunities does not take away from the planner his responsibility as a professionally qualified expert to give his advice, on the basis of the evidence contained in the analysis, as to the best or preferred alternative. It is not normally sufficient for the planner to present only the comparative analysis, leaving it for others to make the choice. From his position as a professional planner, he should be prepared to recommend the best alternative to meet stated objectives and explain the criteria by which he arrived at this recommendation. Also, he should be prepared to justify his choice dispassionately to the public and be prepared to accept other alternatives in its place if it can be shown that other objectives and criteria are more valid. The examination of alternative strategies by the public should ideally be started at an early stage in every major project so that those of the public who are interested can be involved in the step-by-step evolution of the plans and can have the opportunity of making a contribution at a time when it can be of constructive value to the development of successive plans.

This kind of complex and sophisticated planning by testing a large number of alternatives and variables has been made possible by the extensive use of computers, since the computer can process a vast number of different permutations with great speed and accuracy. Indeed computers are being used to provide a wide variety of new and valuable planning tools. The Ministry of Housing and Local Government, for example, developed a computer technique using standard computer line printing to produce diagrammatic maps called 'Linmap' designed to accept magnetic line input. Professor Fisher from Harvard Graduate School of Design has developed the 'Symap' programme whereby contour-type maps can be produced. For example, data concerning land values often available only sporadically can be processed to produce broad contours of land value for a city area.

Other novel techniques are being introduced into planning, for instance cost-benefit analysis whereby costs and social benefits are assessed and compared for alternative strategies. Cost-benefit analysis is a form of appraisal which takes into account all the consequences of alternative policies and where possible measures them. Its purpose is to display, as far as practicable, to the decision-makers the costs and benefits of alternative courses of action thus helping them in their judgement. It is not intended to replace that judgement.

Cost-benefit analysis tries to assess all the results from any course of action, whether advantageous or disadvantageous and regardless of who sustains them. Thus the interest of groups in the community as a whole is considered as well as that of individuals. Secondary effects are assessed in addition to those directly attributable to the project, and the future is given significance as well as the present. This technique certainly provides a useful rationalized list of considerations to assist the decision maker, and could, if developed, provide a comprehensive assessment of the relative merits of different alternative possibilities.

One of the nationally most important recent cost-benefit studies in the UK is that which the Third London Airport Commission (chairman Mr Justice Roskill) undertook in connection with the selection of a site for a third London Airport, and a representative example of evaluating alternative urbanization strategies for one of the four sites considered is described in Appendix 7. However, it must be emphasized that all cost-benefit studies are limited to the extent that many socially important factors cannot be costed as readily as construction or travel costs, and much will then depend on the weighting which is attached to such unmeasured elements. Also, there is no technical way to determine how costs and benefits should be distributed.

An adaptation of cost-benefit analysis intended for planning problems is Lichfield's *Planning Balance Sheet*, which he applies in his work 'Cost-benefit Analysis in Town Planning—a Case Study of Cambridge 1966'. In this, a plan is regarded as a series of interrelated development projects. For each project a list is produced of all parties (public and private) concerned with 'producing' and 'operating' the services, and of all those who will 'consume' them, whether through buying them in the market or collectively with rates and taxes. For each producing or consuming party, a list is made of the costs and benefits that will accrue, each item being measured in money or physical terms as far as possible, otherwise noted as intangible. Thus a complete set of 'social accounts' is produced, normally in a descriptive set table, which shows all the significant costs and benefits arising from the plan as a whole. The accounts are 'reduced' by eliminating double counting, transfer payments and common items. If alternative possibilities are being compared, the account reveals the differences. The final Planning Balance Sheet is thus a summary of advantages and disadvantages to the public and assists in more informed and rational policy decision making.

The Planning Balance Sheet approach, however, fails to assess a project in terms of defined objectives, and relies on somewhat arbitrarily assumed universal values. Hill, in his paper 'A Goals Achievement Matrix for Evaluating Alternative Plans', published in January 1968 in the *Journal of the American Institute of Planners*, suggests an improvement—the *Goals Achievement Matrix*—which he prefers because it relates to the declared goals of a project and assesses how far they are achieved. To construct a Goals Achievement Matrix the first stage is to focus on the goals for the plan in question. The relative value to be attached to each goal must be established, objectives having been defined operationally rather than in abstract terms. Then each alternative course of action must be examined to see how far it satisfies each goal. Thus the overall performance of each alternative in relation to all the goals can be seen.

The compatibility or conflict between goals can be demonstrated in a Goal Compatibility Matrix. This shows clearly when some compromise is necessary. However, the Goals Achievement Matrix is not very useful if weights cannot be objectively determined or assumed. Another problem is also pointed out by Hill: "A major disadvantage is that inter-action and interdependence between objectives is not registered."

Thus, despite attempts to adapt cost-benefit analysis to land-use planning problem evaluation, four significant questions remain unanswered: What weight to attach to groups in the community? What weight to attach to different planning goals? How to measure goal interaction? How to measure unquantifiable components?

A recent interesting development is *Threshold Analysis*. Pioneered in Poland, it has also been applied in Britain, for example in the Grangemouth-Falkirk Regional Survey and Plan produced by the Scottish Development Department in 1968. It produces comparative cost figures for alternative locations and schemes for accommodating given numbers of people. The procedure is to examine the costs involved in providing services for an expanded population. Some of these services cannot be supplied in continuous small increments, but involve periodic large-scale investments—cost 'thresholds'. This is true of such services as roads, sewers, town centres. This form of costing is an advantage on the traditional method of making a decision to locate a certain number of people in a particular area in ways based on 'planning criteria' alone, and then costing that proposal, thus effectively masking any cost thresholds that have been passed.

The disadvantages to a planner of Threshold Analysis, as used so far, are that only certain of the relevant costs have been included in calculations and that there has been no estimating of returns, thus net return is not indicated. However, there appear to be no reasons why these inadequacies cannot be made good.

New management methods are being evolved, in central and local governments, such as a 'Planning, Programming, Budgeting System', or PPBS, which ensure that goals, criteria and costs are identified and that priorities are determined from the outset.

Thus, in the past decade or so, highly sophisticated new techniques have enriched planning methodology and transformed planning from a subjective exercise based on hunches into an objective science-based activity. These new methods have also brought into the planning team, in addition to the planners, architects and engineers, such specialists as transport engineers, urban economists, demographers, sociologists, statisticians, mathematicians and computer experts. The composition of these new planning teams and the methodology they are evolving are beginning to reflect the multi-faceted and open-ended reality of contemporary urban society for whom and with whom we are planning.

However, it must be emphasized that techniques and methodology—however sophisticated —are but means to an end, and we must at all times be in full control of them and think out the directions in which we want to go rather than become bemused and eventually enslaved by them. And since society is extremely unevenly developed throughout the world it will require good judgement as to the degree of sophistication in planning techniques which should be applied to different situations. Above all, we must never lose sight of the essential nature of the planner's contribution. He must bring to bear his creative thinking on the social and economic as well as the physical problems of our society.

Appendix 5

Local activity centres—Milton Keynes New City
Planners: Llewelyn-Davies, Weeks, Forestier-Walker & Bor

In the planning of new communities, centres of activity have been traditionally located in the geographical centre of neighbourhoods. This tends to limit people's choice, restricts social inter-action and makes it often difficult for visitors to find these centres. The principle adopted for the location of local activity centres in Milton Keynes attempts to overcome these limitations.

The local activity centres have been sited at the edge of residential areas of approximately 1 km² at the midway points between the crossings of the main roads from where they are visible and where the main pedestrian spines will cross them safely by means of underpasses (Figure 1). There will be up to four local activity centres per residential area, all within walking distance of each home within the area (Figure 2). Since these centres occur at the safe crossing point, people from adjoining areas will also be able to use them, and social inter-action between adjoining residential areas will thus be encouraged.

The type of activity to be located at each centre will vary according to local circumstances and demand. However, all will have bus stops so that a choice of four bus routes will be available within walking distance of each home. Every centre will also have a first school (children from five to eight years), so that there will be a choice of several such schools within walking distance of small children. About half of the centres will have middle schools (children from eight to twelve years). Some local activity centres will have shops and local employment (Figure 3).

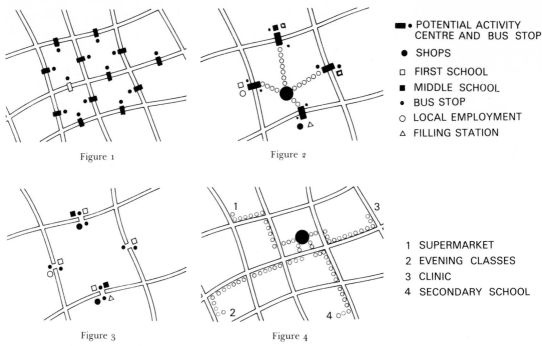

POTENTIAL ACTIVITY
CENTRE AND BUS STOP
SHOPS
FIRST SCHOOL
MIDDLE SCHOOL
BUS STOP
LOCAL EMPLOYMENT
FILLING STATION

Figure 1

Figure 2

1 SUPERMARKET
2 EVENING CLASSES
3 CLINIC
4 SECONDARY SCHOOL

Figure 3

Figure 4

Figure 1. Local activity centre location

Figure 2. One family is able to choose to use different centres for different purposes, meeting people from other neighbouring environmental areas, all within walking distance

Figure 3. Typical distribution of local activity centres

Figure 4. Choice of other activities within a short bus or car ride

Those activities which serve a wider population will be sited in several local activity centres which, like all others, will be easily accessible by private car or a frequent minibus service. These would include supermarkets, clinics and groups of three secondary schools (for 1100–1400 pupils), together with health centres and 'scarce resource' centres with special educational and recreational facilities (Figure 4).

Appendix 6

Merseyside Area Land-Use/Transportation Study (MALTS)

This study, which was jointly sponsored by the Ministry of Housing and Local Government, Ministry of Transport, six Merseyside planning authorities, British Rail and five local bus operators, commenced in 1966. The study dealt with the problems of the distribution of land uses and the associated transport system in an area extending to Formby in the north, St Helens in the east, Ellesmere Port in the south and the Wirral Peninsula (see Figure 1). The study was planned to be spread over a period of three years, at a cost of half a million pounds, and work was planned to maximize the use of local authority staffs so that there would be a transfer of know-how from the consultants (Traffic Research Corporation) to the participant local authorities. Despite a number of difficulties, the study was completed on time and nearly within its budget. Apart from dealing with the problems within the study area described, account was also taken of other factors outside the area which might affect the disposition and type of land uses and transport within the area under consideration.

Unlike a number of other land-use/transport studies, this particular exercise sought to compare a variety of land-use alternatives with a variety of transport solutions, with a view to arriving at a land-use system and a transport plan which are mutually beneficial: the objective being to obtain the greatest benefit from dealing with land use and transport as a single issue.

In the course of the study it became clear that existing commitments in terms of planning permissions granted, and developments already in hand, prevented any significant short-term flexibility. Consequently substantially varied options could only be identified in the long term (i.e. up to 1991).

Figure 1. Diagrammatic map of MALTS area showing proposed land uses and major transport links up to 1991

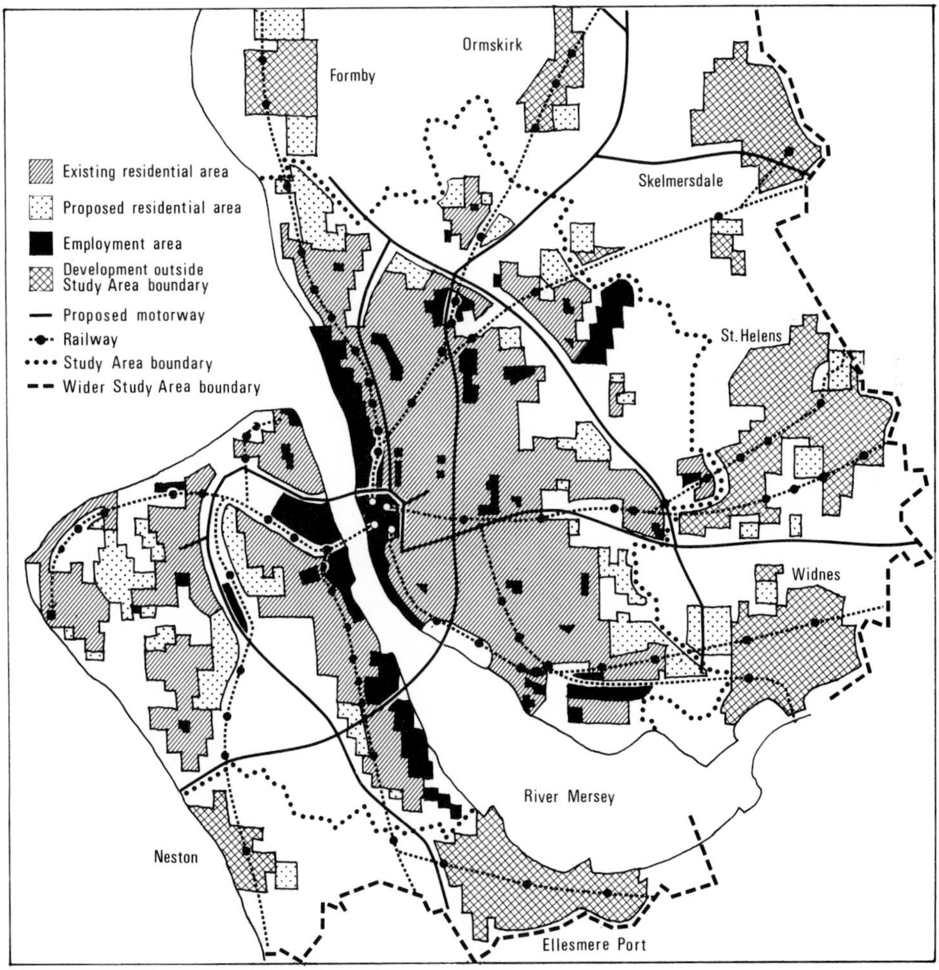

The fundamental land-use variables which were used to construct a variety of land-use hypotheses were different rates of population growth, different distributions of new residential areas and different distributions of employment. It was found that if central-area employment growth continues on a major scale, then the most efficient land-use/transport pattern was one of radial rail routes running northwards into the Lancashire Plain and into the Wirral Peninsula, forming the 'spines' of linear development on townships, each containing local facilities and some local employment. If, on the other hand, employment could be dispersed more evenly through the built-up area, especially at district centres and on the periphery, then development along the radial routes eastwards through Lancashire to St Helens and Warrington would be more efficient.

Two lessons might be drawn from the MALT study. One is that uncertainties about the probable rate of regional population growth can have serious effects upon the validity of some of the economic conclusions necessary to make a sub-regional plan. For instance, if population growth is slow, then there may not be sufficient numbers of people travelling along a particular route to justify its construction or improvement. This being so, it may be necessary either to change the plan or operate the communications system in this sector at well below the optimum economic level.

The second lesson which can be drawn from the study is that, whilst on the transport side it was relatively easy to compare the benefits and costs of one transport scheme with another, it was extremely difficult to compare in any objective way the relative merits of different land-use plans. No one plan could be shown to provide a demonstrably better or worse environment for living, work or leisure than another. Planners were therefore forced back into the position of saying that probably the best course was to produce a plan which gave the greatest variety of opportunity to the individual. At first sight this may seem technically inadequate, but if one accepts the principle that planning should aim at maximizing the human satisfaction, then it may well be that a plan with a wide range of alternatives for the individual has the greatest chance, resulting in a high proportion of the population being satisfied with its environmental conditions and range of opportunities.

Appendix 7

Selection of a preferred strategy for urbanization

A recent example of the evaluation of alternative planning strategies was the work undertaken by the planning consultants to the Commission on the Third London Airport on the proposals for an airport city to accommodate airport workers, their families and their associated service population. These airport city urbanization studies were carried out jointly by Llewelyn-Davies, Weeks, Forestier-Walker and Bor, and Shankland, Cox Associates. The consultants were asked to examine the implications of urbanization at each of the four airports sites under investigation by the Commission.

In their work, the consultants established common performance standards for the urbanization plans at all four airport sites, covering such aspects as journeys to work, acceptable aircraft noise levels, desirable densities for urban development, etc. Using these common principles, a series of alternative strategies for urbanization were developed. The strategies were then assembled and their performance was ranked against a set of comparative criteria. From an examination of these rankings the preferred pattern of urbanization was then selected.

As an example of this method, the evaluation and selection of a preferred strategy for the airport site at Nuthampstead is shown below. This site has been chosen for inclusion here because it demonstrates how one strategy can be selected from a group of eight alternative strategies.

Figure 1 illustrates the eight alternative strategies of urbanization developed for the Nuthampstead airport site. In the left column are shown the strategies in which the new urbanization is located on one side of the airport, while in the right column are shown the strategies where urbanization is on both sides of the airport site. Figure 2 shows the table used for making a comparative assessment of alternative strategies. The criteria under which the strategies were ranked are grouped into three sections. The upper section includes criteria concerning capital construction costs. The performance of a strategy under each of these criteria can be given a monetary value. The middle section includes criteria concerning transportation user costs and these also can be given a monetary value, although not such a precise value. The lower section includes criteria which cannot easily be measured in monetary terms.

The ranking and selection of these strategies were carried out in two stages. The reason for this was to enable a large number of alternative strategies to be examined easily during the first stage, as a result of which about half of the obviously less satisfactory strategies were discarded, leaving a more manageable number of the better strategies to be more closely examined and costed during the second stage of the evaluation.

In the first stage of selection, shown in Figure 2, the performance of each of the strategies was ranked on a five-point scale against a set of comparative planning criteria. No costing was carried out during this stage. Pairs of strategies were then compared criterion by criterion, and where one strategy dominated the other, by having a higher ranking for at least one criterion and no lower rankings, the dominated strategy was rejected. This process continued until about half of the less satisfactory strategies had been discarded, leaving three or four strategies, including the best strategy on transportation user costs, to be carried to the second stage of selection for comparative costing. (As a working example the procedure of pairing the strategies is described at the end of this appendix.)

At the second stage of ranking and selection, shown in Figure 3, crude estimates were made of the capital and user costs and monetary values were inserted in the table of the rankings. The strategy with the lowest total cost was then provisionally selected. The rankings for the criteria in the lower section of the table, which could not be costed, were then examined to establish whether there were any factors that might outweigh the least cost of the strategy which had been provisionally selected. As a result of this examination, which was again carried out by pairing alternative strategies and carefully comparing their performance one

43

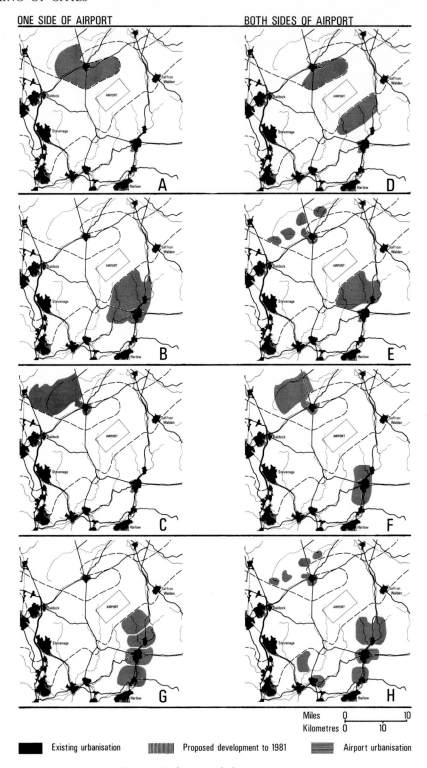

Figure 1. Nuthampstead alternative strategies

Figure 2 : Stage 1—Assessment of alternative strategies at Nuthampstead

Criteria	Strategies							
	A	B	C	D	E	F	G	H
Capital construction costs								
Site development								
Land liable to flood	+	+	−	+	+	−	+	+
Abnormal ground conditions	−	+	−	−	−	−	+	−
Preparation of an acceptable urban environment	+	o	o	+	o	o	o	o
Engineering								
Sewerage and sewage disposal	−	+	−	−	−	−	+	−
Drainage and surface water disposal	−	+	−	−	o	−	+	−
Undergrounding or diverting overhead transmission lines	+	−	+	−	−	+	o	+
Transportation								
Roads from urban areas to the airport	+	+	−	+ +	+	−	+	− −
Other roads	−	−	+	o	+	−	−	−
User costs								
Transportation								
From urban areas to the airport	o	+	−	+ +	+	− −	o	−
Elsewhere in the area	+	+	o	+	+	−	+	−
Unmeasured advantages and disadvantages								
Effect of urbanization on existing environment								
Preservation of landscape	− −	+	o	− −	+	o	+ +	+
Effect on environment of existing urban areas	o	+	−	−	o	o	+	+
Effect of existing environment on new urban areas								
Proximity to fixed installations	+	−	+	−	−	+	o	+
Suitability for housing	+	+	−	+	+	o	+	+
Access to existing recreational areas	equal							
Potential for recreational development	equal							
Contribution to new urban areas by existing urban areas	o	o	−	−	o	o	+	+
Other factors								
Proximity to noise corridor	− −	o	−	− −	o	+	+	+
Potential for long-term growth	o	+	− −	+	+	o	o	+
Barrier effect of airport on social patterns	+	+	+	− −	o	o	+	o
Provision of major service centres	−	+	o	−	+	−	−	−
Losses in agricultural production	− −	−	− −	− −	−	−	+	−

Key : + + Considerable advantages   − Some disadvantages
     + Some advantages   − − Considerable disadvantages
      o Neutral

Figure 3: Stage 2—Assessment of alternative strategies at Nuthampstead

	Strategies			
Criteria	B	D	E	G
Capital construction costs		£ million		
Site development				
Land liable to flood	ø	ø	0·1	ø
Abnormal ground conditions	ø	2·25	3·8	ø
Preparation of an acceptable urban environment		equal		
Engineering				
Sewerage and sewage disposal	ø	1·6	1·8	0·5
Drainage and surface water disposal	0·1	0·8	0·4	ø
Undergrounding or diverting overhead transmission lines	1·25	0·5	1·05	ø
Transportation				
Roads from urban areas to the airport	3·2	ø	2·2	4·6
User costs				
Transportation				
From urban areas to the airport (capitalized)	8·75	ø	7·5	12·5
Total	13·3	5·15	16·85	17·6
Unmeasured advantages and disadvantages				
Effect of urbanization on existing environment				
Preservation of landscape	+	− −	+	+ +
Effect on environment of existing urban area	+	−	o	+
Effect of existing environment on new urban areas				
Proximity of fixed installations	−	−	−	o
Suitability for housing		equal		
Access to existing recreational areas		equal		
Potential for recreational development		equal		
Contribution to new urban areas by existing urban areas	o	−	o	+
Other factors				
Proximity to noise corridor	o	− −	o	+
Potential for long-term growth	+	+	+	o
Barrier effect of airport on social patterns	+	− −	o	+
Provision for major service centres	+	−	+	−
Losses in agricultural production	−	− −	−	+

Key: + + Considerable advantages
    + Some advantages
    o Neutral
    − Some disadvantages
  − − Considerable disadvantages

Note: ø denotes alternative with lowest cost for each criteria. Figures show excess cost of other alternatives in £ million.

against the other, the less satisfactory strategies were eliminated and the preferred or best pattern of urbanization was selected. The working example of the procedure for studying the performance of pairs of strategies at the Nuthampstead site was as follows:

First stage of selection

Strategy A compared to Strategy B

Strategy A required less in the preparation of an acceptable urban environment, but this was a minor factor in this generally attractive site and was more than counter-balanced by the disadvantage of strategy A in the very important criterion of the preservation of areas of landscape value.

Strategy A had an advantage over strategy B in that it would not involve any undergrounding or diverting of overhead transmission lines, but the cost involved would be a very small proportion of the total urbanization cost.

Strategy A had an advantage over strategy B in connection with the proximity of fixed installations, but as this related only to a switching station it was considered to be a less important criterion.

Strategy A had no advantages over strategy B in any other criteria while strategy B had advantages over strategy A in many more important criteria. Strategy A was therefore eliminated.

Strategy D compared to Strategy B

Strategy D was better than strategy B in the preparation of an acceptable urban environment, but had severe disadvantages in the preservation of areas of landscape value.

Strategy D was better than all other strategies on transportation user costs, and was therefore carried forward to stage 2 for testing, as the best strategy on user costs.

Strategy C compared to Strategy B

Strategy C had obvious disadvantages over strategy B in transportation, long-term growth and development on floodland and had no advantage over strategy B in any major criteria. Strategy C was therefore eliminated.

Strategy F compared to strategy G

Strategy F was better than strategy G only on a few very minor criteria. In addition, strategy F had considerable disadvantages in transportation costs. Strategy F was therefore eliminated.

Strategy H compared to strategy G

Strategy H was better than strategy G only on a few minor criteria. It was better on potential for long-term growth, but this was considered relatively unimportant as in theory strategy G could grow to become similar to strategy H. Strategy H had major disadvantages in transportation costs. Strategy H was therefore eliminated.

Strategies B, D, E and G were carried through to the stage 2 comparative costing selection process, strategy D being the best strategy on transportation user costs.

Second stage of selection

Capital and user costs

The variation between strategies in terms of capital and user costs made strategy D the most economical and strategy G the most costly. Strategies B and E were less costly than strategy G but more costly than strategy D. The estimate for strategy D would be higher if the cost of linking the two new urban areas by highways under the central spine or around the airport site were taken into consideration.

Unmeasured criteria

Because the difference between strategies on the basis of costed criteria was not particularly marked, the unmeasured criteria assumed considerable importance in the selection procedure.

1. Preservation of areas of landscape value—strategy G had only marginal advantages over strategies B and E. Strategy D had major disadvantages.

2. Effect of new urbanization on existing environment—strategies B and G had advantages over the other strategies in this criterion, while strategy D had some disadvantages.

3. Proximity to fixed installations—strategy G was marginally better than strategies B, D and E.

4. Suitability of existing environment for residential development—there was no difference between the strategies in this factor.

5. Contribution made by existing urban areas to the new urbanization—strategy G had slight advantages over the others, especially in the initial stages of development.

6. Proximity to the noise corridor—strategies B, G and E were much the same, while strategy D had major disadvantages.

7. Potential for long-term growth—the linear form of strategy G may have some disadvantages in comparison to the others which were all equally good.

8. Barrier effect of airport on social structure of new urban areas—strategy D had severe disadvantages on this respect.

9. Provision for major centres—strategies B and E had greater possibilities for establishing a major new shopping centre by comparison with strategy D, where the divided form of the town would make it very difficult and strategy G where it would be necessary to expand the existing centre at Bishop's Stortford, or develop one or two new centres nearby.

10. Losses in agricultural production—strategy D would incur the greatest loss to agricultural production primarily from the area south-east of Royston. Strategies B and E would also involve some loss and strategy G whilst still incurring a loss to agriculture would be the least costly of any of the strategies in terms of agricultural production.

In summary, although strategy D had the lowest costs, it was eliminated by its strong disadvantages on important unmeasured criteria. Strategy G rated well on unmeasured criteria but involved the highest costs. Also the disturbance to existing towns, social upheaval, and a more costly infrastructure, gave strategy G considerable disadvantages.

Strategies B and E, which were somewhat similar, had distinct advantages over the others in that they rated well both on costs and unmeasured criteria. In addition, strategy E had some important social advantages over strategy B in giving a wider range of living environments from which to choose and could be revised to reduce the higher capital costs which could have been incurred in the northern portion. With this proviso a combination of strategies B and E was selected as the preferred strategy for urbanization at Nuthampstead.

Part 2
Politics and Urban Planning

"An enlightened citizenry, ready and capable of participating in political action and community decision-making, is the foundation of democratic self-government. Is it possible to develop political processes and voluntary associations in large cities through which a substantial proportion of the population can find meaningful participation, a sense of community responsibility, and effective control over their own decision?"

Dean Donald C. Stone

4 Political Framework

The planning of our towns and cities generally and the renewal of their worn-out areas in particular is not only a complex technical and socio-economic but also a political problem. The United States and Britain have by now gained considerable experience in the whole field of urban planning and it may therefore be of interest to compare the practice of planning in both countries, particularly from a political point of view.

In the United States, planning is still not universally accepted as being necessary or desirable, since it is bound to interfere with the rugged individualism which is part of the American way of life. Although many cities have large and well-staffed City Planning Departments, their activities, some notable exceptions like Philadelphia apart, have been limited and circumscribed by what is politically acceptable. Much of their often highly sophisticated work is research rather than action orientated.

However, concerted efforts have been made in recent years to introduce systematic and effective operational urban planning into US cities. First, special agencies were set up —Urban Renewal Agencies—to produce action-orientated plans under Federally subsidized Renewal Programs. This was followed by the Model Cities Program whereby some 150 cities were selected as 'Model Cities' because of the urgency of their urban problems, particularly with regard to the urban poor, and encouraged to submit their proposals for the socio-economic and physical upgrading of the most needy areas and for planning grants to produce action plans to that effect. Having been associated with one such application on behalf of the Negro community in Watts, Los Angeles, I gained the impression that the information and ideas expected to substantiate such submissions were not dissimilar to the planning process in operation in the UK and applicable to all its towns and cities. However, much of this planning data is required to a much greater degree of detail and accuracy to conform with Federal rules, and there is a much greater emphasis on socio-economic aspects rather than on physical planning. In addition to these Model Cities applications, immediate action or Impact Programs are being prepared which take the form of applications for Federal funds for immediate investments to alleviate urgent problems.

The 1968 Housing Act was an important step in freeing private initiative to tackle the rebuilding of the old cities and the creation of new ones. However, the first comprehensive piece of legislation dealing with urban growth policies and new community development is the Housing and Urban Development Act of 1970. This Act aims at a balanced urban growth policy for areas which demonstrate special potential for accelerated growth and includes as its goals amongst other things the reversal of migration and physical growth which reinforce disparities amongst states, regions and cities, and the comprehensive treatment of problems of poverty, employment and housing without regard to race or creed. Under this new Act the President shall transmit to Congress every two years, beginning with 1972, a Report on Urban Growth which would review the progress which has been made to implement the policies set out in the Act.

The Act encourages the establishment of new communities by making guarantees and loans available to public and private developers, which represents a considerable advance on the Housing Act of 1968. Within the Department of Housing and Urban Development a Community Development Corporation will be set up with a Secretary who will be the Chairman and four full-time members. The Secretary will encourage the formulation of plans and programmes as to where growth should take place. This new Act demonstrates clearly the will in the US to alter present patterns of growth to deal more effectively with the problems in existing towns and to create new communities, and as such is a major step towards a national planning legislation. Thus we have been witnessing, during the past decade, a strong resurgence of interest in urban affairs in the US where urban issues, especially decent housing, orderly growth and a good environment, are now high on the national agenda.

US planners have been working in exposed positions in a political climate and under commercial pressures of an almost exclusively market-orientated society which must have been many times more frustrating and inhibiting than the cumbersome but basically more open-minded situation within which their British counterparts operate. For instance, it had been realized very clearly by many US planners that the way urban renewal had been operating over the years in American cities has resulted in a worsening of the plight of the urban poor, who were gradually displaced from their homes to make room for more office space, civic centres and sometimes for better housing for those who could afford it.

Although some farsighted planners were aware of these problems and cried out in the wilderness, the majority went on producing the same kind of plans which became known as 'Negro removal'. However, even if there had been more pressure from professional planners, it would have had little effect until public opinion was ready for a change. Similarly, in the core areas of US cities, American planners had often to content themselves with such blunt planning techniques as zoning ordinances and a by-law like approach to planning, which drew fierce censures from critics like Jane Jacobs, simply because a more positive, better integrated and action-orientated approach was not politically acceptable and could not therefore be realized.

It is no coincidence that the prime movers until recently in action-orientated planning have not been the professional planners but an emerging new breed of 'advocacy planners' who have the full support of the local population on the one hand, and a Federal initiative to enhance the role of urban planning on the other. Thus a new climate of public opinion is being created in which US planners are likely to play an increasingly important role.

Traditions of local government are very different in the two countries and this has a profound effect on planning policies. When political changes take place in the USA they not only affect elected representatives but also many of the most senior officials, making continuity in policies and action fraught with difficulties. The relationship between city government and the local population is even more lacking in mutual trust than in Britain, and genuinely representative citizen participation, particularly by the urban poor, has until recently not been conspicuous. However, great changes are now taking place and the Federal Government makes, for instance, the granting of funds, particularly within the framework of the Model Cities Program, conditional upon demonstrably effective and genuine citizen participation. Yet another interesting recent feature is the emergence of 'advocacy planning' whereby groups of citizens, disenchanted with official planning proposals, hire their own planning teams to produce plans in opposition to official schemes.

The increasing realization that the established methods of urban development and redevelopment in the US have proved to be largely ineffective has led to the creation of new public authorities with powers to make things happen, as for example the Urban Development Corporation in the State of New York (see Appendix 8). Other new organizations have been created in recent years to assist communities of the poor and disadvantaged to provide themselves with the skills and services they seek. One such organization is the Centre for Community Change, whose activities are described in Appendix 9.

However, the basic difference between US and UK practice is that in the United Kingdom the legislation for and the approach to town and country planning is much more comprehensive and fully accepted by the public. The whole of the country is covered by an all-embracing planning legislation and the renewal of slums and worn-out areas is an integral part of a continuous planning process. In addition to this, there are special Slum Clearance and Housing Acts under which much of this renewal work is done. Most problems of urban renewal, especially in central areas of our cities, are primarily economic ones. Since in most non-communist European cities and certainly in all US cities central land values are extremely high, central area redevelopment can only take place if the utilization of the land and buildings can show a return which makes redevelopment financially viable. And since there are only a few uses which are sufficiently profitable to offset the high values, such as offices, shopping and possibly some entertainment like bowling alleys (though their heyday is over), central areas of Western cities have tended to be redeveloped with these uses, while residential uses, cultural and social buildings, notable exceptions apart, were either left to decay or were removed to make room for the more lucrative offices and shops. Only a few enlightened city councils have resisted this obvious temptation to secure fat rates from these new developments, and fewer still have succeeded in striking the right balance between private and public interests.

In these circumstances, the dilemma of elected local representatives is very real. They are usually harassed to provide the maximum amount of housing which has to be partly subsidized from local taxes, and anxious to achieve some physical improvements, like better roads and more parks. Local Councillors are at times driven by these pressures into the acceptance and even promotion of developments which they may not regard as 'good planning' but which would help to pay for other amenities. Thus, many decisions affecting the efficiency and attractiveness of our environment are coloured by local politics, by success or failure to enlist central government help and by a host of personal considerations. A professional planner, particularly one in a senior position such as that of a City Planning Officer, must not only be technically competent to give the best possible advice on how to reconcile conflicting interest, but must have a deep understanding of these political issues. This does not and should not mean that he ought to trim his professional advice according to the prevailing political winds. On the contrary, irrespective of these pressures, his duty is to give his objective professional advice. It does mean, however, that he must tender this advice in a way which combines professional integrity with an understanding of political realities, something, incidentally, which he is unlikely to learn in a school of planning but which he must develop as he gains experience.

The need for good planning, and much of the necessary legislation to secure it, is accepted by all major political parties in Britain and is not a party political issue, in spite of the fact that local representatives are elected on a party political basis. However, it is only natural that there are instances where party political bias favours one planning approach over another, often irrespective of its objective merit in the particular local situation. At local level, usually a plethora of different committees is responsible for different aspects of physical development, such as housing, highways, schools, parks, welfare—each of these committees anxious to make the maximum impact in its own sphere of influence. Thus we get a conflict of interests, often on the same piece of land, in financial allocations and priorities, and the overall objective of renewing an old environment and creating a new one is often distorted, if not lost altogether. For instance, since housing has usually a greater priority than the provision of open spaces and social service buildings, the emphasis has been more often than not on housing as such, leaving the creation of open spaces and the building of community facilities which should be an integral part of the housing 'till later'. There is no surer way of promoting social dissatisfaction and even vandalism than this sort of narrow, short-sighted policy.

Fortunately, however, an increasing number of local authorities have been realizing during the past few years that the activities of these individual committees must be brought together and shaped into a purposeful total effort. They are taking the logical step of setting up single executive management committees which would be responsible for all physical development and redevelopment, like the Boards of New Town Corporations, with all the other committees responsible for different aspects, subordinate to these overall executive committees.

Parallel with this there is also an urgent need at the administrative level to coordinate and progress this physical development by establishing a senior post for an officer who would be charged with these responsibilities. The Maud Report on Management in Local Government published in 1967 emphasized the need for coordination and a managerial approach to local government and saw the clerk of the authority as the chief administrator responsible for the function of securing coordination. The Report was also in favour of greater delegation of technical decisions to chief officers, to enable elected representatives to concentrate on main policy direction. Several major cities have by now adopted and implemented these and other improved management structures. An example of this is the new system adopted by the City of Liverpool, described in Appendix 10. However, since this is a recent development, we must wait some time before we can assess the success of these new management structures.

But if there is confusion and wasted effort at local level, it is even more so at national level, with different Ministries fighting each other just as committees do at the local level. Until recently there has been no one Ministry which was responsible for the total physical environment, and not infrequently individual Ministries responsible for different aspects pulled in opposite directions. Until a few years ago, for instance, the Ministry of Transport's goals in urban areas were concerned with traffic as such with little, if any, regard to planning aspects generally and to the effect on the environment in particular. Fortunately, however, the approach of this Ministry has been radically modified in recent years to broaden its concern and bring it in line with overall urban planning policies. Similarly, the policies of the Board of Trade, responsible for development certificates for industries and offices, have often been in conflict with those of the Ministry of Housing and Local Government. For instance, while the latter Ministry designates new towns, approves their plans and encourages their building, the Board of Trade may withhold development certificates for urgently needed industries in new towns if they are not in a development area, and most of them are not.

Some new towns are partly inside a development area and partly outside it, like Washington New Town, County Durham, where the industrial zoning had to be changed because one of the sites originally earmarked for industry was outside the development area.

An example of a more integrated organization at Government level in Britain has been the Scottish Development Department in which the functions of the Ministry of Housing and Local Government, the Ministry of Transport and the Board of Trade are combined.

In October 1969 a new ministerial post was created in the Labour Government, i.e. that of the Secretary of State for Local Government and Regional Planning to whom the Ministers of Housing and Local Government and Transport reported on environmental planning affecting both Ministries. Thus the first steps were taken in Britain towards greater integration of physical planning and transport.

A further welcome step in this direction was taken by the new Conservative Government when in October 1970 a Department for the Environment was created with a Secretary of State overseeing the activities of three Ministries—for Local Government and Development, for Housing and Construction, and for Transport Industries. Amongst these, from a planning point of view, the most important is the Ministry for Local Government and Development in which local government, regional, land-use and transport planning are combined for the first time. This Ministry has also responsibility for countryside and conservation, roads and road passenger transport, water sewerage and refuse disposal. However, responsibility for the nationalized transport industries, including railways, freight haulage and international aspects of inland transport are with the Ministry of Transport Industries, while new towns are with the Ministry of Housing and Construction and location of industries are altogether outside the Department for the Environment with the Ministry of Trade and Technology. Thus even in this much improved reorganization some important aspects of physical planning and transport are divorced from each other and a good deal of complex coordination will still be necessary.

Basically, however, it is the historical structure of local government in Britain which is frustrating effective planning and is in urgent need of reform. The Labour government recognized this fact by setting up a Royal Commission on local government in England in 1966 under the chairmanship of Lord Redcliffe-Maud. The Commission's Report was published in June 1969 and proposed that in England (outside London) 69 new local government areas be established. In 58 of these new areas the local authorities would be unitary authorities, i.e. they would be solely responsible for all major services. But three very large metropolitan areas around Birmingham, Liverpool and Manchester, like Greater London, have two levels of authority.

These 61 new local government areas should be grouped, with Greater London, into eight provinces each with a provincial council responsible for the provincial strategy and planning framework.

The Labour Government in its White Paper in 1970 accepted the concept of unitary and metropolitan authorities, but it proposed that England outside Greater London should be divided into 51 unitary authorities (instead of the Commission's 58) and that two areas, West Yorkshire and South Hampshire including the Isle of Wight, be added to the metropolitan authorities, making them five in all. The powers of local councils should be strengthened to give them executive responsibility for improving the local environment. The question of provincial government was, however, deferred until the Commission on the Constitution will be in a position to make their recommendations.

The Conservative Government which superseded the Labour Government after the 1970 General Election produced a White Paper in February 1971 outlining its approach to local government reform. Basically, a two-tier system is envisaged throughout the country, with 44 new counties outside Greater London, largely based on existing county boundaries. These new counties, combining urban and rural interests, will be the main executive authorities, and the towns and cities within them will function as second-tier district authorities responsible mainly for local services. Six predominantly urban or 'metropolitan' areas are proposed—three more than by the Redcliffe-Maud Commission: Merseyside, SE Lancashire/NE Cheshire, West Midlands, West Yorkshire, South Yorkshire and Tyneside/Wearside. These will be treated as single entities for major functions such as land-use/transport planning. As in the previous Government's White Paper, the question of regional authorities is referred to the Crowther Commission on the Constitution.

This approach largely confirms the historical accident of existing county boundaries which bear little relationship to the developing pattern of urbanization, abolishes what in my view have been the most effective local government units, i.e. the all-purpose county boroughs, and in an effort to preserve counties metropolitan areas are proposed which are too small to deal effectively with their problems. The resulting two-tier system of local government throughout the country is likely to have many built-in delays and frictions between upper and lower tier authorities. However, at the expense of greater efficiency this may lead to an improvement of services at the local level. At least, this is the Government's hope, whether this will prove to be the case remains to be seen.

The Conservative Government's proposed reorganization of local government, based on a two-tier system largely within existing county boundaries, is not likely to result in a local government system as suitable to respond to the changing needs of our society as that put forward by the Redcliffe-Maud Commission. However, the one over-riding policy common to both the Commission and the White Paper is to do away with the obsolete and harmful distinction between town and country and to recognize that they are one and inter-dependent. Therefore the Government's proposals, although in my view only a second-best, are still, in this and other respects, a great advance on the present structure of local government and, given the political realities, the only ones likely to be implemented, as intended, by 1974.

Appendix 8

The Urban Development Corporation

On February 27, 1968, Governor Rockefeller called on the Legislature to establish an Urban Development Corporation. The Joint Legislative Committee on Housing and Urban Development had already emphasized the need for a statewide development entity. The legislation was controversial, and the month of March was filled with discussion, debate and hearings. Many amendments were proposed—some were accepted. On April 10, 1968, after passage of the New York State Urban Development Acts of 1968, UDC was signed into law. Edward J. Logue became its first President and Executive Director.

The goal of the Urban Development Corporation is to channel and coordinate public and private resources in an effort to:

1. promote sound growth and development in our municipalities;

2. satisfy the demand for safe, sanitary and decent housing for low and moderate-income families;

3. revitalize old and attract new industry to provide jobs and combat deterioration in urban areas;

4. expand educational, recreational, cultural and other community facilities.

The UDC statute

UDC is a public benefit corporation, not unlike other agencies established in New York State during the last ten years to deal with the problems of higher education, mental health, hospital care, mass transportation and water pollution. UDC's statute authorizes:

(a) acquisition of land by purchase or condemnation;

(b) clearance of project land;

(c) the issue of notes and bonds up to $1 billion, as well as the use of other sources of public financing, such as Mitchell–Lama and Job Development Authority programmes;

(d) the sale or lease of projects to private investors, including banks and insurance companies, and leasing back projects for management purposes;

(e) the construction as well as planning of projects;

(f) the creation of subsidiary corporations;

(g) non-compliance with local land-use controls and zoning, when compliance is deemed to be infeasible or impractical;

(h) non-compliance with local building codes, when necessary. UDC is required to follow local codes except when adherence to them threatens project feasibility. To insure the health and safety of future occupants, UDC must build to the State Construction Code whenever it deviates from a local code;

(i) special tax abatements on real property. Like other publicly assisted low- and moderate-income housing projects in New York State, residential projects of UDC and its subsidiaries are given abatements from local property taxes on the value added after site acquisition.

UDC came into existence at a time when there was increasing disenchantment with the older, established methods of urban development and redevelopment, such as public housing, urban renewal and city planning. Its basic mission is to improve the physical environment for low- and moderate-income families, and to improve their job opportunities. As a State agency, UDC's territory is all of New York; it does not stop at city lines, as nearly all other urban programmes do. This coincides with an increasing recognition that solutions to urban problems must be found in the wider metropolitan context.

In its brief span of existence, UDC has put dozens of projects into its pipeline. Indeed, the complete development of every project now being worked on would fully commit the entire initial $1 billion bond authorization.

For 1970 the UDC are aiming to start construction on approximately 10 000 housing units, at an estimated total cost in excess of $300 million, in communities from one end of the State to the other.

The UDC legislation highlights the particular importance of the private sector by calling for the sale or lease of UDC's interest in projects to private enterprise at the earliest feasible time. Clearly, private capital, private entrepreneurs and private experience are crucial if the residents of the State of New York are to receive optimum benefits from UDC.

Guidelines

UDC have evolved some basic policies which guide their activities. In all communities in which UDC is active, it has a working partnership with local civic leaders, local public officials, local community residents and local developers.

UDC housing seeks to provide for a cross-section of age groups and income levels in a diversified community, where the elderly are not isolated from the young. UDC's housing policy has led to a 70:20:10 formula—70 per cent of all housing units on a particular site for middle- and moderate-income families, 20 per cent for low-income families and 10 percent for the elderly. This housing mix may vary, depending on the project and local needs.

Much public and publicly assisted housing has a dreary, institutional appearance and atmosphere. UDC believes that this is unnecessary and that with some effort good design can be achieved on any project. Such an effort will yield both short- and long-run dividends for both the community and its residents. UDC will not attempt to perform functions that other public or private entities can do as well, such as construction or management activities, if others can do the job.

UDC's role is primarily catalytic. After it has done its part, UDC will turn projects over to private enterprise for fees sufficient to keep it self-liquidating. Thus, private enterprise will clearly have the major role envisioned by the statute.

A practical example of the kind of activities which UDC is engaged in is the development of a new community at Amherst, near Buffalo, as described in Appendix 26.

Appendix 9

Center for Community Change

The Center for Community Change, with its headquarters in Washington, DC, is a non-profit corporation established to assist in the development of self-sufficient community organizations.

The Center for Community Change will provide an overall coordinated framework for the delivery of the various technical and professional services necessary to the creation and continued functioning of successful community organizations.

These will range from staff and leadership training and programme development to the creation of a sophistication necessary to shape and manage the economic and physical development of the community. The nature of the services extended to a community will be tailored to fit the local organization's needs and its stage of development. In every case the primary objective of the Center is to enable the members and leaders of the community to develop the ability to achieve their goals.

The Centre began operations by working with the following six community groups:
1. Mississippi Action for Community Education (MACE)—which is building local community organizations in twelve Mississippi Delta Counties by training local leadership and assisting organizations to design and operate economic, education and social projects.
2. National Farm Workers Service Centre (NFWSC), Delano, California—which is training community organizers and paraprofessionals to operate social service programmes for migrant labourers.

3. The East Los Angeles Community Union (TELACU)—which is building community-owned businesses and housing projects in a Mexican-American section of Los Angeles.

4. Watts Labor Community Action Committee (WLCAC)—which has a well-established record of manpower, economic development and housing programmes in the Watts area of Los Angeles.

5. The Woodlawn Organization (TWO), Chicago, Illinois—which is training indigenous leaders to develop and manage housing and economic development projects.

6. North Jersey Community Union (NJCU), Newark, New Jersey—which is concentrating on youth and manpower programmes and the development of black contractors.

The Center for Community Change is organized, through the Citizens Advocate Center to assure equitable treatment of all community organizations in their dealing with the government. It will constantly monitor governmental programmes, their regulations, their procedures and their administration. It will seek to demonstrate the need for a permanent public or quasi-public agency to serve as an impartial monitor between the community with a grievance and the governmental agency.

Through the Social Development Corporation particularly, the Center will encourage innovative projects of job development, training and retraining, and the restructuring of occupations in vital human services such as health and medical care. The projects will aim at expanding job horizons for the disadvantaged worker and, at the same time, improve the delivery of much needed services to the public.

Through the New Community Press, it will also spotlight central issues in the areas of its activities, expose to public view the problems which exist, and publish new and constructive ideas and programmes to attack the causes of poverty and stimulate change.

Appendix 10

New Liverpool management structure

Liverpool Corporation has acted on a report from McKinsey and Company Inc., Management Consultants, and has reorganized the Council's committees and departments according to their recommendations.

McKinsey's point out that in the next ten years the Corporation can expect a revenue expenditure of some £1000 million and that there were limitations in the Corporation's structure of 23 committees, plus sub-committees and 25 departments which existed before 1 May 1969, and in the new structure of ten committees introduced on that date. These limitations are difficulties in fixing priorities and in controlling effectiveness.

It is proposed to introduce a system of programme planning and budgeting and to reconstitute the committees on the basis of programme areas as shown in Figure 1. Each area has been designed to bring together those functions of local government which can collectively achieve sets of inter-related objectives.

In terms of staff and departmental organization, the proposals are radical. There is to be a Chief Executive Officer assisted by a Director of Programme Planning, a tier of executive staff and functional heads, and a tier of programme directors, as shown in Figure 2. Post descriptions for the Chief Executive and the 12 other officers (commonly referred to as the 12 apostles) are summarized in the executive and functional tier in Figure 3. The responsibilities of the programme directors are similar to those of the six programme committees set out in Figure 1.

Programming (the grouping of specific objectives), planning (the development of the strategy of achievement) and budgeting (the control of performance and efficiency in the achievement of objectives) are terms which in this context have meanings which are different from those familiar to many physical planners, but which are intended to be equally applicable to all the programme areas.

It is intended that the technique of management by objectives shall be applied to all levels of Corporation activity. McKinsey's propose that major policy objectives shall be determined by the Policy Committee advised by the Chief Executive, the City Treasurer, the City Planning Officer, the appropriate Programme Director and any other principal officer directly concerned. Programme Committees will make decisions on secondary objectives advised by a similar group and will normally implement their programmes on the advice of the Programme Directors.

The McKinsey report proposes the grouping of several departments or parts of existing departments under the Programme Directors, the executive staff and functional heads, and have emphasized that the Programme Directors should be appointed on the basis of management ability and that they need not have professional experience or qualifications.

The purpose and scope of three posts are worth particular mention because they have far-reaching implications for planners and architects. Firstly, the City Planning Department, directed by Francis Amos since 1966, is to provide a Corporation-wide information service, and is to be the principal adviser on the physical, social and economic development of the city. This role will provide the Corporation with a service for a comprehensive approach to all developmental activities. A group of services is recommended in the Seebohm Report ('Report of the Committee on Local Authority and Allied Personnel Social Services' published in 1968). These can thus be coordinated in terms of service and accommodation with education, leisure programmes and physical development. Similarly plans for economic growth of the area can be used as a means of increasing and allocating resources for other programmes.

Secondly, the Programme Planning Department is essentially concerned with budgetary measures and the achievement of high performance standards. Inevitably this Department

PROPOSED COMMITTEE STRUCTURE AND PROGRAMME RESPONSIBILITIES

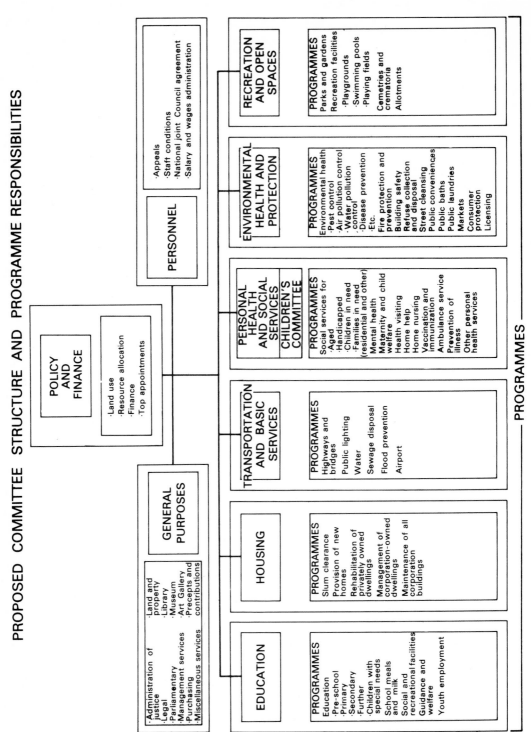

Figure 1

PROPOSED PERMANENT STAFF STRUCTURE

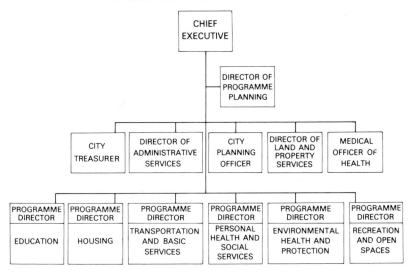

Figure 2

PROPOSED PERMANENT STAFF ORGANIZATION
STAFF AND FUNCTIONAL RESPONSIBILITIES

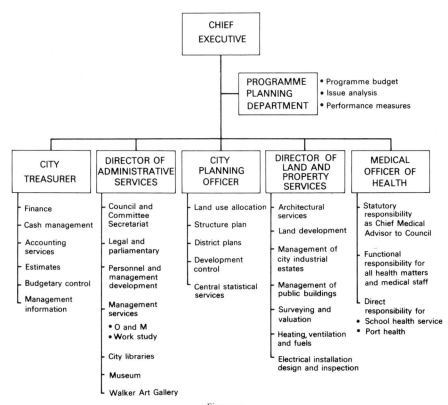

Figure 3

will work closely with the City Planning Department, but its influence over strategic or local policies affecting physical, social or economic development will be confined to determining the restraints of resource availability and continuously assessing the effectiveness of plans.

Thirdly, the Land and Property Service Department will embrace the existing department of the City Architect and parts of the departments of the Director of Housing, City Estates Surveyor, City Electrical Engineer, City Baths, Laundries and Fuels Officer. This means that all these officers will be under a Programme Director, who may be an administrator or a qualified man of any profession, provided that he has management ability.

5 Towards a Greater Public Participation in Planning

Until a decade or so ago people did not appear to care, or at least there was insufficient evidence that they were seriously concerned, about the planning of their environment. But in Britain the last ten years or so have seen a radical change in this attitude. Groups of citizens, frustrated or dissatisfied with the official efforts or the lack of them, have come forward with positive suggestions. One of the main catalysts of this new environmental consciousness has been the Civic Trust and its regional offices.

According to the Civic Trust, there are now over 700 civic societies in the country, 400 of which have been formed in the last ten years, and new such societies came into being at the rate of one a week between 1968 and 1970. The Trust itself has considerably expanded its activities which started originally with 'face-lifting schemes' whereby the Trust organized the cooperation of private owners and local councils in repainting schemes and removal of litter according to concepts worked out by architects. These schemes became very popular indeed, so much so that criticisms were voiced that this was only a superficial way of dealing with much more complex problems. The Civic Trust, realizing that these schemes, however desirable and successful, had only a limited value, proceeded to embark on a series of much more ambitious and comprehensive schemes, all concerned with raising the quality of the environment. Examples of this are the Reports dealing with tree planting, the Rhondda Valley Rehabilitation, the Lea Valley Recreational Parks and North-West Region 'Operation Spring Clean'. A start had been made in opening people's eyes to their surroundings and giving them a new confidence in their power to do something about it.

It should be remembered, however, that these groups of civic-minded people consist mainly of articulate middle-class individuals and the other groups have so far not shown any marked interest, although this may well change in the future. In Liverpool, for instance, recent years have seen a dramatic increase in participation at the local level by working people in the lower-income bracket.

One of the major recommendations of the Planning Advisory Group was that there should be greater participation in the planning process. The Minister of Housing and Local Government, in accepting these recommendations, set up the Committee on Public Participation and Planning under the chairmanship of A. M. Skeffington, MP, to consider ways in which the community might make a greater contribution to the formulation of development plans for their areas. What is involved is nothing less than effective public participation in the planning process from the initial goal-setting stage right through to the evaluation of final proposals, their implementation and subsequent reviews of previous planning proposals.

The Skeffington Committee's Report 'People and Planning' was published in July 1969 and its main recommendations for public participation in planning are:

1. People should be kept informed throughout the preparation of a structure or local plan for their area by a variety of methods and the cooperation of the local press and broadcasting should be secured.

2. When the decision is made that a plan should be prepared, the authority should inform the public, and should propose a time-table showing the main opportunities for participation and the causes for their consideration.

3. Representations should be considered continuously as they are made while plans are being prepared. Local planning authorities should concentrate their efforts to secure participation at the presentation following surveys of the choices which are open to the authority in deciding the main planning issues for the area, and the presentation of a statement of proposals for the area. Where alternative courses are available, the authority should put them to the public and say which it prefers and why.

4. Local planning authorities should consider convening meetings in their area for the purpose of setting up community forums. These forums would provide local organizations with the opportunity to discuss collectively planning and other issues of importance to the area.

5. Local planning authorities should seek to publicize proposals in a way that informs people living in the area in question and should be directed to organizations and individuals to enable those wishing to participate in depth to do so.

6. Community development officers should be appointed to secure the involvement of those people who do not join organizations. Their job would be to work with people, to stimulate discussion, to inform people and give their views to the authority.

7. The public should be told what their representations have achieved or why they have not been accepted.

8. People should be encouraged to participate in the preparation of plans by helping with surveys and other activities as well as by making comments.

9. Greater efforts should be made to provide more information and better education about planning generally, both through educational establishments and for the public at large.

The report illustrates with a flow chart how this public involvement in the planning process would work, both for the strategic structure plan and for the local plan. Although during the preparation of the local plan the public, through their local societies, is expected to take an even more active part, basically the procedure envisaged for the structure and local plans is similar, and runs as follows: the intention to prepare a plan is announced, planners collect data by physical surveys as well as interviews and questionnaires, analyse the data, discuss and comment, publish the survey report together with definition of objectives and sketches of alternative plans, and possibly indicate preferred solution. At this stage the public is invited to view the proposals and hear them explained, to comment on alternatives and submit representations. These are then considered, a preferred plan is selected on the basis of comments, developed in depth and published. Whereas the structure plan would then be submitted to the Minister for approval, and if objections are received would then be subjected to a public inquiry, the local plan would go directly to such an inquiry.

In order to make such public participation fully effective, an appropriate machinery must be set up. In addition to local public meetings on a ward or area basis, schools, colleges, and a variety of organizations should be informed of the broad aims of the authority's policy, and asked to submit comments and suggestions. At the same time publicity should be given to the survey data as they become available, so that an awareness of the factual background of the process can be created. It is important to make this information clearly comprehensible to the lay public and to avoid giving the impression that it is being 'blinded with science'.

Of special importance is the feed-back from the public in response to proposals put to it. Hence the public must be convinced that its reactions are of interest and concern to the authority. For instance, individual comments on exhibitions should be encouraged by questionnaires and interviews, and discussion meetings organized in conjunction with exhibitions and extensive press, radio and television coverage should inform the public fully about proposals.

Successful examples of these methods have been the extensive public participation in the planning of Coventry, the exhibitions of the Liverpool City Planning Proposals, of the Barnsbury Study and of the Piccadilly Redevelopment, where much effort and imagination was devoted to the clear and easily understandable presentation of the proposals. One

This Liverpool City Centre Model formed part of an exhibition which was staged to inform the public and seek its comments in 1966. A tape-recorded description of individual features which light up as they are described is being listened to by several visitors in the background. Over 150 000 people visited this exhibition

of the most recent instances was the interim plan for the new city of Milton Keynes, which was presented in the form of a travelling exhibition and taken to 20 community centres or large halls and schools throughout the designated area and the adjoining communities and discussed with local residents (see Appendix 11).

However, as the Skeffington Report points out, the problem is basically one of public education. A concerted effort should be made throughout the curricula of elementary and secondary schools and universities to concentrate attention on urban issues. In addition, special education programmes should be organized for elected representatives, business leaders and public administrators to inform them in depth about urban planning problems and opportunities. However, more important still, the public should not only be continuously informed but genuinely consulted about current planning issues and evolving planning policies.

Since effective public participation takes a lot of time and effort, planning authorities will have to devote much more financial and staff resources to this end than they have done in the past. Not only will they require more staff, but the personnel involved in this work should be specially trained in the principles and techniques of public participation.

However, greatly welcome as the move towards greater public participation in planning is, there is a danger that, if not fully thought through, it could become counter-productive. First, the public must realize that its involvement is bound to lead to more delays at a time when there is already much criticism of delays caused by planning. Next, the whole problem of blight must be faced squarely: any planning proposals which are published and affect adversely people's property could result in their inability to sell and thus incur serious losses for which they must be compensated. More important still is the need for public participation to be genuine and effective. If it were seen by planning authorities merely as a public relations exercise whereby people are merely informed of what is being planned for them without seriously taking their views into account, it could lead to much frustration and bitterness. However, perhaps the most difficult problem will be to effect genuine representation of local communities. For instance, it is usual for those who object to any particular planning proposal to shout loudest while those who benefit from it tend to keep quiet. The situation can therefore arise when an overwhelming majority would greatly benefit by the implementation of planning proposals but action is stopped by a small but articulate minority. Unless the decision makers have the courage to make balanced judgements even if it involves antagonizing a minority, all positive planning in the interest of the community as a whole could be frustrated.

While citizen participation is a relatively recent development in Britain, it has been in existence for some time in the United States. The requirements for citizen participation established by law for Model Cities and Urban Renewal are as follows:

The Housing and Urban Development Department will not determine the ideal organizational pattern to accomplish public participation. It has, however, outlined performance standards for citizen participation which must be achieved by each Citizen Development Agency (CDA). It is expected that patterns will vary from city to city, reflecting local circumstances. The city government, as the principal instrument for carrying out the Model

Cities Program, will be responsible for insuring that whatever organization is adopted provides the means for the Model Neighbourhood citizens to participate and to be fully involved in policy making, planning, and the execution of all programme elements. For a plan to be approved, it must provide for such an organization and spell out precisely how the participation and involvement of the residents is to be carried out throughout the life of the Model Cities Program.

In order to provide for the citizen participation called for in the Act, there must be some form of organization structure, existing or newly established, which involves neighbourhood residents in the process of policy and programme planning and programme implementation and operation. The leadership of that structure must consist of persons whom neighbourhood residents accept as representing their interests.

The neighbourhood citizen participation structure must have clear and direct access to the decision-making process of the CDA so that neighbourhood views can influence policy, planning and programme decisions. That structure must have sufficient information about any matter to be decided, for a sufficient period of time, so that it can initiate proposals and react knowledgeably to proposals from others. In order to initiate and react intelligently in programme matters, the structure must have the technical capacity for making knowledgeable decisions. This will mean that some form of professional technical assistance, in a manner agreed to by neighbourhood residents, shall be provided. An example of this is a planning workbook for the community prepared by the Research Centre for Urban and Regional Planning at Princeton University (see Appendix 12).

Where financial problems are a barrier to effective participation, financial assistance (e.g. baby-sitting fees, reimbursement for transportation, compensation for serving on boards or committees) should be extended to neighbourhood residents to assure their opportunity to participate.

Neighbourhood residents will be employed in planning activities and in the execution of the programme with a view toward development of new career lines of occupational advancement, including appropriate training and modification of local civil service regulations for job entry and promotion.

This law about citizen participation has resulted in a situation where in most community planning operations it is taken for granted that the local elements of the community are represented. This applies particularly to the black community, since they live in the areas where most of the Urban Renewal or Model Cities Program are taking place. It is of course intended that the boards will be representative of the opinion of the whole community. This, however, is not necessarily the case in practice. Very often the question of participation turns into a question of power. For instance, a recent meeting to present the New York Master Plan, where there were some 2000 people waiting for presentation of the proposals, was broken up by 50 militants, most of whom were black, who stormed into the meeting and systematically broke up each discussion group. They said that they had not been consulted in the preparation of the New York Master Plan and therefore they were not going to allow the meeting to proceed.

The real difficulty is defining what the communities' interests are and who really represents them. For instance, a conservative white community's reaction to proposals for social and racial integration in housing would be to veto the intention to provide housing for lower-income blacks in the area. Yet it may be for the common good to encourage the building of suburban housing near to employment for low-income minority groups. But, the community representing, in this case, a conservative white majority would not agree to this. Who, therefore, represents the real interests of 'the community' ?

Appendix 11

Public participation in response to the interim proposals for Milton Keynes

Preparation for the public presentation of the interim proposals for Milton Keynes began some time before the Skeffington Committee presented its report 'People and Planning', but many of the ideas put forward concerning the Milton Keynes exercise are in full accord with the Committee's recommendations.

The Skeffington report did not, however, cover the planning of new towns where the existing population at designation is only a small part of the target population of a new town and where, for migration to occur at all, major decisions regarding housing, roads, industry, recreation, etc., have to be made in advance of the arrival of new residents.

Of the target population of quarter of a million for Milton Keynes only about 40 000 lived in the area at the time of designation. In so far as they represented a public to be directly and immediately affected by the planning proposals for the new city, these could and should be presented to them for information and comment. This population also included a large number of immigrants to the area, either through the town expansion scheme at Bletchley within the designated area or through the improvement of commuter services to London. As representatives of certain interests and views likely to be evident amongst future immigrants, particularly those arriving during the early years of growth, it was reasonable to suppose that the views of this newer section of the population would have longer-term validity.

Although in the more general proposals on public participation described in the plan a variety of means such as the household survey or the 'consumer panel' were proposed, it was decided that participation at the interim stage should take place by means of public meetings and questionnaires.

The questionnaire was seen to provide an opportunity for reaction to those unable or unwilling to attend public meetings and to allow some private reflection and discussion before views were put forward. The public meeting was seen to be a valuable means for planners to inform the local public in a personal and immediate way of their work, and respond similarly to questions, criticism and suggestions put to them by the public. It was also seen as a way to identify public officials and reduce the facelessness of those authorities which were to affect the lives of local people in such a radical way.

Twenty-five local public meetings were held to obtain public reaction to the interim proposals and a similar series of meetings was arranged for the presentation of the final plan. Announcement of the meetings was made beforehand by public advertisement and the press, which gave supplementary coverage of the proposals, throughout the exercise, and a short popular booklet on the proposals, a time-table of meetings and a simple questionnaire was delivered to every household in the designated area.

At almost all the meetings attendance was high, and at a number of meetings people unable to obtain seats remained standing throughout their duration of two hours or more. Representatives of the Board, the Corporation and the planning consultants comprised the the platform and the programme consisted of an introduction by the chairman of the meeting, a description of the proposals and a question and answer period. Exhibition material was available for viewing both before and after each meeting. At the end of the programme those of the audience who had not already done so were invited to complete questionnaires identical to those delivered throughout the designated area. These called for a few basic personal details in addition to general reactions to the proposals. Many of the meetings concluded with spontaneous informal discussion between members of the platform and the public.

Altogether just over three thousand people attended the meetings, which on the basis of assumptions on multiple attendance and residential location, was estimated as about 12 per cent of the total adult population of the designated area. Though seemingly low, this proportion is well above that at which many electoral or other political meetings, for example, are considered to have been successful in their attendance figures.

Nevertheless the non-attendance of a large proportion of the public at meetings specifically held to encourage their participation will continue to be a common problem in the planning process as a whole. Clearly where non-involvement is a matter of choice, planning authorities can exercise no compulsion, but where such opportunities are not taken advantage of for other reasons it will remain the responsibility of the planning authorities to explore other means of encouraging participation.

The several hundred questions put to the public meetings, not all of which related directly to the planning proposals (some concerned long-standing local issues), have been analysed in depth in 'The Plan for Milton Keynes, Technical Supplement No 2: The Presentation of the Interim Proposals', and it is not appropriate to consider them in detail here. In general, however, they fell into the following main categories.

1. Those requiring simple factual answers.

2. Those requiring technical answers.

3. Those requiring assurances that certain physical factors had been taken into account.

4. Those requiring assurances that certain individual and social factors had been taken into account.

5. Those strictly relating to new city policy.

6. Those relating to the provision of special facilities.

Many of the questions were in fact fully covered in the interim report. This is not to criticize questioners for not having read the report, indeed it probably reinforces the demand for reports aimed more positively at lay readers. However, the fact that these questions were put suggests that they should have been anticipated over the whole range of issues with which the proposals were concerned, and this was not the case.

Such omissions underline the importance, in any exercise in public participation, of the planners' responsibility to expose proposals and their implications as fully as possible and in anticipation of the public's lack of awareness that some issues have implications beyond common understanding and knowledge.

Replies to the questionnaires, made available throughout the designated area and at all public meetings, had a slightly different overall emphasis to the questions put at the meetings possibly because of the greater opportunity which they gave for reflection and considered comment, and a wider range of reaction was possible than in a single question put to a public meeting. Thus a respondent could concern himself with several issues in writing but usually confined himself to a single issue in open question time. (These replies to questionnaires are also analysed in depth in Technical Supplement No 2, to the Milton Keynes Plan.)

In presenting the interim proposals to the public the Milton Keynes Development Corporation declared its intention to take full account of public reaction in the preparation of the plan and its implementation. In those fields where its own action can be effective in allaying fears or meeting hopes it will be able to meet this responsibility directly. Where it is not itself responsible for certain effects such as the quality and extent of various services within the city it can bring public reaction to the notice of the responsible authorities. However, a number of issues were raised at the meetings on which the Corporation cannot act even indirectly since they concerned national or regional policy; and it will remain a task common to all planning authorities, firstly to make clear to a given public the nature and limits of their power to respond to public reaction and, secondly, to bring to the notice, of those in a position to influence them, wider issues (such as national housing policies) about which concern has been expressed.

Appendix 12

Planning workbook for the community

This abstract is based on an article by John Morris Dixon in *Forum*, December 1969.

The Research Centre for Urban and Environmental Planning at Princeton University prepared a 592 loose-leaf page workbook for the State of New Jersey which is the first serious effort to provide for community participants a tool for understanding planning.

To quote its opening paragraphs, the purpose of the workbook is:

"The Planning and Design Workbook is for people who want to take action to make a better life in their community and in their housing. You can use the instructions and information in this book to help you decide what changes you would like to make. . . . "When you use the Workbook, you will be able . . . to make concrete and detailed proposals which describe the specific changes you believe are needed. You will be able to work more effectively with the many officials and professionals who are involved in carrying out any proposal for change."

The book consists of four parts: a 'how-to-use-it' introduction, a section on 'community activity planning', a section on 'site planning' and one on the 'dwelling unit'. Although

Figure 1. Visual index of typical site-planning alternatives

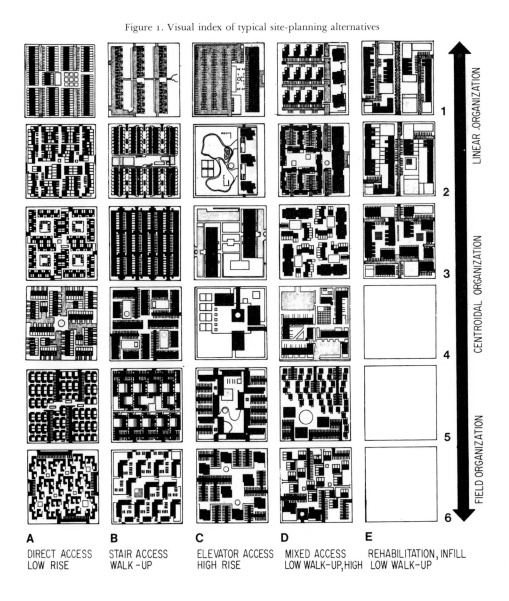

A DIRECT ACCESS LOW RISE

B STAIR ACCESS WALK-UP

C ELEVATOR ACCESS HIGH RISE

D MIXED ACCESS LOW WALK-UP, HIGH

E REHABILITATION, INFILL LOW WALK-UP

all these aspects are explained in layman's terms, it is recognized that any group of interested laymen using the book would probably have a trained adviser or professional consultant.

After the introductory Part I, in each of the planning parts of the book the process begins with identifying issues—'What problems do you want to work on?'—and agreeing on policies for each—'What actions do you want to take to solve your problems?' An extensive list of sample issues is provided, along with alternative policies for each, and some indication of 'results' to be expected from each. The group is then asked to assign priorities to their policies—'How important is each of the actions you wish to take?'

They are then asked to consider a selection of planning solutions—'How have other groups tried to solve the same problems you are working on?' These representative solutions are abstracted so that they can be compared and presented in sections labelled 'catalogues'. For the most part, the catalogue entries are the same prototype solutions that planners and architects carry—or ought to carry—in their heads (see Figure 1).

After considering the pros and cons of catalogue examples, the group is asked to prepare a proposal and analyse it and then, if they deem it necessary, to draw up alternative proposals and evaluate them before making a final selection.

6 Monitoring and Evaluation

If planning in the future is to be guided to a greater extent than in the past by clear and explicit goals or objectives, then an integral part of this process is the measurement of achievement against intention, and the objective appraisal of methods and policies used. This kind of assessment has come to be commonly described as Monitoring and Evaluation and can be defined in the following way:

Monitoring is the periodic recording of selected information to show how a system of plans and policies is performing in the achievement of its stated objectives. The concept of monitoring is that of continuous testing of and feed-back to any plan. It therefore implies a reinterpretation of the decision-making process. A check would be made from the inception of a plan to its completion to ensure that the initial bases for the plan still existed and that it was, in fact, achieving what had been intended. Section 1 of the 1968 Town and Country Planning Act makes monitoring of relevant changes obligatory.

Evaluation is the comparison of the effects or implications of plans against their original objectives, intentions or expectations. Evaluation can occur before plans are implemented, as a method of selecting a best alternative, or after implementation as an assessment of results. Evaluation implies 'putting a value' or 'passing a judgment' on an event whether real or hypothetical against some standard of expected performance or output. Thus evaluation depends both on adequate monitoring and on the availability of output standards. These though politically and technically difficult to establish are essential to the processes of monitoring and evaluation.

Monitoring implies that evaluation must become a continuing process, evolving with the plan to which it relates. It also implies a continuous examination and possible redefinition of the goals and objectives. Improvement of the quality of planning depends on evaluation before as well as after a proposal is implemented. Thus we are progressing towards a situation where assessment of results will be made on 'outputs' rather than 'inputs' from planners. In the past it has been customary to account for local authority or governmental

77

services in terms of the resources allocated to them rather than in the effect of applying these resources in various ways: that is by 'inputs' rather than 'outputs' as in the measurement of housing by numbers of dwellings built rather than the way in which houses of different kinds have met the needs of various family types and life styles.

The idea of testing the value of an activity by looking at its effect in this way has in the past been more readily accepted in other fields than planning. Business firms, for example, tend as a matter of course to measure success or failure by appraising the extent to which their activities achieve particular objectives, whether these be a certain profit level, a change in market shares or a given rate of growth.

Very few government programmes or city services have so far been put to such tests, although recent attempts have been made to use work load as an indirect measure of output, for example in relating the number of children to teachers in a school, or the number of patients treated by a given staff complement in a hospital. Although these have given a better measure than input measures such as the number of school places or the number of hospital beds provided, they remain inadequate since they still fail to measure the quality of service provided and the degree of satisfaction given to its consumers. While moves are under way to widen the application of monitoring and evaluation, these techniques are by no means yet widespread even outside planning. The system of PPB (Planning Programme and Budgeting), developed in the United States and now beginning to be applied in Britain, does however represent a disciplined and analytical approach to the clarification of policy objectives and selection from them on the basis of a quantitative analysis of the costs and benefits involved. The fundamental problem of assessing plans and policies in such a structured and systematic way is that of finding acceptable measures of their success. The problem will be particularly acute in planning which covers such a wide and diffuse range of economic, social and physical, as well as political, factors.

Work is in progress, however, both in Britain and the United States to develop a series of indicators of the effectiveness of policies in various fields. Similar studies are required in the field of planning in order to develop a satisfactory programme of monitoring and evaluation for any particular planning programme. The tests through which such a programme would be put would need to vary according to its nature. Cost-benefit studies could be effective if the programme involved fairly clear tangible factors as in engineering or physical building programmes for examples, whereas in more socially based programmes criteria would have to be established through various consumer assessment techniques such as opinion polls, household surveys, panels of experts and consumer committees.

Part 3

Urban Living and Movement

7 Housing in Different Urban Contexts

Essentially our cities are places where people live and work. Before the industrial revolution there was little physical distinction between these two basic functions and people as a rule lived on top of their place of work. However, as the work places grew in size and importance during the 19th century, large industrial areas were developed, separate from housing and living, and work places became increasingly divorced. Furthermore, as a result of the shift from factory work to employment in offices and shops in the course of this century, housing in city centres was being displaced by commerce to a growing extent. The City of London, for instance, which at one time housed within its square mile the whole of London's population of several hundred thousand people, had after the war only a population of some 5000 people, mostly caretakers. Thus the centres of our cities have become increasingly depopulated. This applies particularly to US cities but has also become a feature of city centres in the UK. On the continent of Europe, however, because of the greater readiness of people to live in high-density blocks of flats, the residential component in many city centres is still strong.

Living in or near city centres enables more people to live close to the greatest concentration of employment and the best provision of shopping, educational, cultural and recreational activities. It reduces commuting and may even obviate the need for a car, which in any case will be difficult and costly to park. This way of life is likely to be more suited to the single person of all ages or to couples who are either childless or whose children have grown up. It is likely to be less suitable for the young family with small children who may have to suffer many necessary restrictions without being old enough to appreciate the advantages of city-centre living. Such families are better catered for in lower density housing with gardens and ample space for children's play and the parked car; the ebbing out of families from the inner areas of our cities and the flooding in of single people is evidence for this. Thus, during different periods of our lives we may well choose to live in different parts of our cities according to our special requirement at that time. Conversely, some people may wish to opt for higher or lower density living contrary to general trends because they consciously trade off the inherent advantages and disadvantages by according priorities which may differ from the preferences of the majority. What is important, however, is to recognize that different forms of urban living are sought and must be provided and that all of them must be of a quality which would ensure human satisfaction.

City-centre housing

Increasingly, the choice and availability of city-centre housing is being narrowed. Some older tenement blocks and other sub-standard housing which has remained provides privately rented homes, flats for subsidized tenants and the poor, while, at the other end of the scale, older small-scale properties originally housing people from different income groups are being taken over for smart conversions by the well-to-do or are being pulled down to make room for luxury apartments. In this way, our city centres have changed radically from places where a representative cross-section of the community lived to predominantly commercial areas with a residue of housing for the rich and mere shelters for the poor.

Sunderland Town Centre. Residential tower blocks on top of a pedestrian shopping precinct provide small flats for single people and childless couples who prefer to live in the town centre. Architects: Llewelyn-Davis, Weeks, Forestier-Walker & Bor. *Photo: Henk Snoek*

However, recent years have seen some attempts at redressing the balance. Because of the considerable financial returns which well-considered city-centre redevelopment schemes can yield, it has again become feasible to reintroduce a residential component into these commercial redevelopments, particularly where such a redevelopment is carried out by the local authority in partnership with private enterprise. A typical example of such a combined redevelopment scheme was recently completed in Sunderland. County Durham, a relatively modest attempt to bring back housing into our city centres. However, one of the most outstanding examples of this operation on a massive scale is the Barbican development in the City of London where homes for some 6000 people are being built as part of a comprehensive redevelopment of 40 acres in the heart of London (see Appendix 13). The densities and rents are of necessity very high and restrict this new housing to people who can afford this way of life.

Housing in the inner areas

The inner areas which adjoin the centres of our cities contain a housing stock much of which as a rule dates back to the last century. Some of this housing has still many years of useful life and could be brought up to modern standards while housing in other areas has to be pulled down and redeveloped. Land in existing towns and cities is expensive and the nearer the city centre the more costly it is. Local authorities are therefore obliged to put as many dwellings as possible on this expensive land in order to bring down the cost of land per dwelling. Because of these high land values, local authorities have found it necessary to redevelop at high densities (between 130 and 200 persons per acre) and these developments have tended to take the form of high residential blocks. However, the social dissatisfaction and high costs of construction have led to a consideration of alternative forms of high-density development resulting in more compact housing without recourse to very high blocks. An example of such a development is the Lillington Street Housing by Westminster City Council.

However, even the most enlightened housing development cannot meet all the social needs unless it is fully integrated with those social, education and recreational facilities which are an integral part of housing. It is true, of course, that in theory new housing is being planned to relate to these facilities, but in practice the housing component has to be inserted often into an existing urban fabric which may be lacking in one or the other, or even all these facilities; it is then extremely difficult to provide the buildings for social and educational functions and the open spaces in phase with the new housing.

There are notable exceptions to this where housing was built as part of comprehensive redevelopment as, for instance, in the East End of London where, as a result of heavy war damage, an area of some 2000 acres was so devastated as to be declared a Comprehensive Development Area (Stepney / Poplar CDA) and the then London County Council

Lillington Street Housing, Pimlico, London. One of the interlocking residential squares with a 19th-century church in the background. The whole scheme when completed will house 2000 people at 200 ppa and will include, amongst shops, doctor's surgeries, pubs, a community hall and a library. Architects: Darbourne & Darke. *Photo: Richard Einzig*

(LCC) took advantage of this situation by planning large areas of new housing as an integral part of and simultaneously with the shopping, social, educational and recreational facilities. Having been associated for over a decade with this massive attempt at comprehensive redevelopment of this part of Inner London, I have been made acutely aware of the opportunities as well as the problems of such an enterprise, and this is outlined in Appendix 14.

Housing in the suburbs

The term suburbia has a negative connotation for many people in Britain and is used to describe large areas of dull suburban housing, usually in the form of semi-detached or

Seventeen-storey blocks of flats and children's home in the foreground as viewed from a new public open place. St George's Estate, Tower Hamlets, London, part of the Stepney/Poplar Comprehensive Development Area. *Photo by courtesy of the Greater London Council*

detached houses, apparently devoid of character and social and other facilities. Many of these misconceptions about suburbia have been disproved by Herbert Gans in his book *The Levittowners*. Architectural pundits and some middle-class professionals who dislike this sort of housing have tended to exaggerate the negative aspects of suburbia and have dismissed too readily the fact that this way of life is sought by an increasing number of people —possibly for lack of attractive alternatives—and that some suburbs attract middle-class professionals and do provide reasonable social and other facilities. In the United States suburban housing usually takes the form of detached houses set in attractive landscape. This, coupled with a high car ownership which brings suburbanites within easy reach of most facilities, has made suburban housing in America a generally desirable objective.

However, whatever some people's subjective reactions to suburbia, there is no doubt that much could and should be done to improve life there, and indeed a good deal has been happening in recent years in that direction. In and around the suburbs of London attractive

Houses and flats in Black-heath, six miles from central London, built by SPAN for middle-income families. *Architect: Eric Lyons and Partners*

sites with mature landscape were developed by SPAN, a private development organization, with housing for middle-income groups. These developments pioneered a new high quality of suburban environment and achieved a good deal of social success by providing for owner-occupier management schemes. With regard to rented accommodation, the former LCC acquired an area of old Edwardian mansions set in spacious gardens near Richmond Park, Roehampton, and developed these with high-quality flats and houses set in beautiful surroundings.

As a result of congestion and high land values, which force an increasing number of businesses out of city centres, there is a build-up of local employment, shopping and even cultural and entertainment facilities in the suburbs which is helping to enrich their lives with new opportunities. Thus some suburbs of our cities are changing from merely dormitory areas to places with their own identity and interest. Croydon, for instance, which until a decade or two ago was mainly a dormitory outer suburb of Greater London, has in recent years developed into a major office and shopping complex with its own theatre and concert hall, and similar developments are taking place in other suburban areas. In other cities, Stockholm for example, a series of new towns like Vallingby and Farsta have been developed on the outskirts of the city as an integral part of the city's planned expansion, with their centres sited on top of underground railway stations.

This trend toward decentralization of employment, shopping and entertainment activities from the centres of our cities is to be welcomed since it helps to take pressures off the central areas and brings new interest and life to the suburbs and offers them alternative employment, obviating long commuting. However, there is a danger that this process, if unchecked, may lead to the other extreme and result in lifeless city centres, as in some cities, for example in Toledo, Ohio (see Appendix 24).

Aerial view of the Roehampton Estate in south-west London some five miles from the city centre. Architects Department, Greater London Council. *Photo: Aerofilms Ltd*

Vallingby near Stockholm. A major shopping centre built on top of the underground railway with housing nearby in tall blocks

Farsta shopping centre, Stockholm. A pedestrian precinct on top of the underground railway. *Photo: Walter Bor*

New towns within the city

Although many of our cities appear to be compactly developed, most cities have in fact thousands of acres of waste land within their built-up areas which for one reason or another have not yet been developed and which could make an important contribution towards remedying some of the deficiencies, for example in housing and recreational facilities. One such area which springs to mind is the Hackensack Meadows in New Jersey, USA, an unbelievable sight of bleak waste and derelict no-man's-land in dramatic contrast with the high-intensity activities of Manhattan, only six miles to the east of it. True, there have been many suggestions for development of the land and many projects discussed, but nothing has actually happened there so far. A similar vast tract of waste land had been embedded in the urban mass of London in Woolwich and Erith in the south-east of London when the Royal Woolwich Arsenal abandoned this site. Because of its marshy conditions, however, this area was not considered capable of development until modern technology proved otherwise and this area is now in process of development by the GLC as a new town, for 60 000 people, called Thamesmead (see Appendix 15).

Thamesmead will be a new town within a large city. Unlike earlier new towns it will not be isolated and set in the countryside, but integrated with the existing urban fabric. This has the obvious advantages that the people living in Thamesmead will be closer to the metropolitan opportunities of London in addition to having their own local facilities. Unfortunately, however, communications with the central area are not as good as one would wish and this advantage is therefore not as real as one might expect. On the other hand, one of the objectives of new towns is green fields, i.e. to give people more space in and about the home, cannot be achieved in Thamesmead, which must be developed to substantially higher densities because of very high foundation costs. Even so, Thamesmead represents yet another alternative way of urban living in a new town within a city.

Living in an expanded or new town

Yet another option, and one which has been developed in the UK very effectively during the post-war period, is life in an expanding or new town. Expanded towns like Swindon in Wiltshire, or Andover in Hampshire, are aiming at combining living at new-town densities with taking advantage of existing and expanding facilities. Town expansion is not without its problems for the newcomers as well as existing residents, and conflicts of interests between these two groups with regard to rents (rents for new houses are invariably higher than for existing ones), school places, etc., have to be dealt with continuously. As the town expands, all the services should be expanded in phase to keep up with the increasing demand and there are often difficulties in ensuring that the provision of these services does not lag behind. What is usually required, if the town expansion is substantial, is a complete restructuring of the town centre to meet greatly increased demands. An example of such a partially rebuilt town centre is Basingstoke, Hampshire, as described in Appendix 16.

Housing in Andover, Hampshire, England, by the Greater London Council as part of their expansion scheme. *Photo by courtesy of the Greater London Council*

However, the possibility of making a fresh start and creating a variety of opportunities which in many ways are different from those in existing urban areas exists to a fully comprehensive extent only in new towns or better still in new cities. Social and economic goals which would provide for many different options can be defined for the people of a new city and physical plans developed in response to these goals. This great variety of options which one can provide in new cities by a goal-orientated planning approach is described fully in Chapter 14, 'Making a Fresh Start'. Britain, although leading in the development of new towns, is of course not alone in this field and attractive examples of new town life are already in existence in other countries like in Finland. The housing in the new town of Tapiola is particularly attractive. In the United States, recent years have seen a renewed interest in the planning and building of new towns which has been kindled by the successful examples of Reston and Columbia.

Tapiola New Town in Finland. Typical family houses sensitively integrated with the landscape makes for gracious living. *Photo by courtesy of the Managing Director, Tapiola*

Housing in Columbia New Town, USA. *Photo: Tadder, Baltimore*

Housing the poor

Although we have seen that in theory there are many different urban situations in which people could choose to live, ranging from city centres to new cities, in practice people's ability to pay for any particular form of housing in any location is often the deciding factor. And while it is true that, with the growth of people's real incomes, the proportion of people able to afford to exercise choice is steadily increasing, a minority remains which is not in this position. This minority is proportionately much greater in the United States where state intervention is much more restricted than in the United Kingdom which is a Welfare State, but in both countries there remains a disconcerting number of under-privileged whose personal resources are too poor to afford decent housing.

The dissatisfaction of the urban poor with their housing conditions and lack of job opportunities has already led to serious rioting in many cities. In Britain their protests have taken the form of squatters occupying vacant premises and of organizations, like 'Shelter', coming into existence whose aim it is to help to house the poor, a formidable task since at present some 18 500 people are in hostels for the homeless. The very need for 'Shelter' is a sad reflection on the inadequacy of state subsidies for those most in need. In both countries some efforts are being made by central and local governments to investigate this problem but neither country is anywhere near solving it. As mentioned earlier, in Britain, some half a million families, involving well over 1 million children live below the established poverty line. The urban poor are made up of families whose breadwinner earns a weekly wage between £10 ($25) and £15 ($37) and has to pay at least £3.25 ($8) per week for a single room. Thus whole families sleep in a single room and in an eight-roomed house there may be between 20 and 30 people living with only one bath and water-closet. Altogether, there are some 155 000 households each living in one room in London. Most of this depressed housing is private housing often owned by unscrupulous landlords. But even where landlords are anxious to provide decent and cheap accommodation, they are in great difficulties for they get no subsidy like Local Authorities, while rent levels are pegged below market level. If they want to modernize their obsolete houses they are likely to incur a cost of about £3500 ($10 500) per house, which would mean they would have to charge a weekly rent of over £5 ($12.50) per week, which half of the private tenants could not afford.

One obvious way to enable these urban poor to live in decent accommodation is to assist them by rent allowances. Since the earnings of a proportion of tenants occupying subsidized council housing are sufficiently high for them to purchase a home of their own—and this proportion has been put as high as 40 per cent—it would seem sensible to encourage these tenants to buy their own houses and release the subsidized dwellings to those in greater need. And there may also be a case for subsidizing the private landlord who wants to provide decent and cheap accommodation for private tenants.

Another possibility which should be explored is to develop some cheap basic housing units which would have essential cooking and sanitary equipment and one or two rooms to start with. These units would be placed on a plot of land and could be bought by people with very modest means, particularly young couples. As they moved up the income scale, further rooms and other improvements could be added so that eventually a good standard of accommodation and convenience is achieved. Much of this work could be done by the owner-occupiers themselves, particularly if prefabricated wall, floor and roof components were used.

This brings me to a third alternative based even more extensively on self-help whereby only the essential services would be laid on and people would be encouraged to build their own homes attached to these services, with some technical assistance. Again, it would be a great asset if suitable prefabricated components could be made available for this purpose. This particular approach is probably more suitable for developing countries and is in fact being considered in Venezuela.

Housing and social planning

Discussions about housing are all too often dominated by statistics of bed spaces, densities and other numerical quantities. These are of course important, but the point they make is rarely related to their wider context, that is to the social function of housing. There is also a tendency to put the main emphasis on the practical and administrative problems associated with housing such as those involved in rehousing a certain number of people in a particular area rather than on its functional qualities such as the opportunities which housing can give to increase choice by the provision of the right kind in the right place at the right time. The most fundamental aim is clearly to provide decent housing for everybody suited to individual needs and well related to job opportunities and educational, social and leisure facilities.

The first provision of housing by the State marked the recognition that housing is a basic need and is therefore of course one of political importance. Since its early days public housing has undergone some profound changes and today some enlightened authorities like the Greater London Council provide public housing of a very high standard. Even so, public housing is still only available to some sections of the community while at the same time the private sector has been increasingly supplying houses in the open market to that section of the community who can afford to buy them as a commodity like cars or television sets. Decent housing is not available to all and its provision cannot yet be regarded as a basic social service.

This issue is of course closely linked with the growth of affluence : in a Welfare State such as the UK, an increasing number of people no longer rely on the provision of housing by a public authority but purchase the housing they want, or rather they can afford. However, we still have a long way to go before these people will be in the majority. In Milton Keynes, for instance, it was found that even in a new city for a quarter of a million, a 50/50 split between housing for rent and sale, which is an objective for the new city, cannot be achieved from the outset. Those who are in a position to buy do not as yet amount to half of the potential inhabitants and special efforts will have to be made to increase the opportunities for people to buy their houses. While the majority of those who cannot or do not wish to buy will be able to rent a house at prevailing subsidized public housing rents, a minority will be too poor to do even that. This unhappy fact reflects the widening of the gap in increasingly affluent societies between the majority who become increasingly better off and the minority who, in relative terms, become poorer, and our society is not doing enough to close this gap. This is illustrated by the following example : 1968 was a record year in building new council houses or public housing, in the UK, but during the same period the number of homeless actually increased.

There is clearly a need to provide a growing variety of good housing for young single people and the elderly as well as families, and to offer them a variety of tenures in the form of publicly and privately rented and owner-occupied as well as housing developed by housing associations. Local Authorities should ensure that there is an adequate mix and volume of house types to meet the needs of their people by providing the required variety in their new housing as well as by improving the existing housing stock. Local Authorities will also have to promote increasingly the improvement of private housing by finding ways of subsidizing, if necessary, some of its owners as well as tenants.

Similarly, it is essential to discover far more clearly what people's preferences are regarding housing and to meet these wherever possible. Although a good deal of further research is necessary, these preferences are being gradually identified by a number of surveys such as that of the Opinion Research Centre and the Rowntree Social Trust Survey by J. B. Cullingworth which indicate, for example, a strong preference for a house rather than a flat amongst households of particular types, with particular aspirations for the detached house

93

with a garden. According to the Ministry of Housing and Local Government's Research and Development Group survey of an estate in Coventry the advantage of attached garages went beyond the convenience of having the car close at hand, they were used as an extension of the house. With regard to densities, a survey of Stevenage in Hertfordshire, which has been developed at an average of ten dwellings per acre, showed that 40 per cent of the people interviewed thought houses were too close together. This suggests a significant preference for houses with more space around them which can of course be provided in new towns more readily than in existing ones. This does not mean that others do not prefer to live in existing towns under tighter conditions in exchange for their many real advantages. In future, as more new towns are built, people will have a genuine choice of living under more spacious conditions in new towns or in compact old ones.

At times even the most well-meaning public housing policy may be at variance with social conditions. For instance, when higher space standards are enforced in public housing, which result in rents which many cannot afford, or when people buy houses with lower space standards provided by the private sector, then clearly the conflict of ends and means demonstrates a basic fault in public social policy. This does not mean that we should not aim at higher space standards, but if we do we must at the same time make sure that people can avail themselves of these higher standards by having the income to pay for them. Indeed, many of our present housing problems would be eliminated if the earning power of people in the worst housing conditions particularly could be increased. In other words, we must consider the social implications in relation to housing much more fully and engage in social planning and development on a comprehensive scale if we are to meet people's preferences and achieve the social goals for housing which our society seeks.

Social planning and the explicit statement of social objectives must therefore be brought fully into housing at all levels by the public authority, both for their own housing and in cooperation with private developers for housing supplied by the private sector, and must underlie the activities of the physical planner and the housing manager. Only thus can we ensure that the housing is provided on a socially sound basis and truly meets the needs of the people for whom it is built. This implies, amongst other things, a new task for the sociologist who has seen his role mainly as a social surveyor and analyser, telling us what went wrong and why, after the event. The sociologist will have to involve himself with the physical planner and the architect in the design process. After all, if planners and architects must and do project themselves into yet unbuilt situations and commit themselves to firm physical arrangements, why not the sociologist who can guide them with his understanding of human behaviour? Unfortunately, however, social planning is still inadequately recognized by housing authorities and most sociologists still prefer the objectivity of academic aloofness to the involvement in social action through participation in the design process.

However, even when social goals have been defined, it will not be easy to achieve them. There is and will continue to be a dilemma between ideal social goals and practice, both in the public and private housing sectors. In public housing, the political pressures for large quantities of new housing to be built quickly will conflict with a more careful and socially more balanced approach which is likely to be slower and yield apparently less spectacular results, while the private sector tends to concentrate on a restricted range of houses which will sell quickly, leaving the Local Authorities to provide for the handicapped, the poor and the old in addition to providing the social facilities. One cannot, of course, expect the speculative builder to think in terms of social goals. It is therefore up to the public authority to construct a socially meaningful framework within which the private developer could be encouraged to make his contribution to the social aims of housing.

The application of social goals for housing will differ considerably, depending whether we are dealing with situations in existing or in new towns. As mentioned earlier, the social goals in existing towns, particularly in the big cities, have become distorted or have been ignored altogether under the relentless pressure to rehouse large numbers of people on scarce and expensive land. As a result, many of them have provided large quantities of new dwellings in the form of extensive areas of single-class high-density, high-rise housing irrespective of the adverse social consequences which have since been identified. Worse still, much of this new housing has been ill-related to people's jobs, to social facilities, and is often poorly served by public transport. As for the individuals involved, their preferences are very rarely ascertained and in the absence of explanation or information they can only feel victim to the heartless processes of bureaucracy.

We shall have to consider more fully the social implications of replacement of obsolete houses and the renewal of outworn parts of our towns and cities which have been causing serious social upheavals. Greater efforts should therefore be made to lay more emphasis on rehabilitation, which minimizes interference with the existing social fabric, than on the administratively convenient but socially often damaging 'clean-sweep' approach. To this end recent Ministry reports like 'Our Older Homes' and 'The Deeplish Study', coupled with the new improvement grants, should be of considerable assistance.

However, if we want to have better schools with more spacious playgrounds, more open spaces and more space in and around our homes and accommodate the motor car as well in our urban areas we shall find that it will still be necessary for large numbers of people to move out of the older parts of our main urban regions to find more space elsewhere, mainly, I suggest, in the new or expanding towns.

The artificial boundaries between county boroughs and county councils, long overtaken by the emergence of city regions, will be abolished when the Government's proposals for local government reorganization are implemented, and this should put an end to the present practice of county boroughs packing the people in as tightly as possible to conserve rateable values, and to their bitter arguments with their county neighbours who have often been singularly reluctant to accept the city's overspill population in the lower income group.

The preparation of detailed action area plans should focus attention on the integration of housing with the full range of social, educational and leisure facilities and ensure that these facilities are provided in step with housing. Social aspects of housing must underlie the physical proposals, including layouts and the detailed design of houses and space around them. Indeed, with the growing recognition of the need for public involvement, these local plans will have to be fully discussed publicly and local residents will be able to contribute with their comments and ideas before the plans are finalized.

In new towns and cities, the preconditions for providing socially more satisfactory housing are more favourable in many respects than in existing ones. Housing does not start with the handicap of a massive heritage of slums and a worn-out environment, and such older houses which there may be in existing small towns and villages within the designated area of a new town are usually more of an asset than a liability in that their relatively small numbers in relation to the new housing may provide cheap accommodation for those newcomers who cannot afford to buy or rent new housing. As land values are low compared with existing towns, people's preferences for more space in and around their homes can be met more readily. It is easier to achieve social balance in new housing, particularly if a substantial proportion is built by the private sector since a wider range of income groups is likely to be attracted. Even so, special efforts will have to be made to attract the minorities like the poor, as well as the executives, the blacks as well as the whites.

However, there are also social problems in new towns which sensitive housing policies can seek to resolve. These problems and ways of meeting them have been discussed in various Ministry of Housing and Local Government publications such as 'The First 100 Families' and 'The Needs of New Communities'. One of the early difficulties will be the relationship of existing communities to the newcomers. Local residents who usually led a quiet, semi-rural existence up to the advent of the new town now have to adjust themselves to the influx of many strangers from old towns, often with a different way of life and culture. With regard to the newcomers, their problems are greater still. Uprooted from their friends and jobs they find themselves in unfamiliar surroundings and often at a loss. They have to rent or buy a new house and often get a new job and their children must go to a new school; all these changes are bound to have an unsettling effect, cause transitional difficulties and are the root of that pattern of dissatisfaction and distress which our journalists have called 'new town blues'.

One of the most difficult problems of new towns is to provide all the necessary schools, shops, social and leisure facilities in step with the new housing. In particular, since the development of a viable new town centre requires a substantial population to support it, town-centre facilities have tended to lag behind people's need and special efforts will have to be made to overcome these difficulties. It is therefore essential for a New Town Development Corporation to be sensitive to the problems of newcomers and local residents alike by mounting information and advisory services from the start which would array the opportunities which the town offers—this is particularly important as far as housing is concerned —inform people about the plans and the facilities which are being provided, and invite people's comments on what is being planned. The Corporation itself needs to be continuously informed of the developing situation by means of a research and monitoring system. It would then know not only of its successes but its failures too, where things went wrong and why, so as to avoid repeating the same mistakes. Although this kind of feed-back from the consumer is of course important in existing towns too, it is absolutely essential in new ones where most of the environment will be created afresh.

If social planning were to guide our housing efforts more positively it would lead to a fundamentally different approach to housing from that which is still the rule rather than the exception. Instead of housing authorities being almost exclusively concerned with numbers of houses and the physical aspects of housing, they would also be vitally interested in providing housing to satisfy individual needs in relation to the life cycle, provide the opportunity for social mix of different income groups and ensure that existing undesirable divisions in society are not reinforced. Housing authorities would plan their housing to maximize freedom of choice and allow for social mobility and would provide a built-in flexibility for people to alter or extend their houses and housing; environmental standards would be governed primarily by social considerations which would in turn strongly influence physical form. It is likely that public authorities would have to take the lead in providing such socially fully considered housing and then encourage the private sector through planning powers to follow suit. The principal task emerging then is to provide new housing in the broader context of social planning.

To meet these objectives, it will be necessary for local authorities to coordinate these various efforts by means of a comprehensive housing service which would bring together a wide range of powers already available in the housing field but which are at present scattered amongst various local government departments, to provide all kinds of people with the housing of their choice.

There could be local representatives on housing estates; residents could be encouraged to talk about their own houses in detail and comment on future projects. Scope could also be provided for people to have a greater say about their houses by leaving them partially unfinished so that new residents can decide how they would like their houses to be completed.

I believe we should think in terms of opportunities as well as problems when we talk about social aspects of housing. Before the turn of the century we shall have to provide new homes for 15 million more people in the United Kingdom so we shall have a unique opportunity to meet one of the most important needs of people, that of housing, in an imaginative and sensitive way which could give them the greatest measure of human satisfaction.

Appendix 13

Barbican Redevelopment in the City of London
Architects: Chamberlin, Powell & Bon

Site

The area of site available for the new Barbican residential neighbourhood was about 35 acres. Warehouses for the clothing trade which, before the war, had occupied most of this land were nearly all destroyed by bombing. The old pattern of streets, housing a complex but obsolete system of underground public utility services, criss-crossed the site and four tracks of underground railway—partially 'in cut' and partially 'under cover'—bisected the site; St Giles Church, the remains of the old Roman Wall and a few other scarred buildings remained. No natural features, landscaping, trees or outlook existed. In short, the site, apart from being largely cleared of buildings, had few redeeming qualities favourable to the creation of a new place for people to live in.

Requirements

The requirements were to provide new living accommodation for as many people as possible within the site available together with those amenities which residents could reasonably expect to enjoy such as open space, shops, restaurants, public houses, garages, etc. Other specific requirements included new buildings for the City of London School for Girls, the Guildhall School of Music and Drama, a theatre for occupation by the Royal Shakespeare Company, a concert hall for occupation by the London Symphony Orchestra, a public lending library, an art gallery and a small arts cinema, a hostel, some commercial warehousing and, in the future, a physical recreation centre. From a town planning point of view, certain traffic and pedestrian routes which cross the available site needed to be retained because they serve adjacent parts of the City.

It was decided at an early stage that it would be important to establish not only a residential precinct which was characterful enough to hold its own against the surrounding high-density commercial and office zones, but also a pedestrian precinct which would protect the new residential environment from the disruptive influences of high density traffic.

Planning and design principles adopted

The need to create a quiet traffic free precinct led to:

1. re-routing the underground railway in new realigned tunnels between Aldersgate and Moorgate stations;

2. closing most of the old streets crossing the site and covering over those which had to remain such as Beech Street and the southern end of Golden Lane;

3. the creation of a new pedestrian level (some 12 acres in extent) about 20 ft above ground level; this new 'podium' level links under cover the entrances to lift lobbies serving all the flats and other buildings with the public rights of way, which connect via bridges across the perimeter streets to the adjacent commercial zones;

4. suppression of all the new service roads ($3\frac{1}{2}$ miles in length of 20 ft wide carriageway) which provide access to garages (2500 in number), service delivery points, etc., below ground or podium levels. The completed scheme will contain nearly 25 acres of service roads and garages planned out of sight beneath the development.

The need to provide as much open space as possible within a high-density development (230 persons per acre over all) led to the planning of most flats and maisonettes with narrow frontages in highly concentrated long terrace blocks rising six or seven storeys above podium level or into three towers each over 40 storeys high. Apart from the 12 acres of podium terrace referred to, there will also be nearly as many acres of landscaped open space, playgrounds and gardens. The scheme as it will appear when completed is illustrated by the model, Figure 1.

Figure 1. Barbican Redevelopment—model 1969. View of model from south-west. The residential area is designed in a series of courts formed by 7-storey blocks above a podium within and under which are accommodated garages, offices and commercial premises. In the centre of the site is the old Church of St Giles, Cripplegate, with the new City of London School for Girls to the immediate left. To the north of the school across the lake is the Arts Centre with the concert hall, theatre, art gallery, library and the new Guildhall School of Music and Drama. Architects: Chamberlin, Powell & Bon. *Photo: John Maltby*

In order to create several local centres of interest significant enough to contribute to the scale of the development, the buildings are grouped to express, or give point to, a particular aspect or characteristic of the scheme. The three high towers are planned along the south of Beech Street, where the axes of the layout change; the polygonal plan forms of the towers stem from these contra-axes. The long terrace blocks are grouped in U and Z shapes on plan each enclosing, or otherwise defining, certain parts of the layout. The areas of the site thus partially enclosed by these long terraces are comparable in scale to some of the familiar London squares. The City of London School for Girls and the row of terrace houses south of the remains of the Roman Wall partially enclose a small square around St Giles Church. All the elements contained in the arts centre are grouped round the common foyers which are sandwiched between the drive-in traffic entrance levels and the pedestrian entrance levels on the podium. These foyers open on to a terrace overlooking the lake, which is the central landscape feature.

The difference in form and character of these spaces and places is contributed to by virtue of their being designed on different levels as well as different positions on plan. The larger

99

landscaped areas are sunk below the surrounding ground level. The new churchyard between St Giles and the girls' school is at ground level. The sculpture court, which opens out
of the art gallery and is embraced by the arms of the horse-shoe block of flats to the north,
is at podium level—as are the squares and enclosures in North Barbican, designed between
the residential blocks above the commercial area planned below the podium. These larger
spatial groupings are also punctuated by smaller elements such as the low blocks of maisonettes planned adjacent to the mews and the arcade below the horse-shoe block, which provides access to the adjacent shops which are to serve the precinct.

The disposition of the space between buildings and its detailed treatment have received
particular attention. The raising of some of the terrace blocks on columns allowing space
to flow, as it were, beneath these buildings is a device employed to express continuity between different parts of the layout and to avoid what might otherwise be, in a high-density
scheme, blunt and oppressive enclosure of buildings forbidding in scale. The continuity of
paved podium terraces extending under buildings and the areas of planting or water which
link and define the open spaces make a significant contribution to the unity of the whole;
the detailing of the hard and soft surfaces of the open spaces will add point to their form.
The central landscaping enclosed by the long terraces of building south of Barbican are to
be laid out on a large scale with grass, forest trees and water gardening, as is familiar in the
London parks and squares.

Conclusion

The Barbican Redevelopment project is an exercise in high-density urban renewal tailored
to meet particular requirements on a specific site. It involves a complete change of use from
the former commercial activity to the new residential occupancy, the purpose of which is
to enable more people to live near to where they work and thus to reduce, however slightly
in the context of London, the journey to work problem. The bringing together of certain
social and cultural needs such as the schools and the activities planned to take place in the
arts centre has provided the opportunity to create a neighbourhood with considerably more
urban character, in the positive sense, than would have been possible if the brief had been
confined to provide only a dormitory 'inner suburb'. The interest of the development may
lie in the decision taken to tackle the problems involved as a single urban renewal project
in which an entirely new infrastructure—concerned with movement and servicing generally
within the City—could be architecturally integrated in a full, three-dimensional sense with
the diverse high-density development arising above it.

Appendix 14

Stepney/Poplar Reconstruction, London

The reconstruction of the extensive war-damaged areas in Stepney and Poplar as one comprehensive development was suggested in the County of London Plan and, after its adop-

tion by the then London County Council, was subsequently confirmed by the Minister of Town and Country Planning in December 1947, when the necessary powers to acquire land for this purpose were granted.

The Reconstruction Area includes part of three communities, Stepney, Poplar and Bow in London's East End. It covers 1945 acres, of which 1312 acres are subject to compulsory purchase. The area has been replanned as a series of twelve neighbourhoods, varying in size from 2200 to 10 700 people, each as far as possible with its own schools, local shopping centres, open spaces and community buildings. One of these neighbourhoods, St Anne's, for whose planning I was responsible, is nearing completion and Figure 1 shows a model of it.

The replanning and rebuilding of Stepney/Poplar, which is still one of the major post-war achievements in London, is fully documented in Percy Johnson-Marshall's book *Rebuilding Cities*. It may, therefore, be of more interest here to evaluate the lesson we can learn from this operation which has now been in progress for over 20 years. However, before I do so, let me recollect the state of leading planning thought in Britain during the late '40s, when the basic structure plan for Stepney/Poplar was drawn up. The neighbourhood concept was then accepted uncritically; land-use planning, though including roads, was thought of more or less independently of overall transport planning and traffic engineering was in its infancy. All data collection and retrieval had to be done manually since computers had not yet arrived on the planning scene.

In spite of the relative lack of sophistication and a tendency towards hunch planning, the planning of Stepney/Poplar broke new ground in many directions and was one of the few forward-looking examples of positive action at that time. The very idea of comprehensive neighbourhood development, i.e. the simultaneous development of housing, open spaces, schools, shops and work places, was new and had to be fought for hard to become a recog-

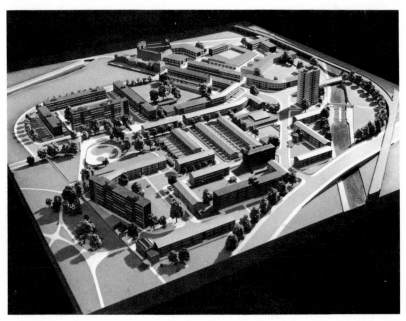

Figure 1. Model of St Anne's neighbourhood, Stepney, shows a new housing area in the form of linked streets and squares with a primary school and a shopping centre in the background. LCC Architects Department, Planning Divison. *Photo by courtesy of the Greater London Council*

101

Figure 2. Play sculpture 'Gulliver' by Trevor Tennant in St Anne's neighbourhood is very popular with the children and gives the place an identity. *Photo: Central Press Photographs*

nized approach. The reconstruction team was one of the first inter-disciplinary teams in a planning office and included even a sociologist. This team pioneered a number of new concepts, foremost amongst them the pedestrian shopping precinct for Lansbury Market in the teeth of violent opposition by the traders who predicted ruin to them. In the event, the planners were proved to be right. This market has now been flourishing and expanding for many years. In conjunction with the LCC housing architects, the team initiated experiments with a large number of different dwelling types to find out in practice which were most popular. When tower blocks of flats were introduced, they were conceived of as integral with the surrounding parkland as in Lansbury (Poplar) and the Stifford Estate (Stepney). The first LCC play sculpture was built by Trevor Tenant in the form of a concrete reclining 'Gulliver' in St Anne's neighbourhood (see Figure 2).

However, many obstacles stood in the way of an even more successful development. To begin with, the tripartite responsibility of the LCC and the Boroughs of Stepney and Poplar did not work smoothly or efficiently, as could have been expected, and resulted in much in-fighting, delay and disruption. The land acquisition policy failed to take full advantage of the low prices at the beginning of the operation, when most of the area could have been bought under the designation order. Instead only blitzed sites and 'soft' properties were acquired. As a result, reconstruction is patchy, existing main-road frontages remained frozen and prices of remaining properties have escalated by inflation and betterment through planning action; the whole operation will now take probably twice as long as anticipated and will cost many times more than it need have done. The planning itself was not only limited to the level it had reached at that time, but was, in addition, frustrated by lack of input with regard to transportation planning, which was the separate responsibility of the engineers. Similar frustrations were experienced in social planning, where well-laid plans of rehousing people locally, as well as enriching the social mix, foundered on the rigidity of the LCC's letting policy and the need to satisfy the housing list priorities. Architecturally, too, Stepney/Poplar is not the success it could have been and one is struck by a lack of architectural cohesion, which is largely due to the number of developing authorities involved and to the considerable differences in the quality of architecture they produced.

If one were to sum up these lessons, one could identify the following five major points:

1. Since the programme called for the substantial restructuring and rebuilding of some 2000 acres with a population of 100 000 people, the task was equivalent to, although in many ways more complex than, the building of a large post-war new town. The appropriate organization for such a massive operation would have been, in my submission, a Stepney/Poplar Development Corporation, composed of members of the LCC, and the Stepney and Poplar Boroughs, with full executive power over all aspects of planning and building, and their own professional and administrative staff to carry out this work.

2. Once the decision was made to proceed with the comprehensive reconstruction of this substantial part of London's East End, the appropriate financial resources should have been made available on a comprehensive basis at the right time and in the right place. This could have been done by means of a rolling capital works programme embracing acquisition of land and buildings and all forms of expenditure on construction, and under the control of the Stepney/Poplar Development Corporation.

3. A more flexible letting policy should have been adopted which would have ensured that a larger proportion of the local residents were rehoused and a wider range of income groups catered for. In this connection, greater efforts should have been made to encourage cooperative house ownership. Thus much unnecessary social upheaval could have been avoided and a socially more balanced community would have resulted.

4. The whole approach was slanted too exclusively upon pulling down and rebuilding. A more selective clearance coupled with a determined rehabilitation policy would have enabled the authority to deal with the up-grading of the whole of the environment more comprehensively and large twilight areas which still stand cheek by jowl with new development could have been substantially improved by now.

5. Reference has been made to the somewhat limited degree of planning methodology prevailing at the time of conception. This particular shortcoming has been largely overcome by now and more sophisticated planning techniques can now be applied during the subsequent stages of completion. There is still considerable scope, since a substantial part of the area has still to be tackled.

Stepney/Poplar is an important object lesson. While the partial reconstruction of this area has many positive features and has pioneered many new ideas and concepts, how much more successful could it have been both socially and environmentally if only the many pitfalls could have been foreseen and avoided. Some of them were, in fact, foreseen, others were not and others still were probably unavoidable at that time.

Appendix 15

Thamesmead—a new town within a city
Department of Architecture and Civic Design, Greater London Council

Thamesmead is a scheme for a virtually new town to house 60 000 people within Greater London. The flat and low-lying site lies about eight miles east of central London on the south bank of the Thames, with a three-mile frontage to the river. The proposed Ringway 2 motorway is planned to pass through the site and under the river in a tunnel. This motorway with its intersection with the main spine road of the development has been a great formative influence in the design of the town.

There is therefore a truly large-scale situation. The decision to design Thamesmead to match this scale is the basic philosophy behind the scheme into which all the other requirements have been fitted. Thus the use of water has been conceived on a large scale, and linked with an extensive open-space system; the three-dimensional form is suggested in bold and well-defined groupings. The other principles on which the scheme is based are:

1. Thamesmead must provide a complete environment with employment and full educational, communal, commercial and recreational facilities.

2. Density will vary from housing areas with large family dwellings at 70 ppa to parts of the town where the density will be at about 140 ppa and provide dwellings for the small family and single persons.

3. Communications between the new development and the neighbouring areas of London have been planned to ensure that the development will become integrated as part of Greater London.

4. It has been accepted that landscaping makes a major contribution to the quality of urban environment; thus the design of buildings and open space have been considered as a single design problem.

The resulting design has a pronounced form with a line of tall buildings which in general run along the river frontage. This line swings away from the river at Tripcock Point where there is a major riverside open space. The centre is planned at right angles to the river with a yacht basin at the northern end and a lake at the southern end (see Figure 1).

The scheme provides about 17 000 dwellings grouped into neighbourhoods which vary in size from about 1500 to 2000 dwellings. They will contain their own primary school and a local centre with shops for day-to-day shopping, churches, pubs and some employment facilities for local workers. The specially designed tall buildings will protect the central part of the housing areas from traffic noise and wind.

The plan makes extensive use of the water on the site. Two lakes will be created which are linked by a canal forming part of a canal system running through the town. The excavated materials from the lakes and canals will be used to create differences in level within the open-space system. The lakes will form part of the general open-space system of the project. The climax to the recreational provision will be the yacht basin which will be of inter-

Figure 1. Thamesmead. London. Model of completed development shows the high blocks in the foreground providing wind shelter for the housing beyond. In the middle of the picture is the new town centre. GLC Architects Department. *Photo by courtesy of the Greater London Council*

national status, and capable of mooring sea-going yachts. It will be flanked by high-density housing and central-area uses.

The central area will contain shopping, office employment, community, recreational, educational and employment facilities. There will also be a comprehensive medical centre and an ecumenical centre. It will have a high-level main concourse with vehicular services and parking and a public transport interchange at ground level.

The development has been planned to take over 15 years and will be carried out mainly by the Greater London Council and private developers. The Greater London Council placed a contract in 1967 for the first 4000 dwellings, using the Balency system of industrialized building. The contractor's first task was to construct an industrialized building factory. This is placed towards the centre of the site where it can best serve the whole development, and it can be handed over from one contractor to another if necessary.

The first stages of the development are at the south-eastern end of the site and include not only housing but a district heating plant, schools, the first lake, a shopping centre and a medical centre (Figures 2 and 3).

Figure 2. Thamesmead, London. Part of model showing first phase of the development now under construction. GLC Architects Department. *Photo by courtesy of the Greater London Council*

Figure 3. Thamesmead, London. Completed housing using balancing system of precast concrete panels. GLC Architects Department. *Photo by courtesy of the Greater London Council*

106

Appendix 16

Basingstoke central area redevelopment
Llewelyn-Davies, Weeks & Partners

Basingstoke, a small town 47 miles south-west of London, together with Andover, both in Hampshire, was selected for expansion by the former London County Council to receive people and jobs from London when the building of a new town at Hook was abandoned. This major expansion of Basingstoke implied the need for a comprehensive redevelopment of the town centre to serve the greatly increased population. The scheme for the central shopping area was a partnership scheme produced by cooperation between the Borough Council who are the landlords and a property company who provided the capital to build, and were responsible for letting the shops to tenants and for the general management of the centre.

Certain essential planning criteria had been established by the development group. Amongst these were the complete segregation of circulation for pedestrians, service traffic and car parking, an uninterrupted pedestrian route linking the old town through the new centre to the station (see Figure 1): the new shopping areas were to be grouped around this route. Short-term parking was to be provided for shopping with easy access from car parking to shopping.

Figure 1. Basingstoke new shopping centre has been integrated with the existing shops in the town centre. Architects: Llewelyn-Davies, Weeks & Partners. *Photo: Henk Snoek*

107

During the study of the problem the following further principles were added as objectives for the design:

1. As the scheme was to be built in two phases, the first plan should be reasonably complete in itself and have convenient access for pedestrians and vehicles before the later phase is added.

2. As the shopping centre was to be about $\frac{1}{4}$ mile long, easy pedestrian access to it should be provided at the sides as well as at each end, linking the bus station with St Michael's Church.

3. The architectural character of the design should harmonize with the scale and character of the existing town. In particular great regard should be given to the area immediately surrounding St Michael's Church.

A group of shops for tenants displaced from the main site, together with a new market square, was put in hand during the finalization of plans for the main scheme.

The project consists of three main vertically separate components:

The service level: this is a semi-basement level connected with the service road and main spine road which run under the shopping centre. All loading and unloading of service vehicles is carried out at this level and loading bays are planned adjacent to each large shop. Some of the smaller shops are more distant from the loading bays and goods are conveyed to them by trolley.

The pedestrian level: this is the shopping level immediately above the service level. The malls which have shops on both sides are completely pedestrian and protection from the weather is provided by canopies or glazed arcades (see Figure 2). The shops are self-contained units, with storage space directly below, so that each shop has access at pedestrian and service levels.

Figure 2. Basingstoke new shopping centre. One of the pedestrian malls with shops on both sides with deep canopies for weather protection. Architects: Llewelyn-Davies, Weeks & Partners. *Photo: Henk Snoek*

Figure 3. Basingstoke town centre multi-storey car park flanks the pedestrian shopping centre below. Architects: Llewelyn-Davies, Weeks & Partners. *Photo: Henk Snoek*

Car parks: the multi-storey car parks for 3300 cars are in three blocks served by two levels of distributor roads, running the whole length of the scheme (see Figure 3). These roads pass above the pedestrian ways and are restricted to private cars and light vans. Access is from the spine road which also gives access to the centre for service vehicles.

Non-retail accommodation: the sports centre and swimming pools, branch library, flats, maisonettes and lettable office space are all located over the shops where they do not occupy valuable retail floor space. Each building or group of buildings has direct access to the pedestrian circulation level and internal lift access to service facilities in the basement.

Actual work on site commenced towards the end of 1966 and the first stage of Phase 1 was officially opened in November 1968. The remaining stage of Phase 1 was completed in April 1970.

8 Urban Transport Problems and Prospects

"We need a wide range of choices and choice means mobility. Choice of jobs and health services, lots of education and recreation in areas different from the home environment. This means transportation."

Delos Five, *Ekistics*, October 1967

Existing and new forms of public transport

Our city streets, particularly in the central areas, are congested with pedestrians and all kinds of vehicles competing for scarce road space. Since the most intractable—though by no means exclusive—urban transport problem is that of the peak-hour commuting traffic, attention is being focused increasingly on ways and means whereby this type of traffic could be brought within manageable proportions. This in turn raises the question of what steps are needed not only to continue to move large numbers of people by public transport but indeed to induce many more private-car commuters to travel to work by public transport.

Public transport in existing cities can operate effectively only if it can have a clear run unrestricted by other vehicles. Provided there are sufficient travellers (approximately 5000 passengers at peak hour) special tracks reserved for public transport use therefore seems the obvious answer. This of course is the case of overhead or underground rail facilities, both of which are in existence in many major European cities, where they make a cardinal contribution to taking people to and from work. In London, for instance, well over half a million people are moved daily by the underground system and some 450 000 by the railway. Such systems are fast and their safety record is high, but they are inflexible and invariably necessitate feeder services to their stations (in the form of buses or private cars) since these must be sufficiently far apart for the systems to operate at reasonably high speeds. These rapid-transit systems are being continually improved and recent developments include the Guid-O-Matic train installed at Houston airport, USA, and the Expo '70 high-speed train from Tokyo to Osaka. The time-honoured tram running on fixed rails embedded in the main street network has by now been discarded in all cities of the United Kingdom because it was found to be slow and inefficient—except for towns like Blackpool

Oxford Street, London. A typical congested central-area street where pedestrians and all kinds of vehicles are competing for road space. *Photo: Tony Brooks*

Guid-O-Matic Train is a small-scale train running on a guidance cable laid in the floor. This system has been installed at Houston Airport and handles 200 passengers in a ten-minute period

High-speed train installed for Expo '70 between Tokyo and Osaka. *Photo by courtesy of 'Architects' Journal'*

111

Trams and station in Stachus Square, Munich. An example of a city where the tram still makes a major contribution to public transport. *Photo by courtesy of Elliot Automation Ltd*

where it still transports holiday crowds along the sea shore. Yet in many cities in Europe, like in Munich, the tram is still one of the mainstays in the public transport system, but, unlike their British counterparts, the modern versions are reasonably fast, comfortable and almost noiseless. In some cities, like Prague, extensive excavations are in progress in the city centre where the trams will be routed underground. It appears that, contrary to British experience, trams still have a useful part to play in many European cities and are likely to continue to do so for a long time.

Another fixed-track alternative is the elevated monorail which, when inserted into an international exhibition like Expo '67 in Montreal or into high-density urban areas like the Wuppertal in the Ruhr or in Tokyo, can be an effective public transport system. To date, however, no monorail system has yet been realized in any city in the United Kingdom where it would have to compete successfully against existing public transport systems. All these types of rail facilities can be viable only if there are enough passengers to patronize them. Our investigation of possible public transport facilities for the new city of Milton Keynes which included 46 equipment types showed that the potential ridership even in a new city for 250 000 was far too small to make any fixed-track system a viable proposition, and that a more dispersed road-based system of small buses would provide a better service at lower cost and would be able to grow with the city as no fixed system could (the Milton Keynes Plan, Milton Keynes Development Corporation, 1970).

All other forms of public transport in the form of buses, coaches, limousines and taxis are road based and have to compete for road space with a host of other vehicles. Reserved bus lanes are one way of overcoming this problem, but not many existing roads are wide enough to accommodate such reserved lanes, and in any case, it may be an uneconomic provision of valuable road space since the average bus lane is used intensively only up to

Light monorail used at Expo '67 in Montreal which ran on twin steel tracks at speeds up to 15 mph and was automatically controlled. This system is very flexible and can be routed through buildings like the US pavilion at Expo '67.
Photo: H. Heiniger

20 hours per week. This is fully described by Sumner Wells in his paper 'The Soft Revolution'; *Architectural Forum,* Jan/Feb 1968. New urban motorways of course provide excellent facilities for express buses or coaches but are less suitable for local buses, since the efficiency of the motorways would be impaired with laybys for bus stops and the admittance of pedestrians on to them.

A further complication is the long period of time required to complete a minimal urban motorway network and the limited value of short stretches of urban motorways in the meanwhile. During the preparation of the Interim Planning Policy for Liverpool, a public transport system mainly based on buses and coaches and using an urban motorway system was priced. It was found to cost about the same amount as a public transport system based mainly on the revitalization of existing rail facilities. The deciding factor, however, was the speed whereby the rail system could be brought into operation (within ten years), while the completion of the urban motorway system which the coaches and buses would use would take up to 50 years to complete.

Buses are, of course, more flexible than fixed-rail facilities but are uneconomic to run between peak periods, even with automatic fare systems, when the crew consists only of the driver. They also fail to stop at one's front door unless one is exceptionally lucky and lives at the bus stop of the bus one wants. A smaller public transport vehicle, which combines ready availability with utmost flexibility of taking one from one's home to wherever one wants to go, is clearly required in addition to the large buses, either in the form of taxis or jitneys (large shared taxis) seating six people and dropping them off wherever they want to go. This latter vehicle is the main public transport facility in South American cities like Caracas, where it is called 'por puesto', and is also gaining in popularity in the USA, particularly for rides to and from airports. European cities, too, could greatly benefit from their service in addition to the usual taxi service, which in any case is usually still inadequate and requires to be developed in most towns. A more readily available and cheaper taxi service (subsidized if necessary) would provide the door-to-door service of the private car without the attendant parking problems.

It is likely, however, that new forms of urban transport will have to be pressed into service

113

to fill the gap which at present exists between fast transit systems requiring feeder services on the one hand and the convenient door-to-door service the private car can provide, but which cannot be used universally in congested urban areas because of its under-use of scarce road space and the parking problems.

One approach would be to invent and bring into operation small-scale systems running above city streets at relatively slow speeds permitting close spacing of stations at about quarter-mile intervals (thus dispensing with a feeder service) and cheap enough to construct and operate so that a fine meshwork of such systems could be provided economically. The visual intrusion of such elevated structures into existing city streets will, however, present difficult problems which will have to be resolved. This family of systems was described by Brian Richards in *Architectural Forum*, Jan/Feb 1968, and is a fast developing sector of modern transport technology.

These novel fixed-track systems, though ingenious, still suffer from the disadvantage, as compared with the private car, that you have to get to the boarding stations, and then from the destination stations to wherever you want to go. They are therefore still not competitive with the convenience of one's own private car. However, it may be possible to develop systems which can give a door-to-door service, and DART (demand-actuated road transit) is attempting to do just that (see Appendix 17).

For the central areas of our cities, we may wish to consider new types of vehicles, since it may be cheaper and wiser in the long run to change the vehicle design than alter the city centre to accommodate the present bulky private car, so inefficient where road space is restricted. These might take the form of automated electrically powered vehicles running on rubber tyres like the small private car or an electrically powered small taxi like those used at Expo '70.

All forms of transport have a profound effect upon the urban environment. If the future can bring new forms of public and personal transport which will be quiet and fumeless, more comfortable and efficient and thus more acceptable in urban areas than are most of the present ones, one of the most important contributions will then be made to the movement of people and goods within urban areas and to the improvement of our urban environment.

Lightweight electric car in use at a shopping centre. *Photo: Tella Photography Ltd*

Electrically powered taxi at Expo '70. *Photo by courtesy of Architects' Journal*

Appendix 17

Demand-actuated road transit (DART)

DART would use a minibus to pick up passengers at their doors shortly after they have telephoned for service. The call is logged in by a computer together with similar origin-destination demands, the computer then selects the right vehicle, despatches it to the caller according to some optimal routing algorithm programmed into the system, and can even give a warning ring on the passenger's telephone a few minutes before pick-up time. Thus DART can go where the demand is and only when the demand is ready to be satisfied. It is likely that DART would serve its passengers not quite as fast as the private taxi but at between a quarter and half the cost.

A practical application of DART is the 'Dial-a-bus' system which 'Tomorrow's Transportation' Report by the US Department of Housing and Urban Development has recommended as having a high expectation of technical and economic feasibility, particularly in a diffused pattern of trip origins and destination. Such a trip pattern is being considered for instance for the new city of Milton Keynes where the introduction of the dial-a-bus is under consideration. The passenger would dial his destination at the bus stop near his home and a central computer would relay instructions to the nearest bus heading towards the passenger's destination.

The hardware system that makes DART economically feasible is an automated vehicle-locating system (AVL) which can establish the location of any vehicle in a metropolitan area 50 miles in diameter. A central transmitter broadcasts regularly and continuously repetitive frequency modulated command impulses each of which addresses one particular vehicle whose equipment recognizes its own coded signal. On receiving it, the addressed vehicle activates a key transmitter which produces a respond-acknowledge signal. At least three receivers pick up this signal and relay it to a data centre where the vehicle's location is computed by triangulation. This system, it is claimed, can keep track of over 1 million vehicles and it can be 'time-shared' by many different users, public and private. It can be operational within three years.

Revitalization of public transport in US cities

Much of the problem of road congestion is due to the greatly increased number of private vehicles, and since in the United States private vehicle ownership and use is the largest in the world—and still increasing—it is important to consider this problem in the light of US experience. However, before we do so, we must realize some of the essential differences between American and European cities.

With very few exceptions, American cities are less than one, or at the most two, centuries old and have almost invariably been laid out on a rectangular grid system of wide straight streets, which lends itself admirably to one-way traffic management schemes and is capable of a traffic capacity greatly in excess of the street network of European cities. Apart from the intensively built-up central areas—though many of these have been emptied of buildings in favour of parking lots—most American cities have been developed to very low densities as compared with their European counterparts

These factors, coupled with a high degree of car ownership (although over 25 per cent of US households still did not own a car in 1960), have had the result of making such public transport as existed increasingly uneconomic to run and even less worth while financially to modernize: that is if solely the economic yardstick is applied and social cost-benefits are ignored, as has been the case. At the same time, great cities like New York have public transport facilities which would be a disgrace to smaller and poorer towns. A ride on one of Manhattan's subways is a degrading experience: the rolling stock and stations are worn-out and obsolete, the noise is infernal and the grime and neglect appalling. Yet they still transport 74 per cent of the working population during peak hours.

As P. H. Bendsten describes in his book *Town Traffic in the Motor Age*, even in Los Angeles, which more than any other city attempted to do without public transport, 57 per cent of those present in the central business district at 15.00 hours came in by public transport. Incidentally, of the total family budget, 9 per cent is spent on transport in New York as compared with 16 per cent in Los Angeles.

In other large cities public transport has been run down to such poor and intermittent bus services that its contribution to shifting the daily commuter crowd has become negligible. At one time, American road engineers were confident that, given the appropriate resources

Los Angeles four-level interchange on the Hollywood Freeway near downtown. *Photo: United Press International*

116

to build the necessary freeways, they could accommodate all the urban traffic, including unrestricted private-car commuter traffic, on their roads. Stupendous efforts were in fact made in this direction in most major US cities and vast numbers of six-, ten- and even twelve-lane freeways were built with two-, three-, and four-level complex intersections extending deep into the urban fabric and often resulting in visual chaos and social disruption.

In spite of all this effort it became increasingly apparent that every additional motorway space tended to become filled up as soon as it was available, while the traffic problems, particularly the peak-hour problems, remained unresolved. The turning point came in San Francisco in 1950 when public pressure succeeded in halting literally in mid-air the extension of the Embarcadero Freeway, which was already seriously marring the views of San Francisco's beautiful bay. Instead of further expensive and unsightly and self-defeating freeway construction, an ambitious $1·2 billion scheme for a new 75 mile long Bay Area Rapid Transit system (BART) was launched in 1957 envisaging driverless trains averaging

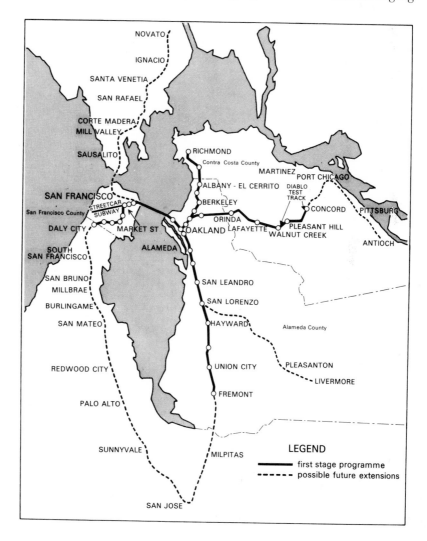

BART (Bay Area Rapid Transit). Map showing first stage and possible future extensions of the new San Francisco transit system

BART. Section through three levels of the transit system. The mezzanine level is pedestrian and shows access to Powell Station. Below this run the municipal trains, underneath are the BART trains. *Photo: San Francisco Bay Area Rapid Transit District*

Specially designed train in use in BART. *Photo: San Francisco Bay Area Rapid Transit District*

speeds of 50 mph and moving 30 000 passengers / rail / hour. This is described in detail in *Modern Railways*, Vol. 22 (1966), and the *Railway Gazette*, April 1965. This reversal of transport policy by revitalizing public transport has since been followed by 35 other American cities.

Chicago, for instance, pioneered the linking of two modes of transportation by inserting a double line of electric railway along the central reservation of the Congress Street Expressway. This electric line can move 11 000 passengers/track/hour at one-third capacity compared with 10 000 persons per four-line carriageway at full capacity. The double-track right of way requires 37 ft, the eight-lane double carriageway 118 ft. A start is to be made soon on the construction of a $600 million 25-mile system in Washington, DC, that may eventually extend to 95·3 miles at the total cost of $2·3 billion.

However, even more significant than the decision by several major US cities to construct new rapid-transit systems is the emergence of a much more comprehensive approach, which sees the construction of these systems as an integral part of an overall transportation plan and a major planning tool in the restructuring of wider urban areas. This concept, which was pioneered by the Stockholm planners, is now being adopted in Seattle, where a multi-professional team of planners, engineers and architects has planned a 47-mile rapid-transit system at the estimated cost of $1·15 billion which will connect downtown Seattle with the majority of the outlying population and employment centres. An integral part of this development will be the physical and social rehabilitation of the central area, the accessibility of which will be greatly improved by the construction of the new transit system. Even the views riders will obtain from the trains have been studied with care.

In some ways it was fortunate that all this happened in the USA, since it is one of the few countries which can afford such monumental mistakes without going bankrupt and where people have minds flexible enough to reverse engines and go off in an opposite direction with the same enthusiasm and drive as soon as they realize that they have been pursuing the wrong course. More important still, here we have the live examples of what happens—under the most favourable conditions at that—when large cities attempt to rely largely or almost exclusively on the unrestricted use of the private vehicle.

Having considered the situation of US cities in relation to private and public transport, let us examine this in connection with European cities. Practically none of the advantages of US cities favouring the unrestricted use of private cars, like rectangular grids of wide streets, low-density suburbs, very high road funds compared with other items of national expenditure and a universally car-orientated society, apply to any substantial degree to European cities. In addition to these differences, European cities are much older and contain a much greater and more vulnerable architectural heritage which could be seriously marred by excessive urban motorway constructions.

On the other hand, most of the essential characteristics favouring a substantial use of public transport exist in European cities as opposed to US cities: great compactness, a long-established tradition to use public transport, a still low though steadily rising private-car ownership, and relatively meagre investment resources channelled into urban motorways. Road expenditure per head of population in 1965 was still only £5·5 per annum ($13) in Britain, £8·5 ($20) in France, £15·3 ($37) in West Germany compared with £25·7 ($62) in the USA (see *Traffic Engineering and Control*, September 1965). A few years ago, for instance, Venice was seriously threatened with massive motorway construction and Stockholm is in danger of losing much of its character by the linking of its islands with motorways. However, one must recognize that such cities as Stockholm are in urgent need of improving overall accessibility by the construction of a limited primary road system, partly in the form of motorways. At the same time, Stockholm, like most other European cities, is improving and extending its existing public transport system. In the case of Stockholm, the city is completing a $37\frac{1}{2}$-mile rapid-transit system linking it with its central section underground, and in the new suburban communities, like Vallingby and Farsta, new centres have been built on top of the 'T' Bana stations. The 'T' Bana has in fact been used in a most intelligent manner in linking the growing new communities around Stockholm and providing them with new centres as part of a well-organized land-use transport plan.

The problem of the parked car

We have so far considered mainly the vehicular traffic on the move and referred to the stationary vehicle only incidentally. In fact, indiscriminate parking can and does also seriously erode the urban environment. Parked cars in narrow central-area streets often protrude on to the footpath and add to the discomfort of pedestrians who already have to pick their way between them and a large assortment of street furniture, lamp-posts, traffic signs and lights, parking meters, telephone boxes and so on. Cars in the form of shiny metal objects of frequently harsh colours can destroy the carefully conceived subtle proportions and colour tones of fine historic streets and squares. Forecourts to cathedrals and other significant public buildings, which should ideally be hard-paved public assembly places for the predominant use of pedestrians, have been turned into a sea of parked cars and coaches, often all but destroying the principal views of these important buildings. It has also become standard practice to use perimeter roads of magnificent parks like St James's Park, or squares like Bedford Square, in London, for extensive parking, thus introducing a visual barrier at eye level between the trees and green and the surrounding urban area and partly destroying the original intention of bringing the country into the town.

Large office blocks, shopping centres and major transportation centres like airports require vast car-parking facilities; where these are provided at ground level, they tend to be a visual problem as well as one of remembering where one has left one's car. Where multi-storey

Piazza Navona, Rome, littered with parked taxis during a protest of taxi drivers in May 1967. *Photo: United Press International*

50 000 parked cars around a stadium in California during Independence Day. Forgetting where one left one's car could be quite a problem. *Photo: United Press International*

San Francisco International Airport. 1400 outdoor spaces and 2700 spaces in multi-storey garaging. *Photo: United Press International*

car parks have been built as part of the street frontage they add little to the architecture with their lifeless appearance and a good deal to local congestion, particularly when used by commuters. However, where multi-storey garages have been well designed and integrated with other buildings as at Toronto International Airport, they can make a positive functional and visual contribution. The best but also the most costly solution is that of removing parked cars out of sight into underground garages, under individual building complexes, as for instance in the new St Paul's precinct, in the City of London.

Enlightened planning authorities like the former London County Council (now the Greater London Council) insisted on such provisions for new buildings in the central area and indeed most post-war buildings have incorporated considerable underground parking provisions. However, in retrospect this policy was found to be a mistaken one since in many instances the car-parking capacity was not geared to the limited capacity of the surrounding roads. The most recent tendency is therefore to discourage the provision of such car-parking facilities as one of the means of reducing the entry of private vehicles into the central areas. A more sensible solution of the central-area car-parking problem now appears to lie in restricting long-term car parking within central areas and in providing a series of major multi-storey car parks around its perimeter, near public transport routes, so that the motorist, having parked his car, can change on to public transport or taxis.

Toronto International Airport. The centrally located multi-storey car park is surrounded with terminal buildings to which easy access is provided. *Photo: Canadian Department of Transport*

Paternoster Square, St Paul's Precinct, City of London. Underground garaging is provided beneath this pedestrian square. *Photo: Walter Bor*

The Greater London Council parking plan for the 40 square miles of Inner London announced in April 1968 envisaged a reduced parking standard for offices from one space for 200 sq. ft to one space for 15 000 sq. ft and a halving of parking standards for shops, together with the provision of 1600 new off-street parking spaces per year. In the absence of higher capacity roads, these parking policies appear necessary and reasonable. Yet this was at once attacked by the Royal Automobile Club and described as "an objectionable threat of traffic dictatorship", adding "This plan can only result in London becoming a carless town in the next decade."

The problem of parking is not confined to the central areas of our cities. It is also becoming quite serious in the surrounding residential areas, where the overwhelming majority of existing houses and flats have inadequate or no garaging facilities and where residents leave their cars parked along the kerbside. Since residential streets are often only three lanes wide, the permanent monopolization of two lanes reduces their usable width to one lane for all traffic, including delivery vans. In many such residential areas the only way to obtain off-street parking relatively painlessly is to sacrifice the front gardens and turn them into parking aprons. This method, though a palliative, is not likely to contribute to the improvement of the environment. The insertion of new garaging facilities is usually difficult, and often only possible by demolishing some residential accommodation and in high-density areas it will be necessary to construct multi-storey garages to meet this parking need. Since the shortage of housing is common to almost all European cities, the authorities will be reluctant to demolish existing serviceable housing for that purpose and there will be a natural temptation to build parking facilities on the remaining open spaces, thereby diminishing the usually already inadequate open-space provision.

Thus we can see that the increasing number of vehicles in our urban areas presents us with some very difficult problems since the existing street network and building stock were not designed to accommodate them. The urban environment is being seriously eroded as a result of our inability to deal effectively with the vehicle, whether on the move or stationary, and a series of measures consisting of restrictions on the one hand and positive

A Los Angeles scrap-metal firm has come up with a partial answer to how America can keep from being buried in unwanted cars which can be converted into usable steel. This photo shows a pile of wrecked cars before going into the machine. *Photo: United Press International*

123

construction on the other will have to be taken to halt and if possible reverse this situation where the vehicle is dominating rather than serving our daily lives.

When we have finished with our cars, their disposal presents yet another growing problem. Modern methods such as compacting cars into solid cubes which are then melted down deal with this problem, but vast storage areas for disused cars are still required and these frequently disfigure the countryside.

The needs of pedestrians

We have been concerned so far only with the vehicle in urban areas. What about the pedestrian, and who is he, anyhow? Probably you and I when we are not driving our cars. The population is often erroneously classified as either drivers or pedestrians, but in fact, to an ever-increasing extent, we are really talking about the same person. It is true, of course, that certain categories of people will never be drivers of motor cars, such as the very young and the very old, and the very poor, people who are disqualified because of driving offences or disabilities and people who simply cannot or will not drive. It is difficult to quantify accurately this category of permanent non-drivers but they may well comprise something like 20 per cent or more of the total population. If no effective alternative method of transport is provided for them, they may turn out to be the new underprivileged class in future, and this is indeed another cogent argument for the need to provide a high-quality public transport in urban areas.

All these non-drivers will walk when they are not riding on public transport to school, to the shops and offices, to the cinemas and theatres, or just stroll in the parks, streets and squares. To these must be added the drivers who walk from their parked car to all these places and those drivers who, for one reason or another, prefer to leave their car at home and use public transport and then walk from the nearest stop or station to their destination or just stroll.

Thus at least in most existing European cities only a small proportion of drivers will actually drive everywhere and the overwhelming majority will walk varying distances. This is indeed borne out by observing our urban streets, particularly those where there is a concentration of activities. The pavements are full of people walking, shop-window gazing, standing in groups and talking—traffic noises permitting—sitting on benches or in parks—weather permitting—lying on the grass. Their requirements in terms of outdoor environment are very different from the much smaller number of people who at any given time sit in their driving seats and who want to get as quickly as possible to their destination.

The environment which pedestrians are likely to appreciate is the one which is most sympathetic to the person on foot—human-scale buildings and spaces, displays of goods, flowers and water, shelter from wind and rain, availability of refreshments, and opportunity to sit and talk or rest in peace and quiet. All this is a far cry from the requirements of the moving vehicle. Yet both these categories must share the same urban spaces, since there are

Pedestrians cross in all directions at East 42nd Street, New York, during a 22-second halt of all vehicular traffic. *Photo: United Press International*

Washington Square, Manhattan, New York, on a spring Sunday morning. Public demand has resulted in this square being made into a pedestrian precinct. *Photo: Walter Bor*

Coventry shopping precinct. People sitting and talking, resting in peace and quiet. *Photo by courtesy of Coventry City Architect*

very few alternatives where they are physically separated. The principle of pedestrian/ vehicular separation has by now been sufficiently expounded to find general acceptance in theory, though the practical implementation has still been only sporadic and isolated. It is particularly important to emphasize the need for a safe and convenient local system of pedestrian ways, particularly for the use of mothers and children who even with a high degree of car ownership will still require it.

Since the major conflict between pedestrians and vehicles occurs in busy shopping centres, town planners concentrated their efforts in the first place on creating traffic-free shopping precincts. The cheapest and simplest method adopted was the rationing by time of the road space of a shopping street, between pedestrians and vehicles, through administrative measures; a road was simply being closed to all vehicular traffic during shopping hours, and deliveries had to take place before or after this period. This method involved only the erection of a few signs. A successful example of this sort of measure was the first stage of the pedestrianization of London Street, Norwich, East Anglia. The two photographs show the street before and after closure to vehicular traffic which resulted in a 300 per cent increase in pedestrians and a 25 per cent increase in the turnover of shops (see Appendix 18).

London Street, Norwich, before closure to vehicles in July 1967, carried up to 600 vehicles per hour and made shopping inconvenient. *Photo by courtesy of Norwich City Planning Officer*

London Street, Norwich, after trial closure to vehicles has become a more pleasant place for walking through and the turnover of the shops has greatly increased. *Photo by courtesy of Norwich City Planning Officer*

The next step is to design for the permanent exclusion of vehicular traffic from a shopping street. This necessitates first the construction of service roads on either side at the rear of the shops and is likely also to require modification to the shops to provide for rear access. Once this is done, the whole ground space between shopping frontages becomes permanently available for pedestrians and the street surface can be remodelled to suit this new function; the separate raised footpaths and kerbs can be removed and the whole street is repaved as a walkway; trees are planted and seats erected to create an intimate and friendly atmosphere and a sense of place in lieu of the previous traffic street. This approach has been particularly successfully carried out, for instance, in Spark Street, Ottawa.

The above two examples illustrate two relatively inexpensive methods of adapting existing shopping streets to pedestrian use and could with advantage be followed in many of our cities. In some European cities Second World War bomb-damage created new opportunities for a more radical approach. In Rotterdam, for instance, an extensive area in the centre of the city was completely remodelled on the principle of horizontal separation of vehicles from pedestrians, in the by now world-famous Lijnbaan, consisting of a grid of pedestrian shopping streets with vehicular rear access to the shops. The two-storey streets are sub-divided into bays by covered ways and are attractively laid out with flower beds, sculpture, seats, kiosks and cafes.

Lijnbaan shopping centre, Rotterdam, with old town hall in the background. *Photo: Walter Bor*

Lower Precinct, Coventry. Two-level shopping precinct. *Photo by courtesy of Coventry City Architect*

A similar principle of horizontal separation was adopted in the Coventry shopping precinct, though here two levels for pedestrians were introduced with shops on two floors. This principle did not prove very successful in the first part of the scheme since it necessitated the climbing of stairs to get up to and down from the upper level. In the subsequent development of the lower precinct this defect was overcome by the skilful exploitation of the sloping site leading people effortlessly to either the upper or lower level of shops, depending from which side one approached.

A little-known but interesting example of an upper pedestrian level in an existing street comes from Morristown, Tennessee, USA, where this upper-level walkway was created by building decks onto the existing buildings and connecting them with bridges.

The principle of vertical separation of pedestrians from vehicles involves an even more massive remodelling and investment and can therefore be undertaken only in the most favourable circumstances. In the Barbican Development in the City of London, following considerable pressure for a comprehensive redevelopment as opposed to the piecemeal approach which hitherto prevailed, a scheme was proposed and is in process of implementation which envisages an upper pedestrian level over a 40-acre area to the north of a new road—London Wall Road—with shops, offices, flats for 6500 people, schools, and a concert hall all connected to it, with vehicular traffic at ground level and underground car parks. When completed this will be one of the most significant attempts to create a total new urban environment based on vertical pedestrian/vehicular separation.

Morristown, Tennessee, USA. Upper pedestrian level is attached to existing buildings. *Photo : Chet Brogan*

Barbican area, City of London, upper walkways in use. In the foreground pedestrian bridges across London Wall Road leading to continuous upper-level walkway system, linking the office blocks on the right with the blocks of flats beyond. *Photo by courtesy of the City Architect*

At the same time as the Barbican Development (see Appendix 13) was conceived, Stockholm city planners designed the Hötorget development in the northern part of the centre of the city on a site previously covered with sub-standard housing. This ambitious development was closely integrated with the extension of the underground system projected to run under the site and consists of three levels of parking and service roads below a ground- and upper-level pedestrian shopping precinct, with five high office blocks above. While the decision to exclude residential accommodation and to superimpose upon the delicate skyline these five closely spaced high office blocks, which merge in many views of the city into a bulky, solid box, can be questioned the purposefulness of this development is impressive and the environment created is attractive and appears to function well.

Hötorget, Stockholm. Pedestrian shopping street above underground car parking and servicing and and underground railway station. *Photo: Walter Bor*

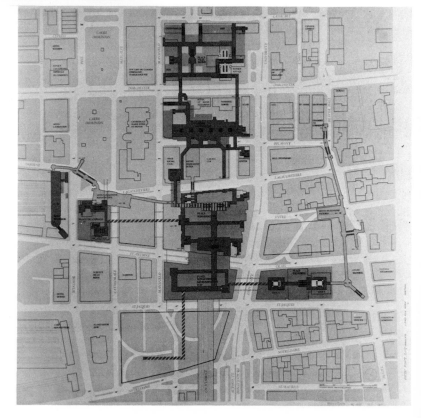

Montreal central area. Plan shows network of underground pedestrian walkways connecting the Place Ville Marie (at top) to the Place Bonaventura (centre), Place du Canada (left) and Place Victoria (right). Planning consultant: Vince Ponte. *Photo: Arnott Rogers Batten Ltd*

130

Canadian planners who have to cope with severe climatic conditions opted for a vertical separation of vehicles from pedestrians whereby both are kept underground in the recently developed Place Ville Marie in Montreal. While there is a slightly raised pedestrian deck above that level, all the shopping is under cover and a very pleasant and appropriate environment has been created which ensures all-year-round functioning. A network of underground walkways connect it to the central station, the Queen Elizabeth Hotel and downtown offices.

Similar climatic considerations which resulted in an underground shopping concourse in the Place Ville Marie, Montreal, have influenced a much older shopping form, the

Place Ville Marie, Montreal. Raised pedestrian piazza in the city centre. From here steps lead down to an underground shopping centre which forms part of an underground pedestrian walkway system connecting the main railway station and other important centres. *Photo by courtesy of 'Architectural Design'*

glazed-in shopping arcade. One of the finest examples of such covered arcades is the Gum Store in Moscow with its three pedestrian shopping levels.

These examples indicate some of the possibilities which exist in resolving, at least within a limited area, the conflict between vehicles and pedestrians, particularly in shopping centres, and in creating a new kind of urban environment with its own identity and character. An attempt to achieve this is being made on a comprehensive basis in the remodelling of the Liverpool City Centre (see Appendix 19).

Gum Store, Moscow. Covered shopping hall with three pedestrian levels. *Photo: Novosti Press Agency*

We shall not succeed in creating a rich and attractive urban environment until we have met the different needs of people living and working in urban areas and moving about as pedestrians or drivers. The conflicts are clearly such that they threaten urban life as such to an ever-increasing degree. We cannot hope to eliminate these conflicts altogether, nor should we, in my view, even try, for much of the vitality and interest in urban existence is due to such conflicts. For instance, the total removal of all vehicular traffic by physical separation in the form of an upper pedestrian deck is not always as successful in practice as one had hoped for and some of these pedestrian decks can be rather bleak and unfriendly. But what we must attempt to do and succeed with is the elimination of violent and dangerous conflicts which are destructive of human lives, health and happiness. And in this respect, the rationalization and improved functioning of the movement of people and goods throughout our urban areas would make the most substantial contribution to the raising of the standards of the urban environment.

Appendix 18

London Street, Norwich—conversion into a foot street
A. A. Wood, Norwich City Planning Officer

London Street is one of the best shopping streets in the city of Norwich and has considerable townscape value, winding between the Market Place and the Cathedral area. Before it was closed to vehicles it acted as a short cut for traffic crossing the central area and carried up to 600 vehicles per hour.

London Street, Norwich, after the permanent adaptation of the street to pedestrian traffic. The raised sidewalks were eliminated, the street was re-paved and seats and kiosks provided. *Photo by courtesy of Norwich City Planning Officer*

The legal powers used to create the foot streets in Norwich are contained in the Road Traffic Regulation Act, 1967. Section One of the Act gives powers to close a street for "avoiding danger to persons using the road". As yet, there are no means of closing streets for purely environmental reasons, but it is hoped that legislation will shortly be forthcoming to make this possible.

The experimental scheme (see page 126) was inaugurated on July 17, 1967, for a trial period of six months at a cost of £1800. Because of the particular layout of the area two sections of London Street were completely closed to traffic and a further section of London Street and several interdependent streets converted to service access only. Servicing to the shops in the closed sections (which for the most part have no rear access) is by trolley or by carry, there being no distance greater than 120 ft from a point where a service vehicle may stop.

The shopkeepers' reaction to the scheme was one of wholehearted approval. They considered the removal of vehicular traffic created a greatly improved business atmosphere and better working conditions. The street became quieter, cleaner and free from diesel fumes. Customers are no longer harassed by traffic and this has led to an increase in impulse buying.

No objections were received at the end of the experimental period and the Minister of Transport confirmed the Order making London Street a permanent foot street. The permanent scheme is estimated to cost £17 000 and includes repaving the closed sections of the street to a uniform level, new street lighting, street furniture and semi-mature trees. Showcases and continental-type cafés will be introduced as outdoor extensions of the shops (see Figure 1).

Besides the refurnishing of the street, the shopkeepers are being encouraged to collaborate in a face-lift scheme. A colour scheme, together with fascia designs and lettering styles, has been prepared to assist the traders.

The London Street project has proved that pedestrian streets can be created without the need to construct rear service networks or relief roads, given *full* consultation with affected parties and given the will of the Local Authority to effect environmental improvement.

The role of interchanges

Amongst the most important elements in a fully coordinated land-use/transport plan are the interchanges—their location, design concept and convenient functioning will largely condition the effectiveness of the system and its convenience to the travelling public. Interchanges are the points where different forms of transport come together to enable travellers to change from one type of transport to another, with convenience and comfort. A good recently built example of an interchange from car to aircraft is Toronto Airport. Since a lot of people use interchanges, ancillary services in the form of shops, restaurants, personal services, etc., if incorporated into an interchange, are invariably a welcome asset. At O'Hare Airport, Chicago, for instance, offices, hotels, barbers and even nightclubs can be found which make up a 'mini-city' where businessmen meet and never enter the city. Finally, since interchanges also represent points of maximum accessibility, it is only logical to concentrate employment opportunities, housing and other uses which benefit from good accessibility, like shopping centres in or near such interchanges.

Combined railway and bus stations form one well-known type of interchange, suburban underground stations combined with car parks and bus stops another. Several recent city plans envisage some of these suburban interchange points as future growth points and nuclei of major district centres with high-density housing, offices and good shopping

Interchange from car to aircraft is made convenient at Toronto Airport where a multi-storey car park is joined to terminal facilities at its periphery. *Photo by courtesy of the Canadian Department of Transport*

Washington Heights, Manhattan, New York, where the Washington Bridge Motorway branches off into a coach station with a shopping centre and residential flats above and an underground station below. *Photo: Walter Bor*

facilities taking full advantage of good accessibility by public and private transport at these points.

The idea of interchanges is, of course, not new and some spectacular examples have been in existence for many decades. Amongst these, perhaps still the most ambitious to date is New York's Grand Central Station. Conceived at the turn of the century and completed in 1913, it has served as the prototype of multi-level distribution complexes of other famous projects, such as the Rockefeller Center in New York, Penn Center and Market East in Philadelphia, Place Ville Marie in Montreal, and, to a lesser degree, the Hötorget in Stockholm. Two underground levels accommodate suburban trains and express trains, with two levels of subway links and a shuttle subway to Times Square on top of it with the pedestrian Grand Concourse used by half a million people per day and acting as the distribution hub of the complex, which serves 21 buildings by means of an underground pedestrian network throughout the 60-acre site. Equally good accessibility has also been

Grand Central Station, Manhattan, New York. Section showing the underground levels of the suburban and express trains, subway links and the Times Square shuttle service. The Grand Central concourse is in the middle of the picture with escalation leading to the PanAm building above. *Photo by courtesy of 'Architectural Forum'*

provided for taxis and private cars by means of an elevated roadway 'collar' around the perimeter of the site, as well as to buses running in the surrounding streets. For good measure, the 59-storey PanAm building, the largest commercial building in the world with its 2·4 million sq. ft of office space housing 17 500 office workers and a helicopter station on the roof, was added in 1963. In spite of this terrific concentration, the Grand Central complex is functioning remarkably well because of the highly intelligent and imaginative way it had been organized and it points the way towards new forms of urban concentrations fully integrated with all modes of transport at the point of interchange which are likely to be the future growth points in our cities.

The impact of air traffic

A report of a memorial service to Carl Sandburg at the Lincoln Memorial, Washington, DC, which was addressed by President Johnson and attended by 5600 people, concluded,

"The program ended with the Air Force Singing Sergeants and mezzo-soprano Jessie Norman singing through the din of passing jet airliners."

This is a telling illustration of how, in addition to the already high noise level generated by vehicles in towns, aircraft noise is beginning to be an increasing nuisance in our cities, disrupting people at work, children at school and people's sleep, and intruding into open-air activities which require dignified silence. It is true, of course, that in the case quoted above Washington National Airport is probably one of the closest to a city centre, but even in London, with Heathrow Airport some 15 miles from the city centre, vast built-up areas are affected by day and night by noise from aircraft about to land or taking off. A further growing problem related to airports near our cities is that of air pollution caused by aircraft taking off and emitting heavy exhaust fumes over built-up areas already polluted by motor-car fumes. Thus many of our cities, already blighted by the noise and fumes from vehicular traffic, are now being increasingly exposed to additional noise impact and air pollution by aircraft.

Yet, we are only at the beginning of an enormous expansion of air transport throughout the world. In the USA, for instance, there was an increase in the passenger volume in 1967 by 29 per cent. The busiest US airports handle up to 10 000 passengers in a peak hour at present, in a few years this maximum could exceed 25 000 (see 'The Airborne Stampede', John Morris Dixon, *Architectural Forum*, Jan/Feb 1968). More important still, the size and with it the noise of aircraft is also increasing. Since the end of 1969 the Boeing 747 'Jumbo Jet' has been in service, probably to be followed by several versions of the jet 'airbus' and the Boeing supersonic, with capacities of about 300. Even before these giants of the air become operational, the British-French Concorde and the Soviet supersonics may be flying, each carrying up to 150 people and causing supersonic booms.

Clearly, if these giant planes arrived in large numbers, in addition to existing air traffic, at any one airport, not only would they saturate the air with a tremendous din but their passengers would swamp all the existing airport facilities. Not only will existing airports have to be radically reconstructed but scores of new airports will be required. For instance, a major search has been conducted by a special Commission set up by the British Government under Mr Justice Roskill for the best location of a third airport for London within a 55-mile radius to the north and east of London (see Appendix 8). Similar location studies are now being carried out amongst other places in New York, Atlanta and Toronto.

It will also be essential to provide alternative inter-city air transport other than by these huge aircraft and a possible solution might be the 'short take-off and landing' (STOL) aircraft carrying up to 60 passengers and cruising at 285 miles per hour, requiring only a 1800-ft landing strip, or the 'vertical take-off and landing' (VTOL) which needs an even shorter landing strip. In other words, these small and relatively slow planes could bring passengers very close in to city centres, e.g. on to a site of abandoned Hudson River piers in Manhattan, only two blocks from the Lincoln Center, or in the Rotherhithe area in East London on the site of disused docks. However, although the noise from STOL and VTOL aircraft is concentrated on relatively small areas compared with traditional aircraft requiring long runways, it is still of such a magnitude and intensity as to be unacceptable for people living in their vicinity. It may well be that the type of Advanced Passenger Trains (see page 110), which are being developed in Japan, the USA and the UK, travelling at speeds of 150 mph and above may prove to be a better answer to inter-city travel than either STOL or VTOL. The aircraft providing a shuttle service between New York and Boston and Washington need as much time to land as an international airliner yet spend only 35–40 minutes in the air. Rapid rail connections could increase the capacity of the airports for longer flights and the recently introduced fast metro liners are a logical step in the right direction.

The task of conveying passengers to and from city airports casts not only a major blight on flying (e.g. at present it takes about one hour by road to get from Manhattan to Kennedy Airport) but adds yet another load on the city road network, unless rapid transit facilities are an available alternative, such as that from Gatwick Airport to London. In the USA, Cleveland is building the first subway line leading directly into an airport terminal. A new rapid rail service is planned to be in operation by the end of 1972 to connect Kennedy International Airport to Penn Station, Manhattan. Los Angeles is planning to get passengers to the airport by a sky lounge which consists of an 'aerial crane' type of helicopter lifting a 40-passenger lounge; this lounge can be towed to passenger pick-up point, then flown to the airport and towed around to sub-terminals. This would be a great advance on existing helicopter services which can carry only small numbers of passengers.

The anticipated increase in air traffic is likely to have a growing influence on our planning in large towns and cities. There will be more pressure for helicopter landing grounds and short air strips for vertical and short take-off aircraft. One of the reasons for building high used to be that the higher you go the further you remove yourself from the street noise; we will now have to add—and the nearer you get to aircraft noise. However, it may well be that more universal use of double glazing and air conditioning will reduce the nuisance of aircraft noise at least within buildings, although outdoor activities will be increasingly affected.

Some of the early railway stations remain to this day great and beautiful monuments to the age of steam. The design of air terminals presents a similar challenge for the age of the fast jet liner, but only relatively few are more than convenient but faceless sheds for the transfer of passengers and goods. There are, however, notable exceptions such as Dulles Airport, Washington, DC, architect Saarinen's poetic masterpiece, whether experienced by day or night. The conveying of passengers from the terminal building to the planes is also very civilized at Dulles Airport, where this takes the form of comfortable mobile lounges.

Mobile lounge used at Dulles Airport brings passengers from terminal to aircraft in comfort.
Photo by courtesy of Federal Aviation Agency

Dulles Airport, Washington, DC, by day. Architect: E. Saarinen. *Photo by courtesy of the Federal Aviation Agency*

Dulles Airport, Washington, DC, by night. Architect: E. Saarinen. *Photo by courtesy of the Federal Aviation Agency*

The need for a balanced transport system

As City Planning Officer of Liverpool my experience—which no doubt I share with most city planners—has been that there is a need for a carefully balanced transport system designed to provide for the use of personal transport where it is most effective (as in the low-density suburbs), the use of public transport to the compact inner areas to shift the bulk of the commuters and the need to establish well-designed interchanges at strategically located points (e.g. at public transport stations, suburban centres, etc.) between the two.

In the case of Liverpool, for instance, major improvements to the city's public transport system were found necessary in the form of an underground loop linking the four city-centre railway stations and thus doubling the capacity of the Mersey railway, as well as the revitalization of an inner suburban rail loop of $19\frac{1}{2}$ miles linking the suburbs with the city centre (see Appendix 19). There is also a need to cater for essential goods and service traffic, fast road-based public transport and to provide better private-car accessibility to central shopping and entertainment facilities and a better provision for short-term parking. It is also desirable to cater for a modest increase of private cars for shoppers and for those who need their cars for business and are willing to pay the corresponding parking charges.

These traffic requirements in turn must be closely related to the location of the main employment areas, shopping centres and cultural and recreational facilities. The wholesale relocation of such traffic-attracting uses is, as a rule, impracticable in existing urban areas. However, there is usually sufficient pressure for growth and change to redistribute these new assets and to re-allocate uses to replace obsolete ones like some marshalling yards and warehouses in a meaningful way. This would help considerably to distribute the traffic load more evenly and to achieve a better integration of traffic generators with the transport system. Resulting from these considerations, a quantifiable need can be established for a limited but high-grade primary and secondary road network which would accommodate essential goods and service traffic, express bus services, through traffic which has been squeezed out of the environmental areas, shopping traffic and some private business traffic, including a proportion of commuters.

The extent of necessary urban motorway construction can only be arrived at after a comprehensive land-use/transport study has been made of the whole city region. This will have to take into account alternative development strategies for the future from which a preferred solution will be selected. Such land-use/transport studies are now under way in most major city regions in Britain and were inspired by similar studies in the USA and Canada carried out in recent years (see Appendix 6).

With regard to detailed considerations of the alignment and construction of the proposed motorways, an essential principle to be followed should be the total integration of the new motorway structures with the surrounding urban areas on either side. In other words, we should reject the idea that motorways, particularly where elevated, can be just inserted into the urban fabric leaving buildings standing on either side, since none of these buildings was designed to stand next door to a motorway which renders working and housing conditions unacceptable and which disrupts the view of the buildings and from the buildings. The only civilized way of dealing with this difficult social and visual problem is to redevelop in depth on either side of urban motorways so that the new buildings and the motorway can be fully integrated but so that buildings may be protected from noise, fumes and vibration.

In Chapter 10 there is a detailed reference to the way this problem is being tackled in Liverpool and it is gratifying to know that the US Highway Department Bureau of Public Roads under the direction of Lovell Bridwell is also thinking in similar terms; under the title Joint Development Concept wide corridors (of up to one mile width) of land are now being acquired for comprehensive redevelopment to ensure better integration between freeways and the surrounding urban areas than has been the case in the past. Great encouragement is also being given to the multi-disciplinary Urban Design Team approach to ensure that the implementation of integrated freeways is also of high visual quality and recently $4·8 million have been earmarked for such a team to work on the Baltimore freeway proposals.

With regard to congestion caused largely by the private motorist, there may also be a need for an economically realistic assessment of road space. At present the private motorist pays a flat rate in the form of an annual tax whether or not he uses his car extensively in urban areas. Since urban road space is expensive to provide and increases in costs towards the centre, it could be argued that the person occupying this space with his car should pay for it. Various methods of road pricing are at present under consideration. Should one or the other come into operation, only experience will show to what extent such pricing mechanisms will help to deter people from driving to the most congested parts of our cities and thus alleviate congestion.

Appendix 19

Liverpool city centre—movement proposals
City Centre Planning Group under the direction of Walter Bor, City Planning Officer, and Graeme Shankland, Planning Consultant

The unusually high degree of dereliction coupled with extensive municipal ownership of land in the city centre provide unique opportunities for a comprehensive redevelopment of the city centre and a radical restructuring of the vehicular and pedestrian movement within it.

The road proposals for the city centre which are an integral part of the proposals for the whole of the city (see *Liverpool Interim Planning Policy 1965*) envisaged an elevated Inner Motorway circumscribing the city centre in a wide loop and linking to a newly formed entry/exit connection of the existing Mersey Road Tunnel and the major existing city radials, and a proposed motorway link to the M6. This motorway will, however, be at ground level near the Anglican Cathedral to avoid a visual conflict with Scott's masterpiece. North of the Inner Motorway a connection is being built to the second Mersey Road Tunnel

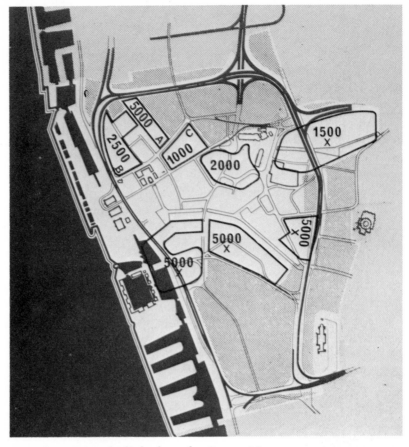

which is now under construction. Directly linked to the Inner Motorway are ramps providing access to a series of large multi-storey garages most of which will form a base for office and other development to be constructed above them (Figure 1).

The main purpose of the Inner Motorway is to distribute major traffic flows round the city centre and to provide better accessibility from the docks to the M6. Having thus freed the city centre of most of this through traffic, it was found that the existing city-centre streets could accommodate the local traffic and that there was therefore, a few exceptions apart, no need for costly and destructive road widenings within the city centre. The existing roads will carry all service traffic and public transport but only a modest amount of private cars, since generous parking provision mainly for shoppers will be made largely in the peripheral car parks. Public transport will be provided by means of buses and taxis penetrating the city centre and a reorganized rail service. The present Merseyside underground railway which links the city to the Wirral and terminates at Central Station will be extended into an underground loop to connect with the existing overhead railway at the four city-centre railway stations. This will also double the capacity of the Mersey railway, an important consideration since it serves a substantial number of the city's commuters who come from the Wirral. Part of this new underground rail loop will also be integrated later with the proposed revitalized Outer Rail loop which will bring passengers from the city's suburbs to the centre.

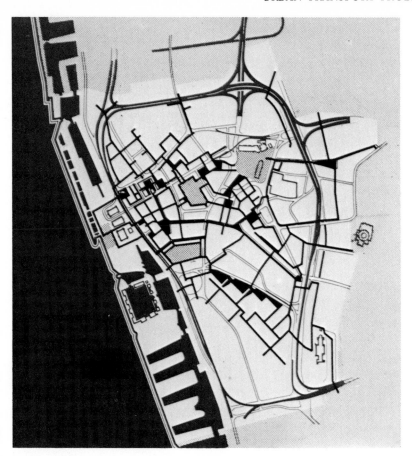

Figure 2. Liverpool City Centre. Diagram illustrates the main pedestrian streets and walkways connecting four central railway stations with major centres of activity, open spaces and public car parks. From: Liverpool City Centre Plan

An extensive and fully comprehensive pedestrian network is proposed to link all the major city interchanges and car parks with the existing and proposed shopping, office and entertainment centres. Pedestrian routes will be at ground level, particularly through existing shopping streets from which vehicular traffic will be withdrawn, and at upper level 20 ft above the ground where they will be built into the new developments. These pedestrian ways will also connect with existing and proposed open spaces and the new civic centre (Figure 2).

Part 4

The Design of our Urban Environment

9 The Urban Design Process

Our historic heritage

Any discussion of the design of our urban environment should start with considerations of how the existing townscape has been created and with an understanding of urban design concepts of the past. Our forefathers created their urban environment, either by an evolutionary and often intuitive process over time, or by a conscious singleminded design effort, in response to the needs and aspirations of their time. We can learn much from their experience and imagination in our efforts to create an urban environment of high quality for the needs of urban society of today and tomorrow. This means a sensitive and intelligent understanding of our fine old buildings and groups of buildings, of the form and character of urban spaces and indeed of whole historic parts of our towns and cities leading to the formulation of action programmes for the preservation, conservation and rehabilitation of our historic heritage.

By preservation we mean essentially the retention of buildings and groups of buildings in their original form, whilst conservation is mainly concerned with the safeguarding of an existing fine urban environment and does not exclude physical changes, modernization and rebuilding providing the character and scale are maintained. An outstanding example of such careful conservation is the historic core of Amsterdam. Rehabilitation is a comprehensive activity which may include selective preservation, conservation and re-development with a view of improving the overall environment of an area by environmental management, tree planting, inserting of such facilities as playgrounds and car parks as well as the modernization of individual dwellings. Rehabilitation is an important and hitherto inadequately used alternative to wholesale demolition and comprehensive redevelopment.

147

Amsterdam's historic core with its unique pattern of streets and canals. The character and scale of buildings in this area have been carefully maintained. *Photo by courtesy of KLM Aerocarto NV*

To begin with we must have some objective criteria according to which an individual building should be preserved, and the five points proposed by the Civic Trust in Britain a few years ago are therefore worth noting. According to these proposals, a building should be preserved if:

1. it is a work of art which enriches the environment;

2. it is a notable example of a particular style or period;

3. it holds an historic place in the community;

4. it has historic associations with great men or great events;

5. its presence lends the surroundings a sense of the sequence of time.

The need to preserve certain buildings was recognized in Britain in the 1944 Town and Country Planning Act which made provision for listing buildings of architectural and historic interest throughout the country. These provisions were written again into the 1947 Town and Country Planning Act and are still in force. This was followed by the 1953 Historic Buildings and Monuments Act.

However, listing alone cannot in fact preserve a building, it only prevents it from being destroyed inadvertently. And since many historic buildings occupy valuable central area sites which, upon redevelopment, could yield considerable profits, historic buildings have been known not only to be allowed to deteriorate beyond repair but the deliberate removal of a few tiles and some flashing has not infrequently helped to speed the course of dilapidation. Thus Britain, which suffered considerable losses of its historic buildings during the war, lost further thousands of them since the war, at the rate of 400 historic buildings per year, through this sort of quiet vandalism. Public demand made itself felt in favour of tougher and more effective legislation for the protection and improvement of buildings of architectural and historic interest which has since been enacted in the 1967 Civic Amenities Act.

The preservation of old buildings of course has its problems. First they are all sub-standard according to modern building by-laws and a conscientious Medical Officer of Health or Building Surveyor could very well condemn the lot as being of sub-standard construction and lacking in modern sanitary facilities. Secondly, their maintenance and repair, improvement and modernization can be a costly business. It is true, some grants are available for that purpose, but they are pitifully inadequate. In Britain, the annual grants for the repair of the most outstanding historic buildings has been only half a million pounds for the whole country. This sum was increased to £700 000 in 1970. However, Local Authorities and private individuals have contributed quite substantial sums of money since the war for the restoration of historic buildings.

A difficult but by no means insoluble problem can arise when a new building is to be built next to or close by a historic building. An example of such a situation is in Blackheath, London. Another example comes from Prague, where houses around the Gothic Tyn church are being restored. In this case a new house had to be fitted between two old houses.

A successful example of happy coexistence of old and new buildings in Blackheath, London. On the left is the flank wall of the 18th-century Paragon (Michael Searle) which has acquired a new neighbour in the form of a sympathetically designed block of flats by Eric Lyons. *Photo by courtesy of Eric Lyons and Partners*

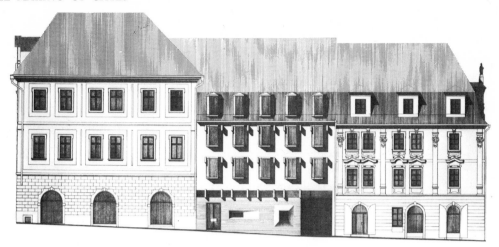

Reconstruction of the 'Ungelt' houses around the Gothic church in Prague. The middle house on this drawing had to be rebuilt and its design filled between two historic houses on either side. Architects: Vavra and Flasar

The sensitive integration of new buildings with an historic townscape is probably one of the most difficult tasks for the urban designer. However, when he succeeds, the results can be very attractive indeed. Perhaps one of the most interesting recent examples of a happy integration of a new building complex into a historic town is the city hall of Bensberg, West Germany, designed by Gottfried Boehm. Built on the site of a mediaeval castle, the city hall contains the council chamber, meeting rooms, offices and public spaces which can be reached from the main entrance at the base of the craggy tower which echoes the preserved tower of the old castle.

Bensberg City Hall, Germany. A successful example of imaginative design and integration of a modern building complex within a historic setting. Architect: Gottfried Boehm. *Photo: Hamburger Aero-Lloyd GMBH*

Wells, Somerset. The market square with cathedral towers in the background. Buildings from different periods merge into a harmonious whole. *Photo: Walter Bor*

Yet, much more important than the individual historic building—however fine an example of its period it may be—can be the whole urban fabric of an old area with its original road pattern and sequence of urban spaces. One of the unique features of many English towns is the casual yet graceful and harmonious way streets, squares and groups of buildings of many periods fit together. A thoughtless widening of a tight corner, insensitive rebuilding of individual houses and the introduction of unsympathetic materials can cause havoc.

In the context of the total urban environment with which we are concerned here, one can think of at least five good reasons for wholeheartedly supporting the principle of preservation and/or conservation (i.e. retention of the essential character and scale while allowing for changes and even rebuilding within it).

1. The retention of whole old areas enriches our visual experience, provides us with a meaningful link with the past and gives people a welcome choice to live and work in these buildings and their environment should they prefer it to contemporary development.

2. In these days of rapid growth and change with few, if any, stable common denominators, such older areas have a refreshingly permanent atmosphere about them which many people find reassuring and attractive.

3. The logic of larger building sites, to make better economic use of modern building technology coupled with organizational changes which favour the larger unit over a multiplicity of small ones, drives contemporary development inexorably towards a large-scale and to some extent an anonymous, diagrammatic form of architecture. At best this is acceptable, at worst it could lead to a boring sameness. The retention of sizeable and homogeneous parts of our towns and cities built to an intimate scale with character will help greatly to retain a sense of place and identity and a welcome contrast to the new development.

4. Our old areas and towns are one of our greatest commercial assets. Britain's rapidly growing international tourist trade is dependent on visitors being able to experience the unique environment of these old places.

151

5. Last, but not least, it is a responsibility to future generations. Clearly we cannot just discard old buildings and towns indiscriminately, but should want to look after those we value with loving care.

The historic heritage the British Isles still possesses is amongst the finest and most extensive in Europe. The Council of British Archaeology published a list in 1965 of no less than 324 historic towns (232 in England, 57 in Scotland and 35 in Wales) of which 51 are considered of special importance. The general public which only a few years ago was somewhat indifferent to this issue is now voicing increasing concern and interest in the preservation of this historic heritage. The Ministry of Housing and Local Government commissioned studies of four different historic towns in England (York, Bath, Chichester and Chester) and published reports on each of these which give detailed evidence of all the issues involved (see Appendix 20).

Many historic towns are also thriving regional centres trying to adapt themselves to modern conditions; their attempt to accommodate new growth and change could lead to the erosion of the historic fabric and their intrinsically closely knit small-scale character. One way to reconcile the preservation of the historic core with the need to accommodate growth and change is to divert the commercial pressures and associated parking problems from the historic core to a new centre or an expanding existing centre not far from the historic centre, as the city of Cambridge is planning (see Appendix 21).

Other European countries have already led the way in the preservation and restoration of historic areas and even whole towns. Czechoslovakia, for instance, is working through a systematic programme of conservation and urban renewal of 39 historic towns where every house is restored externally to its original design, including baroque sculpture, gilded angels and all, and modernized internally. Perhaps the most successfully restored, to date, are the South Bohemian town of Cesky Krumlov, the Hussite town of Tabor, the Moravian town of Telc and much of the historic core of Prague.

Cesky Krumlov in Southern Bohemia. The baroque castle tower still dominates the skyline of this historic town which has been fully restored

Tabor, the 15th-century town of the Hussites with the Gothic town hall in the top centre overlooking the town square. One of the best-preserved mediaeval towns in Europe. *Photo: E. Vasiliak*

Telc, a historic town in Moravia; 16th-century houses, grouped around the town square, have all been restored to their original form. *Photo: M. Sukup*

The gothic church in the old town of Prague surrounded by old houses which are being restored. On the left is the historic Orlow clock restored after the Second World War

The Poles have rebuilt the historic core of Warsaw out of total ruins and have restored a large number of their historic places, and in the Soviet Union Leningrad was restored to its old glory after its wartime ordeal and many historic places like Petrodvorjets have been completely rebuilt and the magnificent collection of churches and palaces in the Moscow Kremlin have been restored with loving care. In Spain and Portugal, too, careful restoration is in progress in many towns and particular attention is paid to their unique walled hill towns like Avila and Obidos. In France, since the passing of the Malraux Law in 1962, for the protection of the historical and aesthetic heritage of France, much has been done by the Commission Nationale des Secteurs Sauvegardes in maintaining the character of particular urban areas, sometimes whole villages and towns. Perhaps the most important aspect of this activity is that up to 80 per cent of the cost of restoration is paid to the owners. Tenants unable to afford increased rents after restoration are found alternative accommodation. This scheme is costing £3½ million per year.

Thus we can see that the peoples of Europe are at work to preserve their historic heritage, in spite of their otherwise considerable political and economic differences.

In the United States, of course, individual historic buildings and whole old towns are much rarer than in Europe and have played a less significant role in people's lives. Yet, Americans are just as attracted to old towns as European people, as the steadily increasing flow to Europe's historic towns shows. Recent decades have seen an emerging interest in the great American architecture of the 17th, 18th and 19th centuries, and some of these fine groups of old buildings like George Washington's Mount Vernon have been restored with great love and skill, particularly because of their historic importance. Indeed, whole historic areas like Georgetown in Washington, DC, have been meticulously preserved and have become prestige residences. During the past decade concerted efforts have also been made to preserve some of the great late 19th-century pioneering examples of America's first

Mount Vernon, George Washington's home, has been restored with great love and skill. *Photo: Walter Bor*

Williamsburg, Virginia. A street of rebuilt historic houses. *Photo: Walter Bor*

skyscrapers like the great architecture of Sullivan, Adler and Burnham in the Chicago loop. Perhaps the most unique example of an historic American town is Williamsburg in Virginia ; whereas most historic towns tend to lose some of their historic buildings over time, Williamsburg, which is being almost completely reconstructed with great scholarly attention to every detail, displays more historic houses as reconstruction proceeds !

Appendix 20

Four reports on historic towns in England

These reports were commissioned jointly by the Minister of Housing and the city and county councils concerned. They seek "to discover how to reconcile our old towns with the 20th century", and taken together, they highlight some of the most significant problems and opportunities of English historic towns. The reports were prepared by Colin Buchanan & Partners (Bath), Viscount Esher (York), Donald W. Insall & Associates (Chester) and G. W. Burrows, West Sussex County Planning Officer (Chichester). All reports are published by Her Majesty's Stationery Office.

These four historic towns reports provide guidance on conservation policies for historic town centres throughout the country. An important aspect of conservation is the devising of appropriate methods of evaluating those factors that contribute to the quality and character of a town and hence its capacity to absorb change. Conventional static techniques, such as 'listed buildings', though important, are not enough; the sense of sequence walking through certain areas, the rhythm and atmosphere created by certain activities must also be considered for a comprehensive assessment, and this has been done by varying methods in all four cases.

Between them, the reports cover a comprehensive range of techniques for the evaluation of historic towns. In their traffic assessments and proposals all the reports develop the principles of *Traffic in Towns,* the Buchanan Report, published in 1963, and the report on Bath develops the concept of environmental management schemes, based on surveys to supplement material on traffic movement data and environmental conditions. An important aspect examined in this report is the visual capacity of the study area in relation to parked and moving vehicles.

The York report is particularly concerned with the problem of visual intrusion which is illustrated with photographs that dramatize the effect of traffic on the surroundings. Proposals for servicing business premises include restriction of access to specific times, thus allowing many streets to be made available to pedestrians during peak shopping hours.

The Chester report concentrates on safer and more convenient pedestrian movement. Imaginative proposals to this effect include bridge links between the upper levels of individual rows with the characteristic two-level shopping and the improvement of pedestrian access into the town centre as a whole.

The role of public transport is seen by all the reports as being closely related to pedestrian movement. The York and Chichester reports discuss new types of vehicle (mini-buses, battery-driven cars, etc.) which may well provide some of the answers in the effort to improve access within the environmental capacity of historic streets.

The Chichester report comes to grips with some of the administrative and financial problems involved and shows that Local Authorities will need many additional powers to safeguard our historic heritage. For instance, they should be empowered to carry out works necessary for the successful implementation of a programme of conservation without the need to acquire a legal interest in the property. Provision should be made for the payment of compensation for any diminution in the value of the property affected, and an implementing organization should be set up to recover betterment. The York report makes a case for a special grant to historic towns of national importance.

In three of the reports—on Bath, York and Chester—the need is stressed for good hotels and additional cultural facilities which would provide a greater momentum for the tourist industry. Another recommendation in the Bath and York reports is the conversion of the many unused upper storeys into student accommodation for the universities. This would have the added advantage of creating a young and lively atmosphere.

Appendix 21

Fitzroy/Burleigh Street Shopping Centre, Cambridge
Planning Consultants: Llewelyn-Davies, Weeks, Forestier-Walker & Bor

Cambridge is not only an historic city of great beauty and of world renown but also an important regional shopping centre. Although the growth of the city of Cambridge has been deliberately restricted in the post-war period, the surrounding communities have grown considerably and are likely to continue to do so. This increased population, together with people's greater spending power, has resulted in great pressures for the extension and modernization of the existing city-centre shops. To meet this need for an increase in shopping facilities, the Council decided to implement a Ministerial decision not to expand the city-centre facilities since this would endanger the historic centre, but to develop instead the nearby existing shopping centre at Fitzroy/Burleigh Streets into a sub-regional centre complementary to the historic centre.

A major challenge was the need to accommodate a link road across the area which was required to meet overall traffic considerations, to accommodate traffic diverted from the historic core which will be pedestrianized, and to improve access to this area. These requirements are being met by an underground cut-and-cover road which would minimize the demolition of existing buildings and the impact on the environment, and which was selected as the best solution from several alternatives. When the road is completed, New Square will be returned to grass, and accessibility to the area and the environment in New Square will be greatly improved (see top left of model, Figure 1).

Figure 1. Fitzroy/Burleigh Street shopping centre, Cambridge. Model shows the rebuilt centre and new road under New Square in relation to the surrounding area

157

Figure 2. Fitzroy Street, Cambridge. Sketch shows existing shopping street transformed into a pedestrian mall. *Sketch by Brian Bunting*

The proposals envisage the retention of substantial existing shops and the gradual re-development of others with new shops of varying sizes and including large multiple stores. Fitzroy Street and Burleigh Street will become pedestrian shopping streets (see Figure 2) with a possible third shopping street extending eastwards. At the rear of the shops provision will be made for service access and for parking of 2000 cars in three multi-storey garages with upper-level enclosed pedestrian bridges giving direct access across the service yards to the shops.

A major new housing development to the south of the shopping centre will provide accommodation for most households displaced by the redevelopment. This is proposed in the form of four- to five-storey maisonette blocks, the deck access of which connects with the shops and car parks, and of two-storey houses and single-storey patio housing giving privacy and taking advantage of the southern aspect. An hotel and arts centre form an integral part of these proposals.

The main pedestrian link across Christ's Pieces between Fitzroy/Burleigh and the historic centre will be by means of a ground-level, tree-lined path, uninterrupted by any road. A mini-bus service connecting the historic centre with Fitzroy/Burleigh is suggested as an aid to pedestrians and a re-routing of local and country buses will provide as good a service for this area as for the historic area. Fitzroy/Burleigh, with its high degree of accessibility by public transport and private car in close proximity to the historic core, can thus develop into a viable complementary centre which will deflect the pressures on the historic centre and assist in its preservation while catering for the necessary increase in shopping facilities.

The role of the urban designer

"Architect-planners are often inclined to suppose that the design of the physical environment—which is their particular *métier*—will automatically secure the social ends which their idealism leads them to desire. This has often resulted in their adopting a set of assumptions that can be called 'architectural determinism', i.e. that architectural design has a direct and determinate effect on the way people behave and largely removes the social factors that also affect environment and which a properly formulated theory of 'the total environment' must surely incorporate. Social organization *and* physical design need to be considered as complementary aspects of the total environment."

Although an architect-planner myself, I share these critical comments of sociologist Maurice Broady. Having observed, for instance, how unforeseen changes caused through people's activities and use had played havoc with what had originally been conceived as an ideal environment I, in company with many other architect-planners, have become increasingly aware of the fundamental importance of the social and economic forces which shape our environment first and foremost. Any town design to be meaningful and to be successful as a living organism must therefore be built upon these considerations. Nevertheless, when all the social and economic factors have been analysed and the appropriate conclusions reached to define the brief for the urban designer, his task still remains to be done with intelligence, skill and imagination. And since in the last analysis it is the built environment in which people will live, work or play, his responsibility is great and his contribution essential.

The urban designer must therefore not only understand the socio-economic forces which shape the environment, but he must also be fully aware of the whole range of possibilities at his disposal to give this content the appropriate form. Many excellent books have by now been written on town design (though not enough about its socio-economic aspects) and there is a wealth of material upon which students of urban design can draw. But even when they have mastered the whole vocabulary, a high degree of skill, imagination and sound judgement is still required to translate theory into practice since each urban design problem is different according to local circumstances.

All too frequently the role of urban design in the planning process is misunderstood. Some see it simply as aesthetic control concerned mainly with the appearance of buildings and this is one of the hoariest old chestnuts, which perhaps has done more than anything else to give planning and planners a bad name. Others veer to the opposite extreme and expect to prepare three-dimensional layouts for the whole town according to which redevelopment should take place. I cannot subscribe to either of these interpretations. Urban design, as I see it, from the point of view of what our cities require has four or five main functions.

It is an integral part of the design process which starts with land-use/transport planning and urban form, and finishes with the built environment. Since one cannot really make many planning decisions which in the ultimate do not have urban design implications, it is wrong to exclude the urban designer from the basic planning process and to call him in only after certain land-use and transport decisions have been made.

159

Urban design must make its contribution to the formulation of policies for historic buildings and rehabilitation not only of architecturally significant groups of buildings but whole areas which are too good to be demolished but not good enough for 20th-century living. It should be concerned with evolving visual policies ranging from such city-wide aspects as the location of high buildings, landscaping and townscaping, to the detailed design of spaces, street furniture and planting in the local environment.

The urban designer must be fully involved in day-to-day guidance of on-going development to ensure that such visual policies, apart from other planning policies, are in fact implemented. In order to be effective and also to avoid head-on collisions resulting in refusals and appeals, close cooperation between developers and their architects on the one hand and planners and urban designers on the other throughout the design stage is essential and is being increasingly practised.

What is perhaps still inadequately realized is the need for clear planning briefs which the planners should prepare to guide developers and their professional advisers. This does not mean fully worked-out designs or even sketches, but diagrams illustrating the main planning criteria such as vehicular and pedestrian circulation, relationship to adjoining uses and buildings, land-use distribution and intensity of use, high buildings policy and the listing of performance standards, general planning requirements and their quantification. Having thus clarified and defined the planning context, developers' architects would have maximum freedom to develop their design within this planning framework. In certain situations, however, for instance in parts of existing city centres or complete town or district centres, the urban designer may have to initiate three-dimensional designs on behalf of the Local Authority, since such an overall concept will be essential where several developers with different architects will operate. Such designs, however, should be seen as illustrations of three-dimensional principles rather than as finite proposals, so that they can be adapted to individual developers' needs without compromising the principles involved. Examples of such comprehensive three-dimensional proposals for redevelopment are the Liverpool City Centre Plan, and the three-dimensional concept for the downtown area for the city of Toledo, Ohio, USA, which is described and illustrated in Appendix 22.

Appendix 22

Toledo : renewal of the core area
An urban design report for the Urban Renewal Agency, Toledo, Ohio, USA, by Llewelyn-Davies, Weeks, Forestier-Walker & Bor

Between 1958 and 1963, retail sales in the central business district of Toledo declined by 22 per cent in absolute terms while sales in the eleven major suburban retail centres increased by 15 per cent during the same period. This was one of the many aspects in relation to the decline of the city's core area which caused concern to the City Council.

Early in 1967 the city of Toledo, Ohio, USA, commissioned my firm to act as urban design consultants in conjunction with two American consulting firms in the preparation of a General Neighbourhood Renewal Plan for the core area of the city, under the auspices of the US Department of Housing and Urban Development. The brief included the preparation of an independent report covering an environmental survey of the study area, the definition of planning and urban design objectives in the re-arrangement of land-use zoning and the highway network, and the preparation of a three-dimensional study of the central business district covering, initially, a 15-year development period and involving the construction of about 1 million square feet of office space, 900 000 square feet of retail space including three new department stores, and between 11 000 and 12 000 new parking spaces.

Among the major problems which had to be resolved in the course of this work were:

1. The need to provide adequate facilities for the separate movement of vehicles and pedestrians in the face of heavy demands for vehicle circulation and parking space caused by, among other things, a projected journey to work of 80 per cent by car and 20 per cent by the public transit system.

2. The need to provide links between the downtown surface streets and the end of the River Maumee and, at the same time, to incorporate a proposal to route a six-lane primary distributor along the river between the central business district and the river, and the need to build into the conceptual framework of the three-dimensional scheme sufficient flexibility to allow for uncertainties in the rate of increase of private investment in the core area.

The General Neighbourhood Renewal Program (GNRP) represents a determined effort by the city to check the dispersal of shopping, business and entertainment interests to suburban centres, and the failure of building investment in the core area to keep pace with the deterioration of structure and the availability of building land. Under the GNRP programme, funds are made available by the Department of Housing and Urban Development (HUD) for the acquisition by the city of selected areas of the core which are underbuilt or which contain a sufficient proportion of sub-standard structures. The city matches these Federal funds either directly or in the form of public works such as parking structures and recreation facilities. Once land ownership is pooled, parcels are re-sold to public or private developers with the condition that the main objectives of the planning study are fulfilled.

The acquisition and development of the weaker areas of the core will result, in the long term, in five major developments in the central area (see figure 1).

1. A new regional shopping centre in the heart of the central area based on the designation of a major street to use by buses and pedestrians only.

2. A civic plaza on the west side of the core incorporating a new administrative building for the city, combined with parking for about 1700 cars.

3. A river-view plaza overlooking the Maumee River on the east side of the core and consisting of office and residential developments over parking for some 3000 cars.

161

Figure 1. Toledo City Centre renewal. Sketch illustrating part of the core area, with Maumee river, the proposed six-lane distributor and a new plaza in the foreground. *Sketch by Gordon Cullen*

4. A new convention centre south of the core linked to a complex of hotels and entertainment facilities.

5. A new residential area on the south-east edge of the core based on the construction of a yacht marina on a site presently occupied by railroad marshalling yards.

In July 1968, interim proposals were submitted to and approved by the city authorities, and discussed at length with the business communities and other representative groups in the city. A final plan and report was presented to the City Council in December 1968.

Urban design elements

The vocabulary of the urban designer is vast and ranges from individual elements such as the floor and the wall, over a variety of spatial arrangements and movements and through these to overall urban design concepts. In designing the floor of a space, for instance, he must consider the different functions the floor will have to perform. Will it carry vehicles or pedestrians or both, should it be straight or curved, what kind of pavement is most suitable for these movements and should there be differences in level between them? Will there be other areas of soft landscape, trees, water features, sculpture, street furniture, and if so, what would be their most appropriate form in relation to the whole design? Which areas will be public and which will be private, which will be sunny and which will be shaded, which exposed and which sheltered? Should he aim at formality or informality, at robustness or gentleness or a combination of both?

162

Above 'Sleeping Policeman'—corrugated strip across carriageway to slow down traffic in London Street, Norwich. *Photo by courtesy of the City Planning Officer*
Above right Detail of pavement, London Street, Norwich, in concrete flagstones and bricks. *Photo by courtesy of Norwich City Planning Officer*
Right Urban Design Elements: the floor. A charming example from Sidgwick College, Cambridge, of circular paving incorporating bicycle stands round trees. Designer: Sir Hugh Casson. *Photo: Walter Bor*
Below Liverpool City Centre. Water feature in the form of mobile sculpture by Richard Huws consisting of buckets emptying water into a pool. Below this is an underground car park. *Photo: Walter Bor*
Below right Street furniture. Brick box with shrubs and wooden seats on concrete supports in London Street, Norwich. *Photo by courtesy of Norwich City Planning Officer*

The walls which are the most important elements of an urban design may take a variety of forms—they could be parts of the building enclosing the space, a row of trees, solid or perforated walls of different heights and materials, or grassed embankments. Where the walls are parts of buildings, they should be designed according to the functional and aesthetic requirements of these buildings and they can take a variety of forms from a simple flat elevation to a strongly modelled one, in a great variety of materials, textures and colours. The designer's task will be to unify floor and walls into spaces which will meet all the functional requirements and are pleasing and attractive.

From the space-forming elements the urban designer's vocabulary extends to spaces and their character. With a street, for instance, the proportion of the heights of the walls to the distance between them is all important. The exquisitely proportioned Architect Rossi Street in Leningrad gives a feeling of dignity and repose whereas a typical street in New York is an oppressive canyon by comparison.

Essentially urban design is a kinetic art in which the three-dimensional concept is experienced by moving through it in the fourth dimension of time. The spaces which are created are therefore closely related to the movement through them. There are special forms which correspond to directional movement, like the street. Other spaces, like the

The Wall. Early 19th-century terraces of shops and houses above. The different functions are clearly expressed in the elevation. Woburn Walk, London. *Photo by courtesy of the Greater London Council*

Architect Rossi Street, Leningrad, leading to the Pushkin Theatre. The proportion of the height of the street to its width is exactly 1 to 1. *Photo: Novosti Press Agency*

Typical canyon street in lower Manhattan has oppressive effect which dwarfs people and older buildings

165

The square denotes a sense of arrival. Shopping square in Tapiola New Town, Finland. *Photo by courtesy of the Managing Director, Tapiola*

square, are apparently more static and restful and denote a sense of arrival. However, if such squares continue through one corner into other spaces the apparent enclosure dissolves into a closure and they too become an integral part of a movement through inter-related spaces within a constantly changing urban scene.

Gordon Cullen, in his book *Townscape*, makes a valuable contribution to this subject when he analyses what he calls serial vision. If all is revealed at once, serial vision cannot exist. If buildings are grouped to produce ever-changing serial vision as one proceeds through spaces, the visual results are more complex and unpredictable and much richer and more interesting. Cullen also argues for the need to intensify differences between places (the *genius loci*) to heighten sense impressions rather than dull them in such a manner that all places become alike.

One of the most attractive possibilities in urban design is to manipulate the sequence of spaces in a way that enriches one's visual experience, and creates an element of surprise. Monumental vista planning, impressive though it may be at first sight, lacks this element and can become very tedious, particularly as one proceeds along one of the axes at pedestrian pace. One such example is the monumental street which Mussolini bulldozed through in Rome from St Peter's to the River Tiber. Instead of bursting, through gaps between old houses, upon Bernini's colonnade enclosing the space in front of St Peter's,

Washington, DC. Monumental vista planning. The Mall from the top of the Washington Memorial. *Photo: Walter Bor*

as was the case before Mussolini's intervention, one now trudges along a boring street lined with fascist-style architecture towards St Peter's, which turns out to be an anticlimax as Michaelangelo's dome sinks behind the main façade the closer one approaches.

Red Square in Moscow, on the other hand, though nothing if not monumental, has a tremendous surprise in store for the visitor as he approaches, particularly from the end of the Historical Museum. Because it lies on the brow of a hill, the vast expanse of the square unfolds only gradually as one proceeds through it past the spires of the Kremlin churches towering above the massive wall towards the picturesque St Basil's.

Red Square, Moscow, unfolds gradually as one proceeds through it over the brow of a hill. St Basil's is on the left, the Kremlin on the right of the picture. *Photo: Novosti Press Agency*

Piazetta San Marco, Venice. San Marco and the Doge's Palace on the left, the island of San Georgio in the background. *Photo: Walter Bor*

Probably the world's most famous example of urban spaces is Venice's Piazza and Piazetta San Marco approached through narrow alleyways and bursting dramatically on to the Lagoon and beyond it to the island of San Georgio with such splendid buildings as San Marco, the Campanile and the Doge's Palace on the way. Most European towns and indeed many towns throughout the world contain splendid if somewhat humbler examples of such space sequences.

The range of spatial enclosures, closures and sequences is unlimited and the variety of different kinds of character which they evoke is very rich indeed. Strict formality and utter informality are the extremes of a whole spectrum of different spatial possibilities. Similarly, different emotional responses are evoked by spaces which are constricted, like narrow streets or archways, as compared with vast boulevards and squares.

Blackheath, London. Its attraction is due to the informality of the winding village high street. *Photo: Tony Brooks*

It is difficult to be precise as to the extent to which our environment shapes us and we in turn modify it by the way we use it. We need to know more about this interaction, but there can be little doubt about the close inter-relationship of people and places. The urban designer uses his skill and imagination to manipulate the physical environment with a view to combining functional efficiency with aesthetic appeal to achieve maximum human satisfaction. He designs for social groups and he must be able to predict the consequences of his planning and urban design decisions. At the same time, he must leave, at least to some extent, room for unplanned action and improvisation for people to be able to adapt and change their environment according to their own preferences.

Amos Rapoport and Robert Kantor, in a thoughtful article 'Complexity and Ambiguity in Environmental Design' (*Journal of the American Institute of Planners*, July 1967), argue convincingly for greater complexity and ambiguity, i.e. admitting more than one interpretation, in urban design. The problem as they see it is that much of contemporary architecture and urban design has been simplified and cleaned up to such an extent that all it has to say is revealed at a glance. If all is designed and settled, there is no opportunity to bring one's own values to the forms. Rapoport and Kantor therefore suggest that the environment should be open-ended, unfinished to a degree so that the necessary completions, the expression of many different people, will result in a degree of diversity, and hence complexity and interest, not possible through conscious design. They also feel it essential to relate the design of complexity to the speed of motion. A great deal more complexity is needed at pedestrian or low speeds than at high or automobile speeds.

This approach is of course at variance with the traditional view of those designers who have been trying to create a completely determined and finite environment. Their hitherto accepted formula has been that form follows function. However, if the form is too closely tailored to function and the original function later on changes as it frequently does, the form may no longer follow the new function and therefore become inconvenient or even obsolete. Reality points thus in a different direction. For instance, the uses to which physical space has been put have been changing over time and most of these changes were beyond the control of the designer—they were accidental and not designed. This unexpectedness of use at any one time and changes of use over a period of time can be met if, instead of rigid single-use zoning, one allows for multiple use, interpenetration of different activities and different uses at different times. This would also bring a greater range of participants and observers into a given area, and the sum total of different experiences within an area would be greatly increased. A similarly flexible approach can also be developed with advantage in the design of buildings to allow for changes within and alterations and extensions of them. Much thought has been given to this subject by such architects as John Weeks, who developed this approach in his article 'Indeterminate Architecture' (*Transactions of the Bartlett Society 1963/64*) and his paper on 'Hospitals for the 1970s' to the Royal Institute of British Architects in October 1964.

The real challenge for the urban designer is to find a happy medium between relying on the one hand exclusively on the unforeseen and unexpected, thereby inviting chaos, and on the other designing everything to such a tight fit and with such finality as to inhibit change and people's individual contributions and expressions. What is therefore required from the

169

urban designer is an imaginative, well-planned framework as a strong overall design concept which will act as a unifier of an environment and which will be used and modified in detail in different ways over time.

The secret may be in inventing new versions of such time-honoured concepts as the Georgian square, which is a unified and satisfying spatial enclosure of terrace houses round a central open space and which can be readily adapted to different uses ranging from the one-family residents with servants to flats, public buildings and professional offices, as the history of many a London square shows. Another possibility might be the construction of frameworks within which people can rent or buy space and fill it in as they please, as was envisaged by Le Corbusier in his Algiers project.

Before we consider some of the significant new elements in the townscape such as high buildings and urban motorways, it is important for us to realize that urban design has in the past tended to be related mainly to comparatively compact situations where buildings come close together in towns and cities. As we move to the low-density outer suburbs, trees and landscape tend to take over and the buildings and spaces assume secondary importance. As we shall demand more and more space in and around our houses and as we endeavour to plan for growth and change, we shall find that increasingly we have to reserve space for future extensions and alterations. This in turn will mean that the fully designed and finished environment, which is still the aspiration of most urban designers, may have to give way to a less finite and a more ambiguous and open-ended design which may have its own quality and which will have to rely strongly on good landscaping. We have not yet fully mastered new urban design techniques which would meet the emerging space requirement and the need to plan for unforeseen changes which would nevertheless result in an environment of high quality.

10 The New Scale

Comprehensive redevelopment

One of the most dramatic changes in contemporary city development has been the emergence of the new scale in layout and individual buildings—many times larger than we have been used to in the past. It is true that scale in city development has been changing over the centuries, but these changes have been more dramatic and quick during this century than during the whole history of cities. The scale has not always been increasing. For instance, the scale of the Roman structures like the Colosseum, the Baths of Caracalla or the aqueducts gave way to the small and intimate scale of the early Christian era which was perpetuated throughout the Middle Ages, with the exception of castles and cathedral spires, some of which admittedly soared to well over 300 ft. But these tall structures were significant public buildings and the outstanding exception rather than the rule.

It was not till the Renaissance period that the scale increased again to something like Roman proportions. Whereas the Renaissance scale can be attributed to the new power of merchant princes and the Pope, the increasingly large scale in modern times is due to economic forces and new construction techniques which, to be viable, must be applied to large tracts of land. Today we have a building technology at our command which can produce great quantities of large-scale structures within a few years rather than decades or even centuries as has been the case with some of the large-scale structures in the past. The skyline of a city like London, for instance, has been dramatically transformed within a single decade by many scores of tall buildings.

A multitude of small individual properties are nowadays amalgamated into one large building site and often covered with a single multi-purpose building including parking garages, shops, offices and flats at different levels. Some of these comprehensive developments are

171

Left The mediaeval Ulm Cathedral, Germany, still dominates the skyline. *Photo: Walter Bor*

Below The massive scale of the Renaissance Palazzo Pitti by Brunelleschi symbolizes the new power of the princely merchants. *Photo by courtesy of the Mansell Collection*

Model of Liverpool City Centre displays dramatically the changing scale. In the background the small scale of the older development, in the foreground the new large scale of the mid-19th century St George's hall, with the proposed civic centre beyond and the now completed St John's precinct complex of shops, car parks and hotel on the left. *Photo: Liverpool City Centre Plan*

of high quality but many are not, and people may be excused for wondering whether what has been put back is really that much better than what has been destroyed. The most disappointing aspect of these operations is that by and large they tend to end up looking all very much the same. The character of the old buildings has gone, but only rarely has a new character and identity been created.

This lack of thought, sensitivity and imagination which is often apparent in so many so-called large comprehensive redevelopments is equally characteristic of the design and siting of the new large elements in the townscape—high buildings and urban motorways.

High buildings

To build high and to escape from the frustrating earthbound limitations has been a human aspiration ever since the biblical attempt of people to build the Tower of Babel. Today there are many additional justifications to build high: high central-area land values call for

173

the maximum exploitation of the building site—the classical example is of course Manhattan—large corporations and developers hanker after prestige offices by which they invariably mean tall blocks of offices, hard-pressed housing authorities have to build high-density housing which has increasingly tended to take the form of high buildings, and the safeguarding of daylighting in intensively developed parts of central areas has also tended to up-end long slab blocks and thus end up with tall tower blocks. Where foundations are costly, as again in Manhattan with its rocky subsoil, it is more economic to concentrate them on relatively small areas and then exploit these to the full by going as high as possible.

All these are on the face of it not unreasonable grounds for building high, but since the market forces and the incidence of individual land ownership are stronger than visual townscape consideration—if these have come into the picture at all—the impact on the townscape has been at best dramatic if haphazard, at worst positively disastrous. The most elementary advantages of building high, as proclaimed by Le Corbusier, like the freeing of ground space and using the roof of the tall block, the provision of spacious setting and consequent optimum sun and daylighting conditions, have been conveniently ignored. In Manhattan, for instance, many office skyscrapers are so closely spaced as to rob each other of sun and daylight from the 20th-storey or so downwards where artificial light must be used permanently. Little if any space has been freed, with notable exceptions such as the base of Mies van der Rohe's Seagram building and few if any of the roofs are accessible except as a landing platform for helicopters like the roof of the PanAm building. Residential tall blocks, again with few exceptions, have likewise failed to produce the full potential benefits of tall buildings—the spaces between them are often a windy and unfriendly no-man's-land, increasingly littered with parked cars, and few are designed to use the roof. One such exception is the tall block in Golden Lane in the City of London.

(Left) The ground space under the building is freed. Unité d'Habitation in Marseille. Architect: Le Corbusier. *Photo: A. E. J. Morris*

(Below) Regained space on the roof of Unité d'Habitation, is used for a nursery, a running track and other recreation. Architect: Le Corbusier. *Photo: A. E. J. Morris*

Right Public open space created at the base of the Seagram building. Fifth Avenue, Manhattan. Architect: Mies van der Rohe. *Photo: Walter Bor*
Below In the middle of the picture is the PanAm building with a helicopter pad on its roof. To the left is the Seagram building and right is the Chrysler building with its romantic spire. *Photo: United Press International*

Roof terrace of Great Arthur House, Golden Lane, City of London, with a fine view of St Paul's Cathedral. Architects: Chamberlin, Powell & Bon. *Photo by courtesy of Architectural Press*

The truth of the matter is that we have rushed into building high without the full realization of what we are doing. One would have thought that so important an element as a high building in the townscape would receive the most careful consideration with regard to its location, design and its impact on the environment. Yet little, if any, such thought has in fact been given to the siting of tall buildings in most cities.

In 1964 I conducted some research into high buildings for an article, 'High Buildings: a Blessing or a Curse?', I wrote for *Architectural Design* in September of that year. My enquiry showed that at that time out of 29 cities in 24 countries very few had evolved anything like a high-buildings policy. Only seven cities had a three-dimensional concept, four cities worked to height zoning and several had minor ineffective controls, others had none whatever.

As a result of this lack of effective high-buildings policies, town after town, city after city, is being marred by a senseless proliferation of undistinguished high buildings, often ruining fine views and making nonsense of the well-established scale of whole historic areas. However, on the credit side, some cities have not only been concerned about the use and siting of high buildings but are in fact implementing a well-thought-out high-buildings policy. Such a policy is bound to vary according to the character and requirements of particular towns. What may be appropriate for one may be disastrous for another; each town must work out its own destiny. Some cities with unique existing skylines and a scale like Prague have rightly banned all high buildings from the historic core. Some small towns like Cambridge are so exquisite in their present form that an imposition of an alien scale, however imaginatively conceived, could only do harm. We must really learn to be more humble at times and realize that past generations have succeeded in some cases in achieving perfection and any radical tampering by us, for instance by inserting tall buildings, however well designed, would be tantamount to sacrilege.

Prague's unique skyline. View from Charles Bridge tower over the many church spires of the old town. *Photo: Walter Bor*

The PanAm building in Manhattan blocks the view of Park Avenue. *Photo: United Press International*

Examples of unsuccessful siting or form of high buildings abound. Reference has already been made to the Hötorget development in Stockholm with its five closely spaced high blocks, the silhouettes of which tend to merge into an ungainly huge box crudely dominating the otherwise still delicate Stockholm skyline. Another example of an unhappily conceived tall building is the PanAm block on top of Central Station in Manhattan. One might have thought that yet another skyscraper there could not possibly make a difference, one way or the other. But this is not so. The main saving feature in the forest of Manhattan skyscrapers, as one looks along their serried ranks, is the cheerful crack of bright sky one invariably glimpses, which owes its existence to the rigid grid of the streets which remain unbuilt upon—with the unfortunate exception of PanAm which rudely and overbearingly blocks the view along Park Avenue and leaves one with a feeling of powerless depression that even this chink of light has been thus extinguished.

In recent years, however, some cities like Liverpool, Oxford, Cambridge and Edinburgh have realized that the location of high buildings requires careful consideration and have developed high buildings policies. Rather belatedly, the Greater London Council, has advocated detailed principles for the siting of high buildings which it is hoped will be more vigorously enforced than the largely ineffective high-buildings policy of the former London County Council. However, much of the damage is by now done in Central London.

The Liverpool City Centre Plan contains amongst its visual policies one for the location of high buildings. It was considered desirable to maintain the traditional scale within the city core against which the Liver Group of high buildings on the waterfront stand out dramatically. Two major groups of new high buildings are envisaged, one along the northern

Model of Liverpool City Centre illustrating the high-buildings policy for the city centre. The Liver Group of buildings (top right) will continue to dominate the old core with groups of high buildings emphasizing the southern (top of picture) and northern (bottom right) edges of the city centre. *Photo: John Mills*

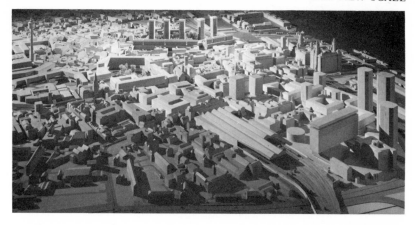

and one on the southern edge of the core area where they would help to define visually the city centre. The southern group will take the form of five high tower blocks of flats, whereas the northern group will consist of office towers in a backland area where redevelopment is desirable and where a higher plot ratio (4:1 as against 3:1 in the rest of the central area) expressed in high buildings will be an encouragement to developers. (Plot ratio is the relationship of floor area to site area. A 5:1 plot ratio means five times as much floor space as site area. This can be achieved for example, by covering the whole of the site with a 5-storey building, or half the site with a 10-storey building.) The northern edge of the core area is marked by the new 16-storey Littlewoods block and a group of tower blocks for the *Liverpool Post* and *Echo* newspapers. It is hoped that this high-building concept will result in meaningful groups of high buildings significantly sited while at the same time the existing scale and character of the core area will be maintained.

In Philadelphia the creditable efforts at rehabilitation of some of the fine Georgian streets is marred by the insertion of several skyscrapers nearby which make nonsense of the Georgian scale and succeed in making the rehabilitated terraces look puny and rather silly. In Hansaviertel in West Berlin a residential area has been developed with carefully grouped high blocks. However, since every one of these was designed by a different architect from a

Hansaviertel, Berlin. Group of high residential blocks each designed by a different architect from a different country. A fine international gesture resulting in a polyglot visual chaos. *Photo: Senator for Ban- und Wohnungswesen*

different country, the result is a polyglot visual chaos. Thus striving for variety can be misplaced if applied to groups of large-scale structures.

Another example comes from Athens, one of the oldest cities in Europe, with its magnificent Akropolis still dominating the skyline. The London *Times* correspondent reported from Athens on January 14, 1968: "The city council was told last week that the Cabinet was in favour of abolishing all town planning regulations which have limited the Athens skyline to seven-storey buildings. Mr Pattakos, the Deputy Prime Minister, told the Council: 'It is a shame that this city of light should have become a city of darkness.' And he ended his address by advocating the creation of vast open spaces by bulldozers with rams at least 100 metres wide. Once this is done, there should be no limit to the height of Athen's buildings, the sky is the limit."

These few examples illustrate the special care which is necessary with regard to the location of high buildings in the vulnerable historic cores of our towns and cities where their impact could mar or even destroy some of our most valuable architectural heritage.

At the other end of the scale are towns and cities which are dull and undistinguished and which could benefit from well-sited and well-designed tall blocks. Indeed, the concentration of skyscrapers in the downtown area of the average US city, although fortuitous and dictated mainly by high land values, does make a meaningful and positive contribution to its townscape, provided this concentration takes a civilized form. Apart from the obviously dramatic visual impact, such a concentration succeeds in giving these cities a clearly recognizable centre with the functional advantages of concentration which promotes face-to-face contact within short walking distance.

Most of our suburban areas are also singularly lacking in character and distinction and well-conceived groups of high buildings, assuming they are socially and economically desirable, may well add visual interest, particularly if these new tall structures can lend visual emphasis to those parts of the urban areas which are of special significance like shopping centres, major interchange points and major open spaces or if they dramatize a hill, a significant part of a river or similar physical characteristic.

There can therefore be ample opportunities of using high buildings in our towns and cities in a meaningful way without clashing with our architectural heritage. They could contribute greatly to enriching the skyline and the character of cities and towns, provided their location and design are accorded the thoughtful and imaginative approach they merit.

We have considered some aspects regarding the location of high buildings and only mentioned in passing the need for high-quality design. But their architectural quality is also of great importance. After all, when a building forces itself upon one's attention through sheer bulk, one has a right to expect more—a quality which lifts the architecture out of the ordinary—and one feels let down when the high block is simply the visual run-of-the-mill stuff, only higher and more of it.

The reasons why the design of only so few high buildings is of high quality are not difficult to find. Since most of these are office blocks, which are usually built as a speculative investment, the developers prefer to select architects who are experienced in producing the maxi-

City-centre housing in Coventry. A tower block of flats overlooking the lower shopping precinct designed by the Coventry City Architect. *Photo: Hompson, Coventry*

mum return in terms of floor space, rather than someone over-concerned with the architectural quality. Thus architecture frequently turns into accountancy and the resulting product clearly reflects this approach.

However, even if all developers and their architects were intent on a high quality, the design of high buildings has many inherent difficulties to resolve which require exceptional imagination and design ability. Because of the sheer size of the buildings, a simple repetitive grid all the way up to 30 or 40 floors, often finishing abruptly when the maximum floor space has been attained, tends to become tedious. Le Corbusier solved this problem in his 'Unité d'Habitation' in an exemplary manner by manipulating different sizes of flats and maisonettes, by interposing a shopping floor halfway up and by modelling the roof structures of the usable roof (see page 174) to create an interesting skyline.

The circular Marina Towers in Chicago not only express a spiral with the car parking ramps below but with the bow-shaped terraces, the whole producing a rich overall texture of light and shade. It is, however, also possible to produce a high building of outstanding quality by the simplest of means—the rectangular prism with repetitive fenestration—but it requires exquisite detailing and the use of high-quality materials. Mies van der Rohe's Seagram block on Park Avenue, New York, is an example of this extremely disciplined approach. Another recent example of a distinguished high block is the Hancock Center by Skidmore, Owings & Merill in Chicago which, however, now dwarfs earlier skyscrapers and

181

Marina Towers, Chicago, with 42 storeys of flats, each with its own deep bowed balcony, above a spiral ramp of car parks. Below the twin towers is a marina. Architects: Bertrand Goldberg Associates. *Photo: Walter Bor*

Hancock Center, Chicago, brings a yet larger scale to the townscape, dwarfing earlier skyscrapers such as Mies van der Rohe's Lakeshore Drive Apartments (right foreground) and SOM's apartment block behind. Architects: Skidmore, Owings & Merill. *Photo: Hedrich Blessing*

illustrates dramatically yet another new scale which it will be increasingly difficult to integrate with an existing townscape.

There are by now many distinguished examples of high buildings in existence, although their sum total represents only a small fraction of all the high buildings built in recent years. Most of the best examples take the form of tall tower blocks rather than slabs. Tall towers are, as a rule, visually more satisfying, are more easily integrated into the urban fabric and reduce problems of over-shadowing and light infringement of adjoining neighbours compared with those resulting from high slab blocks. An example of such a successful integration is the group of towers of the *Economist* building in St James Street, London, by the Smithsons.

While similar townscape and architectural considerations apply to high residential blocks as to tall offices, the social considerations are so important that they may tip the balance when decisions are made whether or not to house people in high buildings. Reference has already been made to the problems arising for young mothers with small children and for old people in such buildings. Careful letting policies, such as avoiding the allocation of flats in tall blocks to young families and reserving some of the flats nearer the ground to old people frightened of lifts, can overcome these difficulties at least to some extent. The sense of isolation some families suffer in high buildings can be overcome by designs incorporating

Economist group of towers, St James Street, London, illustrates a sensitive integration of the lower tower in the foreground with the scale of the street. In the background is the *Economist* office block. There is another residential tower block to the left of it which is outside the picture. Architects: Peter and Allison Smithson. *Photo: Sam Lambert*

Park Hill, Sheffield. High-density, high-rise housing which pioneered the idea of pedestrian decks giving access on every second floor to the front doors of the dwellings, providing safe and covered play spaces and an opportunity for a gossip with the neighbours. *Photo: Walter Bor*

pedestrian access decks backing the flats, as in Park Hill, Sheffield. Imaginative layouts and good landscaping can and do produce very attractive developments with high residential blocks like the Roehampton housing by the former London County Council, where high buildings have been used to their full advantage giving magnificent views and allowing the retention of fine mature trees.

In spite of all these positive features, even in Roehampton some of the dissatisfaction, to which reference has already been made, has been voiced by tenants of the high blocks. However, it is the indiscriminate use of high residential blocks, often on unsuitable sites, which has resulted, in many towns and cities, in socially and architecturally deplorable developments. Local housing authorities in these places have used high buildings for the

Roehampton, London, where high residential blocks take full advantage of the magnificent views. *Photo by courtesy of the Greater London Council*

main purpose of 'achieving high densities' or, to put it more crudely, to 'pack them in', often by making 'package deals' for batches of standard high blocks as the apparently quickest and most effective way of dealing with their housing problems. These blocks lack, as a rule, compensatory amenities such as playrooms or double glazing, essential at least in the upper parts of high blocks, and heating is often inadequate to overcome the excessive cooling down of external walls. Finally, it is often insufficiently realized that living in high blocks calls for a certain degree of sophistication and restraint which it is unreasonable to expect from people who have lived in by-law houses with back yards and whose normal style of life can be seriously inhibited by the constraints imposed upon them in high flats. It is not surprising, therefore, that a growing number of people are having second thoughts about the wisdom of using high blocks to solve our housing problems.

Are high buildings really inevitable?

This is perhaps the main question one is tempted to ask in the light of the many formidable difficulties implied in the design and location of high buildings. The usual answer has been that they are if we want to 'achieve' high commercial plot ratios and residential densities. Leaving aside whether this 'achievement' is a desirable objective or not, the facts are that what are by British standards very high plot ratios (5:1) and high residential densities (100 persons per acre) can be attained by development which does not have recourse to high buildings, as will be shown later. If these facts had been known and accepted earlier many an undesirable high building development could have taken an alternative form with buildings of traditional height accommodating the equivalent amount of space.

The deep office block

Although the first massive wave of new offices has just passed over many European cities, a good deal more office space will yet be required and built in years to come. It is therefore wise to take stock of the office development we have carried out so far and ask whether we should continue to build offices in this way or whether some other form may not be more appropriate. The average European office block is based on the natural assumption that it will be adequately lit by normal daylighting. This means that light is assumed to penetrate up to 20 ft in depth into offices. Allowing for an internal core of lifts, staircases and corridors and a grouping of 20 ft deep offices around it, a total depth of some 50 to 60 ft results, and since offices tend to be located on expensive land, which encourages intensive exploitation, these offices tend to take the form of high buildings, often in the wrong position. Thus the way office blocks are conceived also has a direct bearing on the question of the siting of high buildings.

US practice has for some time now developed an alternative approach—the 'deep office block'. Daylighting, it is argued, though psychologically desirable and still obtainable in the normal way, is by no means adequate to give uniformly good internal lighting conditions. The office worker sitting near to external windows suffers from excessive glare (unless tinted glass or venetian blinds are used, which, however, lower the intensity of daylight in the rear parts of the office) while his less fortunate colleagues further back from the window receive inadequate daylight and have to supplement it by artificial light most of the time.

A deep office block does not rely on daylighting but ensures an equal and high standard of artificial lighting and incidentally also air conditioning throughout the whole of the deep office area. Furthermore, it is claimed, the large uninterrupted floor space with its flexibility in layout is more appropriate to the working of modern office organizations. It allows for a large variety of spatial alternatives ranging from the large uninterrupted office space (Büro-landschaft) to one which is sub-divided by movable partitions according to the needs of the organization.

There has been deep suspicion of and a strong resistance against this American practice in European cities, particularly in London where it was held that the conditions in a 'deep' office blocks were inferior to those designed for daylight penetration, but these views are based on hunches rather than on any objective investigation. R. G. Hopkinson, Professor of Environmental Design and Engineering at University College, London, in writing about windowless buildings in *New Society* (June 6, 1968), says this about the psychological and physiological aspects:

"One of the most controversial questions is the effect of lack of windows on physiological and psychological health. No reliable evidence seems to have emerged so far to show that short-term physiological harm results from lack of natural daylight. Nor can the constant and exclusive use of fluorescent lighting be shown to be a short-term hazard. It is too soon to establish if any long-term effects will eventually show themselves. Psychological effects do manifest themselves, and the dislike, fear and even panic which can sometimes arise in enclosed spaces must not be discounted. But so many people are now working in so many windowless buildings that the seriousness of these psychological effects can be grossly exaggerated. If people can be reassured that they will come to no harm, and if they can be taken into confidence about the need for a windowless controlled environment, they will, as a majority, consent to tolerate it. The reluctant or adamant minority must seek shelter elsewhere. The only strictly factual arguments against the windowless building are the fire hazard and the possibility of panic."

Peter Manning of Liverpool University has studied this problem as a research project supported by Pilkingtons. He reached the conclusion that most prejudices against deep office buildings are ill-founded. Inevitably a good deal of artificial lighting is involved, but there is no evidence that this had any ill effects on health or efficiency, and provided there was a clear and unobstructed view of a window there was no psychological effect. The study also indicated that the fairly widespread objection to the open-planned office and the expressed preference for a small office came mainly from those who had no experience of working in such offices. Whilst smaller offices tended to encourage competitive spirit, the larger office fostered a greater cooperation.

Detailed comparative costing was found to be scanty, but in spite of the necessity for air conditioning in the deeper office block, it would generally appear to have cost advantages, and heating could be more efficiently controlled. The noise level, whilst higher, was generally not excessive, and was frequently reduced by permanently closed windows, associated with air conditioning. The study concluded that the likelihood of increasing needs for flexibility and for inter-office communication, the use of mechanical or electronic procedures and the findings that the lighting requirements of clerks can, in suitable circumstances, be adequately met by well-designed lighting, indicate the suitability for more widespread use of deep, artificially lit buildings. These will need to contain open-planned office space, with a minimum of partitions and a maximum size of window, so that staff working in the interior space have an adequate view to the outside world. If Peter Manning's conclusions are accepted, the 'deep' office block could become a normal feature in the UK, reduce the need for high office towers by affording the possibility of attaining a 5 : 1 plot ratio in a five-storey building and would bring office development within the manageable situation when high office buildings become a matter of choice rather than necessity.

High-density low-rise housing

Just as the deep office block is a viable alternative to the high office block, so there are alternative ways of developing with residential high densities without recourse to high blocks of flats. There are many advantages in this both socially and economically. The more dwellings can be provided at or near ground level, the greater the opportunities for residents to meet and for children to play in the open; the scale of the development could be more human and friendly, and draughty no-man's-land areas between high blocks can be avoided. The cost of low-rise development is usually considerably lower than that of providing the equivalent number of dwellings in high-rise blocks unless special foundation costs outweigh these savings. And since less money needs to be spent on construction, more can be spent on elements which contribute to the quality of the environment like play facilities, lighting, seating and planting. For these reasons a greater interest is now developing in high-density low-rise housing.

An attractive example of such high-density low-rise development is the Milton Road housing scheme built by the London Borough of Haringey which consists largely of two-storey houses with private gardens. The scheme has been developed at 108 persons per acre and includes garage provision for every house and for visitors, a ground-level toddlers' playground and one for older children above a covered car park. The '5M' system of construction has been used, which is a kit of components for building houses designed by the Ministry of Housing and Local Government.

Yet another possible development in this category are the proposals for new housing in Glasgow at 100 persons per acre. Single-aspect housing facing either east or west has been grouped to form short intimate streets on the entrance/kitchen side of the dwelling running in a north/south direction. This has been achieved with a basic four-bedspace terrace house, having a south-facing living room extending into a small walled garden leading through to local open space which can either be laid out as a communal garden with toddlers' playspaces or the individual gardens extended. Garages are grouped at the ends of

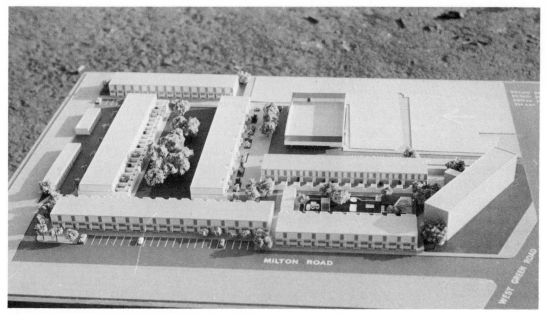

Milton Road, Haringey, North London. Two-storey houses grouped around internal greens. Density 108 persons per acre. *Photo by courtesy of C. F. Jacobs, Borough Architect*

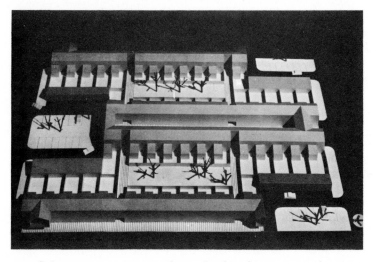

Summerston Housing, Glasgow. Model shows typical unit made up of 2-storey pedestrian street creating intimate and sheltered space for front-door gossip with generous space on private side for long gardens or communal facilities. Architects: Llewelyn-Davies, Weeks, Forestier-Walker & Bor

300 ft long access courts along the local access roads. Two secondary pedestrian ways link the access courts at right angles and connect to the main pedestrian spine to form a mesh with many possible routings between any two points. These pedestrian ways, and the links to the garage courts, are partly covered where they enter the access courts, by the additional bedroom of the six-bedspace houses in the development. Thus a high degree of protection from the elements and a clear definition of public and private open space can be achieved.

There will, in any case, be new forms of housing evolving in the near future which will break away from traditional concepts. An example of the possible shape of things to come is 'Habitat', the housing development by the young Canadian architect Safdie, for Expo '67.

'Habitat', Expo '67, Montreal. Prefabricated house units assembled in a highly imaginative way to provide optimum living conditions at high densities. Each dwelling has its own private open space. Architect: Moshe Safdie. *Photo: Walter Bor*

'Habitat', Expo '67, Montreal. Close-up view. *Photo: A. E. J. Morris*

Although only a modest fragment of a much more ambitious project, the pyramidal cluster of prefabricated superimposed house blocks is a highly original way to house people at high densities with fine views in many directions and a good deal of privacy. There are, however, some drawbacks: the pyramidal structure creates a wind tunnel which on the exposed island site in the St Laurence river accentuates the climatic difficulties particularly during a Canadian winter, the cost of construction was very high since this one-off job was produced by mass-production techniques requiring a much greater market to be economically viable, and full privacy has not been achieved as there is a good deal of overlooking. Even so, 'Habitat' is certainly an important and imaginative breakthrough in housing design.

When sufficient such housing developments have been built and used over several years it will be interesting to compare the social satisfaction of people living in them and compare them with high-rise housing for similar groups of people in similar locations.

189

Urban motorways

Like high buildings, urban motorways have overwhelmed some cities, particularly in the United States, before it was fully realized what was happening. Here we have again precedents from the past to learn from—the railways which had been built in the course of the second half of the 19th century to bring people and goods into the very centres of our cities. These railroads were often cut ruthlessly through the existing urban fabric with well-known damaging results, be it the loss of the loch at the foot of the castle hill in Edinburgh and its substitution by a railway belching steam and smoke (now mercifully converted to diesel traction) or the ruthless routing through Newcastle Castle or the unsightly bridge at Ludgate Hill in the City of London slicing through the principal view of St Paul's Cathedral. Houses just outside the path of the new railway lines were left standing, with living rooms and bedrooms often within a few yards of the rail track; alternatively rows and rows of supposedly private back gardens were exposed to the view from passing trains.

However, though marring the urban environment, these railway lines were not anything like as destructive of it as their urban motorway successors. Their tracks were relatively narrow and economic in space, except where they multiplied in railway stations and mar- shalling yards; junctions of two lines were as a rule at the same level, their points being signal controlled; the railway tracks were at all points grade separated from the existing road network (mostly flying over it) and it was not necessary to merge one with the other except at the stations. The most important aspect on the credit side, however, was and still is the ability of railways to shift large numbers of people quickly (because of the reserved track) and safely (because of automatic signalling and other controls greatly reducing human failure) without creating major problems, such as parking, at the arrival point in the town centres.

The impact of the new motorways, particularly where elevated, on the urban environment has already been colossal and in many instances disastrous, especially in American cities where the building of urban freeways has been most extensive. Amongst them, probably one of the most beautiful, San Francisco, has suffered severely, with the Embarcadero Free- way at high level being interposed between the city and its bay. In Caracas, an eight-lane urban motorway effectively slices the city in two (although in the last few years attempts have been made to reunite the two parts by building over the motorway), while in London a recently constructed part of the elevated west cross route (Westway) runs parallel to three-storey terraces of houses at a distance of less than 10 yards. Since the opening of Westway, very strong protest by the occupants of these houses has led to the belated decision of the Greater London Council to rehouse them. In Paris, considerable stretches of the Seine Embankment, which until a few years ago were quiet pedestrian retreats, have now been converted into noisy motorways. Thus a unique feature of Paris has been sacrificed to the motor car.

But even greater than the visual disruption has been the social one, splitting whole, and previously homogenous, urban areas into fragments which rarely had any social meaning. The demands on urban space of the six- to twelve-lane urban freeways with their two-, three- and even four-level complex intersections has been tremendous. To this must be added the vast acreage required in or near the city centre for the parking of vehicles once

Embarcadero Freeway, San Francisco, ruining the view of the bay from the city and disrupting the urban fabric. *Photo: Walter Bor*

Eight-lane motorway through Caracas with buildings and decks over it in the foreground re-uniting the severed parts of the city. *Photo: Walter Bor*

they have arrived. Thus urban motorways, unless very carefully sited and integrated with the surrounding urban areas and unless built as part of a comprehensive transport plan which integrates all forms of transport, can create more problems in urban areas than they solve. These are the sort of problems which worry for example, the many people who object to the London Motorway proposals.

While it has by now been established that public transport in most major cities will have to play a predominant role, particularly for the commuter traffic, it is likely that these cities will also require a limited primary road system in the form of urban motorways to improve the flow mainly of the commercial and service traffic and to collect the through traffic which should be eliminated from environmental areas. Let us assume then that some urban motorway construction will be found necessary and that we must therefore face this challenge.

Before one considers how this problem can be tackled satisfactorily, it is necessary to be clear about the possible forms an urban motorway could take. Since its main function is to carry large capacities of smoothly flowing vehicular traffic at reasonable speeds, all the usual obstacles to this must be eliminated; there must be as few side streets as possible entering, no traffic lights stopping the main flow of traffic, no 'U' turns, no loading and unloading, no stopping or parking and no pedestrians or cyclists. Furthermore all intersections between motorways must be free-flow grade separated, with turning movements carried over or under the main flow. To meet all these requirements, an urban motorway must be constructed entirely independent of the existing road network. This can be done in three ways: either at least 20 ft above or below the existing street level, or at street level, depending on a number of considerations like the configuration of the land, soil conditions, underground services, the local road network and of course costs.

Obviously a ground-level motorway is the cheapest to build but necessitates the sealing off of all roads on either side of it and causes the maximum social disruption, since it severs physically the adjoining areas from each other. Some road and pedestrian bridges or underpasses will be required to re-connect the severed parts. The elevated motorway is

Acklam Road, West London, where Westway, the new urban motorway has been built parallel and within 10 yards of 3-storey houses. Since this photograph was taken the motorway has been completed and is now open to traffic. The noise levels in the adjoining houses have been measured and, predictably, are well above the acceptable levels.
Photo: Tony Brooks

more costly and presents the largest number of visual and social problems as can be seen from the many bad examples where these problems have not been resolved. There is the difficulty of reconciling a continuous wide bridge and its resultant linearity with the townscape on either side, the problem of what to do with the areas underneath when they are not used for roads or footpaths, the raising of the noise and air-pollution level in more senses than one, and the ramping problem to connect to ground level to provide access at limited points to the existing street network as the example from Boston shows. Socially the elevated motorway is still disruptive, though rather more psychologically than physically since the cross movement of vehicles and people may be possible underneath, but the massive construction of the motorway may inhibit the extent to which this takes place.

Urban motorway with on- and off-ramps in Boston, while providing a smooth-flowing road for through traffic, illustrates the disruptive effect on the townscape. *Photo by courtesy of British Road Federation*

193

A sunken road through the heart of Rotterdam illustrates that this type of road minimizes the environmental impact. *Photo by courtesy of the Cement and Concrete Association.*

The sunken motorway, on the other hand, clearly minimizes both the visual and social problems in that it practically buries them. If cleverly handled, such sunken motorways are quite unobtrusive like the sunken approach to the Maas Tunnel through Rotterdam, and the life of the town flows over it largely as before it was built. Unfortunately, except for bored tunnels this is by far the most expensive solution since all existing underground services in the path of the sunken motorway have to be diverted and costly excavations and retaining wall construction and many bridges are entailed. However, some recent studies indicate that the extra cost may not be as high as is usually assumed.

These are but some of the very real visual and social problems arising from the insertion of motorways into the urban fabric. Yet if this operation is performed with great care and imagination, urban motorways can make positive and visually creative contributions to the townscape. Some of the first principles in choosing an alignment for an urban motorway are similar to those relating to the location of high buildings. Areas which form socially and architecturally homogeneous units must be identified and their character and scale respected. An urban motorway, particularly in an elevated form, would play havoc with such areas and is therefore unacceptable in or close to them. Thus any urban motorway alignment must steer well clear of such areas even if it means a detour.

On the other hand an alignment of urban motorways should, ideally, follow 'cracks in the urban fabric' such as existing railway lines which are also already accepted as major noise generators and wherever possible be located through areas which are slums or of poor quality. The renewal of these areas could then be conceived as an integral part of the motorway construction and the comprehensive reshaping of these areas could then be achieved in positive social and visual terms. Buildings, even housing, could be designed to live happily with the new motorway. The Liverpool Inner Motorway, for example, was routed wherever possible through areas which required redevelopment. In order to ensure the fullest possible integration of the Inner Motorway with the surrounding development a policy was adopted for redevelopment in depth on either side of the motorway. With this in mind an extensive land take of 275 acres for the motorway and adjoining land was secured by a Private Member's Bill which received Royal Assent in 1967.

Single-aspect housing with imperforate walls on to the motorway can, as in Heston Grange near the M4 motorway 12 miles from London, create viable living conditions close by. Alternatively a new open space pattern and earth embankments can be designed to act as a noise buffer. Buildings which are less vulnerable to motorway noise like industry, storage and service buildings could form buffer walls against the motorway. The decks of urban motorways can be pleasantly landscaped as on East River Drive, New York. Shops and offices can be fully integrated into urban motorways and become a fully accepted part of the street scene as the very successful example of the Sukiyabashi motorway in Tokyo shows. These and many other means can be employed to minimize the detrimental effects of urban motorways and to integrate them successfully with the urban environment. Such an integration is much more readily achieved where an area is being developed for the first time

Right M4 motorway leading out of London to the west flanked by single-aspect housing looking away from the motorway and providing acceptable living conditions. Architect: Ivor Smith. *Photo: Walter Bor*

Below left East River Drive, New York, where the roof of the urban motorway has been pleasantly landscaped. *Photo: Walter Bor*

Below right Sukiyabashi motorway, Tokyo, with shops and offices fully integrated into the urban motorway, which becomes a fully accepted part of the street scene

195

and where the alignment of a future motorway is known and can, therefore, be fully taken into account at the layout stage (see Summerston Area, Glasgow, Appendix 23).

The impact on the environment and the problems and opportunities arising from urban motorway construction have been discussed with special reference to London in a report 'Motorways in the Urban Environment' by Llewelyn-Davies, Weeks, Forestier-Walker & Bor, and Ove Arup & Partners, published by the British Road Federation in 1971.

Conclusions

Socio-economic and visual considerations interact in their influence upon the environment, and the urban designer, whose job it is to mould these influences into a cohesive entity, has an increasingly important role to play. To date we have not been spectacularly successful generally in achieving urban environments of high quality, notable exceptions apart, and much more attention and skill must be devoted to this aspect of urban planning if we are to succeed in building new towns and rebuilding parts of old ones to give us anything like the visual delight we get from some of the best examples of the past.

Appendix 23

Proposals for Summerston, Glasgow
Planners: Llewelyn-Davies, Weeks, Forestier-Walker & Bor

Summerston lies on the northern fringe of the city of Glasgow and is one of the last remaining unbuilt areas within the city boundary. The brief asked for plans to be prepared for a residential community of 20 000–22 000 persons, a new district centre to serve these people and a wider area of housing at present under-provided, and to integrate this development with the projected Trossachs motorway which was located through this area.

The basic problem was therefore to create viable living conditions for this new community which was threatened to be bisected by the motorway. This situation clearly presented a major conflict between the needs of traffic and good living conditions which had to be resolved.

The proposals (Figure 1) are attempting a solution by locating two primary schools and a secondary school with their playgrounds in a broad open space belt on either side of the motorway. The housing areas are then grouped beyond the open space and schools at a considerable distance from the motorway and further protected from noise by single-aspect deck-access maisonette blocks looking away from the motorway. The bulk of the housing takes the form of two-storey housing which is arranged in the form of single-aspect houses

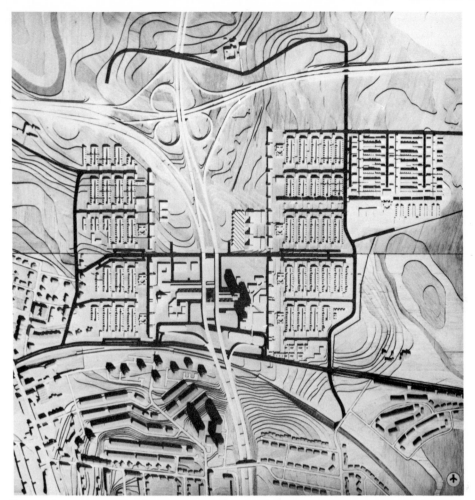

Figure 1. Summerston area, Glasgow. Air view of model of whole area showing the north–south Trossachs motorway bisecting it. The proposed housing is set well back from it and a new district centre under the motorway links the two parts together again

Figure 2. View of model from the north

along 15 ft wide streets with bridge blocks creating a sheltered public approach with a more open aspect towards the gardens and communal play spaces (see page 188).

However, this arrangement, although minimizing the impact of the motorway and providing sheltered living conditions, mostly in low-rise buildings, could still result in two separrate communities. The district centre is therefore located in such a way as to link the two

197

housing areas together in the most effective way (Figure 2). Since the Trossachs motorway would be elevated in the southern portion of the area, the low shopping blocks can be slotted in under the motorway and the shopping streets can be designed to link with the major pedestrian spines. Thus a strong link can be re-established between the two housing areas so that the community can function as a whole in spite of the motorway. Ample car-parking facilities, a church, health centre, primary school and a community centre, local industries and a police station are proposed as an integral part of this district centre. A group of three residential tower blocks for childless couples and single people provides an opportunity for those who prefer to live close by this centre.

Although the location of the Trossachs motorway was moved further to the east after these proposals were submitted, and this scheme was therefore not implemented, this study may nevertheless be of interest in the way it attempted to resolve what will be an increasingly typical conflict between the needs of motorways and those of adjoining new residential areas.

Part 5

Towards Comprehensive Urban Planning

"Planning can introduce ideal concepts—not how the city will be but how it could and should *be. A vision of successful change becomes part of the present reality, the basis for analysis and examination from which the planner devises authentic and realizable alternatives. Community acceptance turns them into actual, concrete changes. Successful change in turn becomes a new reality from which public reactions can be gauged and further extrapolations carried out."*

Delos Five, *Ekistics,* 1967

11 Pre-conditions to a Comprehensive Urban Planning Approach

So far, individual aspects of our urban environment and the changes they are undergoing have been discussed. To complete the picture, we need now to look at the way our urban environment operates as a whole. And not just how it operates but what sort of comprehensive urban planning approach is necessary to ensure a meaningful interaction of individual policies which would achieve the best possible life and environment for the people in our cities.

I believe that there are five basic conditions which must be met to ensure the effectiveness of urban planning and its full public acceptance. There must be:

1. A clearly understood and workable concept of planning at national and regional levels

We in Britain have yet a long way to go before we can be satisfied, particularly with regard to planning at national and regional level.

At the national level, Britain has at long last taken some major steps towards the integration of various aspects of physical planning and development by the creation of a new Department for the Environment to oversee the activities of the Ministries of Local Government and Development, Housing and Construction, and Transport Industries. In particular, the bringing together of land-use and transport planning within the Ministry of Local Government and Development promises a better integration of these two inseparable aspects of physical planning, although some other aspects still remain separated in other Ministries (see Chapter 4).

At the intermediate level between national and local planning, that is, at the regional level, the position remains a good deal less satisfactory. At this level, physical planning has been divorced altogether from economic planning and the twelve Economic Planning Councils are only concerned with economic planning. Furthermore, these Councils are advisory bodies only and have no executive power. It is little wonder, therefore, that by and large their work has not been a spectacular success and has to date not produced a single effective regional plan which could give real guidance to Local Authorities within the regions.

The Redcliffe-Maud proposals for the restructuring of local government (see Chapter 2) envisaged provincial authorities which would be responsible for regional planning. The Conservative Government deferred a decision on regional matters pending the Report of the Crowther Commission on the Constitution. If this Commission recommends strong regional authorities and if this is followed up by the establishment of effective regional government, then regional planning may yet become a reality in Britain.

In the meanwhile, the Ministry of Local Government, in an attempt to guide regional planning policies in the South-East has produced a South-East Plan in 1970 in collaboration with the constituent authorities in the region. Thus the Ministry is now beginning to accept responsibility for regional planning in the absence of effective regional planning authorities and further such strategy studies for other regions are to follow.

2. A corresponding structure of local planning authorities

The Conservative Government rejected the principle of the large unitary authorities as recommended in 1969 by the Redcliffe-Maud Commission and opted for a two-tier system of local government to supersede the present fragmented and ineffectual County and County Borough structure. This new structure is in my view only a second-best solution as it will result in many built-in frictions. Even so, local government reorganized in this way will be better suited to carry out the new planning functions as envisaged in the 1968 Town and Country Planning Act (see Chapter 1). However, this hopeful change has yet to be enacted by Parliament and put into operation. There will, no doubt, be many teething troubles, particularly during the transitional period before the new structure of local government is fully accepted and becomes effective.

3. A full integration of social, economic and physical planning at all levels

While physical planning has been in operation throughout the country since 1948 Britain has had to do without a Ministry responsible for Economic Affairs during most of this time. And though a Department of Economic Affairs was set up in 1964 it was dismantled again in 1969 and was therefore too shortlived to make a lasting contribution to the planning process. However, economists are nowadays playing an important role in multi-disciplinary planning teams and we are moving in the direction of closer integration of economics with physical planning. We have not got nearly as far yet on the social side, mainly I believe because there are as yet not enough social scientists trained and ready to contribute effectively to the planning process. Yet their role is likely to grow as we are becoming increasingly aware of the importance of social aspects in planning generally and in urban planning in particular.

4. The appropriate financial organization and support to ensure phased implementation of planning proposals

Just as planning has to be carried out at central, regional and local level, financial resources for the phased implementation of planning proposals should correspondingly be allocated at these levels. At present, since regional planning is not operational, responsibility for finance is shared between central and local government authorities. At national level, a national budget, divided up into the regions, would give some indication of the total national resources available. At local level, the local budget, supplemented with certain grants from central government, is usually split up and portions are allocated to various service committees, the investments of which are then often inadequately coordinated.

A more effective method is to work to a capital works programme which can ensure the allocation of financial resources on a geographical basis so that new housing, open spaces, schools, shops and social facilities are provided simultaneously within a given area. Such programmes are most effectively implemented by management methods which are relatively new to local government such as the Programming, Planning and Budgeting System (see Appendix 10) which requires goals, cost criteria and priorities to be identified and investment to be allocated in a meaningful and coordinated way. With regard to the private sector, much needs to be done to encourage private enterprise to play a more effective and useful role in the redevelopment of existing cities and the building of new ones.

5. Planning must be fully integrated with the political apparatus and the public be given an opportunity for active participation

Planning is a continuing process and therefore requires assured continuity in operation. This is only possible if the major political parties, who may alternate in forming governments, see planning as an essential and indispensable instrument for guiding development. This does not of course preclude party-political differences on certain planning issues, which are inevitable and a healthy sign of a vigorous democracy. Within a framework of general political support for effective planning much more should and will be done to make it a more democratic process than it has been in the past. Some of the principles for effective public participation in planning have been stated in Chapter 5. Since basically an educational process is involved here, it is likely to take several years of concerted effort to establish a firm and realistic basis for informed citizen participation. However, a start has been made. Equally important are programmes of monitoring and evaluation (see Chapter 6) to ensure that decision makers are informed of the way in which their decisions affect people's lives and to assist them in continuously improving on their performance.

These five pre-conditions, if they were met, would go a long way to improve the effectiveness of planning and achieve better integration of inter-related planning issues. At present, these conditions exist only partly and much of our planning effort is therefore not producing the best possible results. Although we must continue to strive for a better overall framework for planning, we cannot wait for perfection but must work within this framework as best we can. Let us therefore now concentrate on the major planning issues, particularly with regard to urban planning with which we are here concerned.

12 A New Approach to Planning

Planning of new cities, and to a more limited extent, the re-planning of existing ones, is therefore not just a mechanical projection of present trends but the formulation and adoption of goals which may well lie outside predictable trends but which would constitute a more desirable state of affairs. These goals, while apparently ideal at the present time, must nevertheless be within the realms of reality and must be capable of periodic revision. Effective and forward-looking planning policies will then connect the present situation with the ideal goals, and will be constantly reviewed and adapted in the light of experience and of changes which occur or are introduced in the course of implementing policies. This in turn requires sophisticated forecasting techniques which must be intelligently and imaginatively applied, as well as a reliable system of monitoring events and feeding back the findings into the planning process to check to what extent past policies have been successful or otherwise.

Such an approach is fundamentally different from the notion that we can produce finite plans for future generations to realize in detail. The baroque concept of city planning, for example, sees the city as a finite artefact of magnificent squares and streets connecting fixed points of major significance. Such plans often forced several generations to their rigid adherence if they were to be realized as originally conceived. One of the last such plans, l'Enfant's late 18th-century Plan for Washington, although far-sighted for its time, has suffered considerably under the pressure of inevitable changes which the author could not foresee. Yet the changes during the period between the concept of this plan and today were relatively small compared with the changes likely to occur during a similar period from now on, since the rate and extent of change is increasing so rapidly.

We must be content therefore to sketch out broad policy objectives for our cities with regard to the distant future in the form of a framework or system within which foreseen as well as unforeseen changes can be readily absorbed. This in turn means the abandonment of the notion that we can ever plan our cities in a finite way. Planning must instead be seen as a continuous iterative process and our cities as ever-changing organisms, certain aspects of which may change more rapidly than others but in which the most important single factor is the people, with their continuously evolving needs and aspirations. As Edmund Bacon, Philadelphia Director of Planning, said at the Ditchley Foundation Seminar, in March 1968: "You cannot make a plan—you can only grow a plan."

The practical application of this flexible and open-ended approach can best be illustrated by an example of how an urban structure plan might be produced. The process would start with the formulation of social and economic goals and objectives and of physical performance standards to meet these. Alternative hypotheses of physical structures of integrated land-use/transport patterns are then prepared to meet the agreed objectives. From these, two or perhaps three alternatives are subjected to comparative testing and the most promising alternative is selected for development in depth. Throughout this process a data bank of relevant information is built up and the data processed as required. Such data would include information about population changes, age and income structures, employment, educational and leisure facilities, the local economy, the building stock, etc. The structure plan which is eventually evolved becomes the overall long-term policy framework, within which the more detailed plans are prepared for areas in which early action is contemplated. Through a monitoring and evaluation system planners keep the plan under constant review and obtain information as to how the plan is working out in practice; from this they can conclude what new policies or modifications to existing ones are necessary to meet these changing circumstances.

In terms of specific planning techniques, planners will prepare their work programme graphically to record the significant steps required in this planning process. The data at each step are then defined, collated and put in a data bank which is based on an efficient data-storage–retrieval system, making use of modern data-processing equipment like storage on punch cards or magnetic tape. A computer programme would be concurrently prepared for the analysis. This modified concept of planning is greatly more complex and sophisticated than the traditional approach of survey–analysis–plan. It not only involves the decision makers to an unprecedented extent at various stages of the planning process but requires well-trained and sophisticated planning staff.

Reference has already been made to the multi-disciplinary nature of the new planning teams. The training of planners is gradually being modified to fit them for the new tasks and those who had been trained prior to the development and application to planning of these new techniques would benefit from mid-career refresher courses. Planners in public and private practice and in the academic field will be called upon to use and develop the new methodology. Different situations require a different kind of planning service and there are many ways of achieving worthwhile results. There is also a strong case for encouraging a much freer interchange of planning staffs between different levels of government, public and private offices, and between these and universities, with likely benefits not only to those concerned but, what is more important, to the work they produce and the service they give.

13 Urban Planning Policies

In order to make a concerted and comprehensive attack on our urban planning problems, it is essential to produce and implement a series of interlocking urban planning policies, the most significant of which are outlined below.

Comprehensive housing policies

The most important component in our cities is the housing of its people, the human habitat, and the relationship of individual homes to each other and the community at large, their links with jobs, schools, shops, social and leisure facilities. Our housing policies must therefore take social and economic needs and aspirations of the people as a basis upon which the physical home environment is developed.

Housing areas must be planned in an optimum relationship to all the daily functions of residents such as going to work, to school, play or shop. Some activities like the primary school, the corner shop and some local employment must be located within walking distance of all homes, while major employment areas, places for secondary and higher education and major shopping and entertainment centres must be easily accessible to all residents, by public or private transport.

We must discard many post-war dogmas which in the event have been found to be ill-conceived. There is, for instance, no need to keep all employment out of housing areas. Many light and service industries and small office developments are clean, noise-free and are often housed in attractive modern buildings. They can therefore be integrated with housing, not only without detriment to the environment, but with considerable advantages. It would add interest to otherwise largely dormitory areas and provide opportunities for some people, especially mothers with children, to find work locally.

The concept of the inward-looking, quasi-independent neighbourhood with its own shopping, schools, etc., has proved socially too restrictive and unreal. The pattern of development should provide for a much freer social interchange than the traditional neighbourhood
allows for. In the planning of Milton Keynes new city, for instance, local schools, shops,
community buildings and local employment have been grouped into local activity centres
and sited at the edges of the residential areas where safe pedestrian under-passes cross main
roads and connect to bus stops. In this way all the adjoining residential areas share in these
facilities and residents have a greater choice of service and a better opportunity to mix (see
Appendix 5).

We must plan for an increasingly affluent society. While one can only guess how people will
spend their extra income, it is, I think, fair to assume that they will buy more cars and will
want to have more space in and around their homes. Both these considerations lead to
lower rather than higher residential densities in the future. It should therefore not be
assumed too readily that people will be prepared to go on living at the high densities they
accept today. One of the reasons why voluntary migration from the inner areas to the
suburbs and out of big cities altogether has been increasing steadily in recent years is
people's preference for more space, which at present they can only get at the price they can
afford by moving out.

However, while the majority of people in this country and the USA are likely to become
more affluent, a minority is likely to remain poor, perhaps not so much in absolute as in
relative terms; the gap between the have and have-nots may well widen unless society makes
a special effort to close it. This fact is already only too evident in the USA, where estimates
of disadvantaged people range between 30 and 40 million, i.e. one-fifth of the total population. In terms of housing this means that provision must be made to house this under-
privileged section of the community decently. Personal subsidies and the use of the older
stock of our houses which could be modernized may well prove important resources for this.
Hand in hand with this provision for shelter, schooling and the other necessities of life,
which must be brought within reach of the poor, should go training and retraining schemes
which would equip them to raise themselves to higher economic levels and enable them to
rent or buy better houses.

Because of growing specialization, people tend to change jobs and move houses more
readily nowadays. Such moves are relatively straightforward for people who own houses
which they can sell and buy another one nearer their next job. Similar ease of movement
should apply to rented accommodation but does not at present. On the other hand, if a
family simply wants to move into a larger or smaller house because their space requirements
have changed, there should be sufficient choice of different types of accommodation and
tenure within their locality for them to move house without having to change schools or
patronize different shops.

We must avoid building large single-class communities. While it would be unrealistic to
expect cheap and expensive housing to be acceptable cheek by jowl, groups of, say, 200–300
houses attracting one income group could with advantage be built next to a group of houses
for a different income group. Children from both groups could mix in the local school and

housewives in the local shops. A variety of different house types and designs would provide people with choice and attract a range of income groups and people from different walks of life. Social factors of status, prejudice and group solidarity are also important aspects which should be faced and tackled as an integral part of housing. If such an approach were adopted the result would be a better integrated community than is possible in very large areas of single-class housing, be they vast council estates or extensive middle-class suburbs. If the same principle were applied to race and colour, particularly in American communities, it could be an important practical step towards racial integration.

Another form of balance which is equally important is the need to provide all the essential services which are an integral part of the home environment, such as schools, shops and open spaces, in phase with housing. The adverse social repercussions of charging ahead with housing while leaving these other essential facilities 'till later' are well known. Such short-sighted policies cause much inconvenience and distress to people and as a rule result in higher costs later.

We should aim at providing people with the greatest possible variety of different kinds of home environment to choose from. Some will prefer to live near the centre of things in high-density flats, others near open spaces or along river banks, others still in an Arcadian-type low-density suburban environment. Some may like to live near major transport interchanges or even urban motorways provided we plan, as we could, the new housing as an integral part of the motorways.

We must establish housing advisory services in all communities, as recommended by the report of the Seebohm Committee on Local Authority and Allied Personal Social Services published in 1968, which would inform people of opportunities of housing for rent or sale and advise them generally on housing matters. The provision of a variety of different types of housing, both with regard to space and value, rent or sale, would also result in a better social mix in terms of age and income groups.

Our approach to costs of development should not just be 'How much?' but 'Is it best value for money?' It is because we have failed to look at the picture as a whole that we have not always achieved the best possible results and often have not even had good value for money. In our cost-benefit studies it is frequently the unquantifiable elements like the degree of human satisfaction with the end product which should rank highest. In other words, we should be at least as concerned with the output of what we provide for people, how it works and whether they like it and if not, why not, as we are with numbers of new houses built or old ones demolished, and with space standards and cost yardsticks. This in turn means that we must be fully and continuously informed about the performance of the built home environment and feed back this information to the designers and decision makers so that mistakes are not repeated and better solutions are constantly evolved (see Chapter 6).

Turning now from these basic principles to detailed considerations of the home environment, I would like to see the same open-ended approach of providing options, allowing for growth and change, replace the present tendency to regard the environment as planned and built in its finite form for all times. One only has to revisit even some of the best housing developments after a few years to realize how people's use of them has changed their character, sometimes for the better, sometimes for the worse. And these changes usually occur in spite of rigorous restrictive rules. Would it not be better to plan and build in such a way that these changes happen naturally and gracefully, and are seen as indications of vitality instead of spoilers of the designers' preconceived image?

The application of this open-ended approach to the detailed design of the home environment means that we are not only concerned with the traditional three-dimensional aspects but equally with the fourth dimension of time as an important factor. We should therefore aim in our design at simple buildings which can be easily altered or extended without detracting from their appearance, and at space which can be used without restrictive rules for a variety of functions including reserves for as yet unforeseen requirements. Let us at the same time attempt to design real live places with their own identity and get away from the impersonal provision by some authority, however well meaning, of a supposedly finished product. Instead, let us encourage a much greater personal involvement and participation of people to take part in the shaping of their own environment.

A balanced transport system

One of our primary objectives in city planning should be the greatest possible choice for its citizens: freedom to choose from a variety of job opportunities, educational, cultural and recreational facilities, and different kinds of urban environments, with a full range of housing for different income groups and household structures. If these goals could be achieved, the unimpeded choice would greatly enrich urban life and would make it an even greater attraction than it is today. All this means greatly improved accessibility to enable people to avail themselves of these opportunities since choices are meaningless unless they are fully accessible. This implies a comprehensive transport system which caters for all types of movement of people and goods from high-speed inter-city travel by air and express trains to slow-moving local traffic, vehicular as well as pedestrian (see Chapter 8).

One of the most difficult traffic problems in cities, the journey to work, will have to be tackled in a variety of ways. Broadly speaking, the larger an existing city the greater the opportunities to serve it with an efficient public transport system combining various forms such as a tram, underground railway, and large and small buses and taxis. With the size of the city, however, the degree of restraint on the use of the private car for commuting is also likely to increase by parking restrictions, discs or road pricing. Where, for a number of reasons, an efficient public transport system based on line haul, e.g. a train or bus on its own right of way, cannot be created, concentration of work places will have to be avoided and as even distribution as possible of the major traffic magnets will have to be the aim, served by a public transport of a diffused type, e.g. fleets of small and frequent buses.

Every major city will have to make the choice about the extent to which it will be able to accommodate private cars in or near the central area. It will also have to determine what the scale of investment should be into attractive and efficient forms of public transport. New types of public vehicles will have to be evolved to supersede the present cumbersome buses and often outdated fixed-track rolling stock. The greater flexibility of mini-buses, limousines (large taxis with fixed routes) and a more generous provision of taxis will approach the convenience of the private car without the attendant under-use of road space and parking problems. One of the greatest contributions towards the improvement of the urban environment would be the eventual substitution of the combustion engine with the electric battery or some other noiseless and fumeless method of propulsion. Such a change, if it were to come about on a significant scale, coupled with the determined enforcement of the Clean Air Act, would practically eliminate the fumes and greatly reduce the noise which at present casts a major blight on town life.

The interchanges, i.e. the points where different forms of transport are brought together to give passengers a comfortable and attractive environment in which they can change from one mode to another, are likely to be the future growth points in our cities. Because accessibility is at its optimum, such places will act as powerful magnets and will attract additional facilities like shopping, offices and entertainment and high-density housing. Thus interchange points are likely to play a major role in urban structure plans of the future.

Closely allied to the subject of accessibility and vehicular movement in towns and cities are comprehensive car-parking policies which can have a vital effect on the control and distribution of private cars used for a variety of trips. Major and convenient car-parking facilities at the interchange points of primary roads with rapid-transit systems on the principle of 'park and ride' will enable people to drive their cars from their homes to the nearest such point and proceed to town by fast public transport. Further in, a ring of car parks around the perimeter of the central area will cater for similar functions but at higher charges for those who want to leave their cars nearer the centre. In the central area itself, a more limited provision of car parks geared to the capacity of the roads serving them will also help to improve accessibility for private cars, particularly of shoppers. The priority of shoppers can be ensured by regulating opening hours. These parking provisions and other parking opportunities like metered streets should be planned as an integral part of the overall transport system and preferably also controlled by the Local Authority. Finally, the safe and attractive movement by pedestrians through and between centres of interest and within easy walking distance of public transport stops is a most important aspect of any comprehensive system of movement of people and goods in urban areas.

Imaginative townscape policies

Towns inevitably consist of collections of buildings, streets and spaces between them and one would expect them to be very similar to each other. Yet thousands of towns throughout the world vary to an extent which gives each an identity of its own. The uniqueness of a town or city results from the way it has been organized, its streets formed, buildings grouped and adapted to the micro-climate, national and local traditions absorbed, changes of levels exploited, important buildings retained or given prominence, the spaces landscaped and people's habits catered for. Some towns are still almost perfect examples of past periods, while others owe their vitality to a judicious mixture of several building periods. But they all have one great thing in common—they are unique, and while certain of their features have a family likeness with similar features in other towns, they have an identity of their own.

However, this uniqueness of different towns is increasingly threatened, and the dangers of ending up with town after town looking very much the same are very real since the pressures which could bring about this dreary monotony on a monumental scale are very powerful. If we are to preserve what is still left of the character of some of our towns and to create new character and identities upon rebuilding and building new ones, very carefully thought out three-dimensional planning policies, both with regard to the overall conception and to local implementation, will have to be worked out and firmly applied.

One of the main reasons for the rapid loss of identity of many cities is their failure to adopt and implement consistent visual policies. The confusion and lack of determined policies with regard to historic buildings has already resulted in many irreplaceable losses not only of individual historic buildings but of whole areas. Such important elements as high buildings are allowed to proliferate without rhyme or reason in city after city and often to blur and distort fine existing features on the skyline. Very little, if any, overall concept usually exists with regard to the city's landscape. Similar failures of a mistaken policy of *laisser-faire* or of *ad hocery* and hit and miss also apply to the control of development generally.

Above all, clear and bold decisions must be made regarding the degree of motorization any city can accommodate without destroying itself, and the design of roads and buildings must be much more imaginatively integrated if we are to absorb the motor car in our cities without visual as well as social disaster. It is therefore essential, in an endeavour to retain and enhance existing identity and foster the creation of a new one, for cities to work out and apply overall policies for such vital aspects of the urban scene as historic buildings, landscaping, advertisements, high buildings, and new structures to accommodate the motor car.

Many towns and cities in Britain have old and unique historic cores with a strong identity, yet few have really fully worked out and firmly administered policies for them. It is not just a question of preserving a few listed buildings but more often one of preservation and rehabilitation of whole areas with their street network, pedestrian alleyways, scale, colour and texture. However, the preservation and/or rehabilitation of historic buildings and the conservation of historic areas and of whole historic towns can be planned effectively only within a regional and sub-regional framework. Only thus can one ensure that, where necessary, undue pressures are diverted from them to those surrounding towns most suited to accommodate future growth.

The design of the spaces between buildings is often carried out—if it is done at all—with insufficient skill and understanding of urban landscaping, of the right balance between hard and soft groundscape and the role trees should play in our cities. In many industrial 19th-century cities nothing could raise the standard of the urban environment more dramatically, particularly in their inner areas, than generous and imaginative planting of trees. Other cities in Britain have certain landscape features which are often more memorable than their buildings (e.g. Paxton's Park in Birkenhead, Cheshire). Policies are needed not only to preserve such features and safeguard them from mutilation and disturbing intrusions, but also to develop others as part of an overall landscaping policy.

In practice, separate Parks Committees are usually responsible for the laying out and maintenance of individual existing and new parks and are rarely advised by landscape architects on a coherent design policy. All too often a suburban garden approach prevails and municipal parks in towns and cities throughout Britain have an uncanny similarity and are more often than not out of tune with the character of their own cities. And how few cities have a tree-planting policy and know what to do with the trees they possess. An increasing number of new buildings will be system-built in future with the consequent possible danger of dreary sameness unless handled with great skill and imagination. Indeed, the main redeeming feature in helping to establish some character and a new sense of identity may then well be the quality of landscaping of spaces between the buildings.

Since both by day and night the character and even identity of certain parts of cities are very much affected by outdoor advertisements, it is important that areas where these should be encouraged and discouraged should be defined. Not only would such a policy, if intelligently applied, safeguard from intrusion those areas where advertisements are undesirable, e.g. in residential areas, but, equally important, the impact of advertising could be dramatized by greater concentration in those areas where it contributes vitality, colour and sparkle to the urban scene, as in shopping and entertainment centres and at transport interchanges. Such a policy could also strengthen their character and identity.

The high building has become as much a symbol of our age as the motor car and is an equally ingenious invention which, however, misused, can cause havoc in our cities. Yet, very few towns and cities have carefully considered policies for either (see Chapter 10). While a policy on the use of motor cars in a city is, of course, an integral part of the strategic plan for the city, a high-buildings policy is one of the most important aspects of a city's visual policy. To start with, plot ratios and residential densities should be such that high buildings remain at all times a matter of choice rather than necessity. This choice element would be further strengthened if the deep office block and high-density, low rise housing were developed further and accepted as viable alternatives to high offices or blocks of flats. Areas where high buildings should be encouraged or discouraged could be defined in most cities and some of them, at least in their historic core, may well end up with no new high buildings or very few.

Assuming a basic network of urban motorways and main distributors is likely to be needed for major cities, one is then left with the difficult visual and social problem of where to route the new roads with the least disturbance and how to integrate these vast, new and complex urban structures into the townscape. Many American cities demonstrate clearly that no single urban element could do more harm to our cities, destroy more of their character and make them look more alike than ruthlessly routed and unsympathetically designed urban motorways and seas of car parks. We must at all costs avoid the cheap and expedient but socially and visually disastrous solutions of littering acres with open car parks and of inserting elevated motorways insensitively between existing buildings. The new road structures and associated car parks should be planned as part of comprehensive redevelopment in depth. They must be designed as integral parts of whole building complexes which would be built sideways to, under and over these new roads. Here is a unique and unprecedented challenge to create a new kind of contemporary townscape with its own character and identity.

At the micro-scale, we need to know more about the impact of the urban environment on man, not only on his five senses but on his physical and psychological well-being, and his activities. There is a danger that some urban designers and architects with their highly developed sensitivity for aesthetically pleasing spatial arrangements may at times lose sight of the deeper meaning of the physical environment. In particular, to the orderly mind of the designer, unplanned incidents and unforeseen 'misuse' by the consumers of what had been designed for them in good faith and with much imagination and sensitivity is so painful as to make him dismiss these as undesirable human frailties which somehow or other should not be allowed.

Today and even more so tomorrow, we are not designing just for the privileged few but for the whole of our people, the rich and the poor, the highly sophisticated and the less sophisticated. The best way for urban designers to overcome this real difficulty is not to design 'down' to the lowest common denominator but to evolve designs that can be appreciated also by the less sophisticated and to persist patiently in persuading them to accept good design, like it, and eventually demand it.

At the same time, it is essential to evolve design concepts which are strong enough to allow for the unplanned incident; particularly since these can only be prevented through rigid control and at the expense of suppressing what may well be a delightful and amusing individual contribution. Such popular embellishments can range from some paintwork in violent colours to elaborate fencing and trellis work, so popular with tenants of English council housing estates, or the solar-heat paraphernalia gracing the roofs of houses and flats in Israel to the dismay of their architects. One cannot help feeling that either these do-it-yourself enrichments are positive signs that people take enough interest in 'improving' their houses, even if these improvements may at times have doubtful aesthetic qualities, or that the designers failed to meet certain needs in the first place. But however humane an approach one may wish to adopt, the urban environment could easily degenerate into unplanned chaos—indeed this has happened in so many parts of cities, particularly in America —unless a strong design concept holds it all together. In other words, we must aim at urban design concepts which are clear and firm on the major visual policies and issues and strong enough to accommodate at the micro-scale the unpredictable irrationalities of human behaviour.

In a society which is increasingly emphasizing the importance of material gains over visual ones, the aesthetic side is bound to be regarded of lesser importance—if indeed of any importance at all. Therefore unless we reassert the fundamental importance of high visual quality much of the urban development efforts could and indeed do result in visual mediocrity, if not worse. And since in the last resort man 'does not live by bread alone' and since the visual satisfaction is also an important factor in his well-being and happiness, we shall have failed if we do not meet these demands. One cannot therefore escape the conclusion that aesthetic and social considerations must play an equal part with economic ones and must in certain circumstances even be decisive.

213

Better husbanding of our resources

Apart from taking greater care of our historically and architecturally significant buildings, there is a more general need for a better husbanding of our existing assets and resources. There are few towns where there are not acres and acres of waste land and buildings which no longer serve their original use but have not been converted or rebuilt for new requirements. Examples abound: disused railway sidings and marshalling yards, derelict warehouses and workshops, closed theatres and churches, empty and unkempt sites, disused docks and waterways. At the same time we are crying out for more urban land. Let us first put to effective use all the existing urban land and buildings; this would cost relatively little and achieve much to provide new accommodation for a variety of uses and would considerably improve the urban environment.

Once we have accepted the need to take greater care with fine old buildings as well as to convert empty sites and buildings to new uses, we have embarked upon a more thoughtful and sensitive approach to the reshaping of our urban environment. We shall then look at the large stock of housing which we cannot as yet classify as slums and which our resources do not permit us to demolish for many years to come. The structures may be 50 or 60 years old but are still solid; the internal planning may be out of date but could be modernized; the layouts may be tight but could be opened up by judicious demolition of intervening blocks; the streets may be bleak but could be humanized with generous tree planting and imaginative landscaping.

In other words, these vast 'twilight' areas of obsolescent housing should be more carefully analysed to discover how they could be revitalized by methodical rehabilitation. The relatively few instances where this approach has been adopted have shown that such an approach is practicable and likely to meet with more approval from the people concerned than wholesale demolition and displacement. If, in addition to this more sensitive and modest approach to urban renewal, we adopt transport policies in our cities in which imaginatively designed public transport plays an increasing rather than decreasing role, we shall find that we shall also be able to economize considerably on new road works. Major new roads, some of urban motorway standard, are still likely to be required, particularly for fast long-distance goods and service traffic, rapid public transport and some private-car traffic, but they would have to accommodate very much less traffic than if they had to carry a vast proportion of private-car traffic as well, particularly at peak hours. This in turn would entail a much more modest degree of urban surgery, resulting in less social upheaval and visual disturbance.

A modified approach to urban renewal

One has now arrived at a modified approach to the whole question of urban renewal. Instead of wholesale demolition and massive rebuilding, and futile attempts to cater for a maximum of private-car trips by building vast amounts of urban motorways and associated car parks, we are now considering the adoption of a less radical and more modest approach to the renewal of our cities. Twenty years of post-war reconstruction have taught us that the radical approach has, with few notable exceptions, not really been as successful as we hoped it would be. Too many drastic urban surgeries have not only been desperately slow and painful but have resulted in ugly scars and piecemeal caricatures of dreams of brave new cities. Our resources have been pathetically inadequate to perform this complex and difficult task successfully, except where physical and political conditions were highly favourable like, for instance, in the blitzed centres of Coventry and Rotterdam, where determined City Councils embarked quickly on comprehensive purchase and redevelopment before it was too late.

This does not mean, however, that we should in any way withdraw from urban renewal, but rather that we should redistribute our efforts and resources in far more modest improvements over wider areas and concentrate our comprehensive redevelopment activities where they would make the best contribution. The over-concentration of resources on spectacular central-area redevelopment schemes has in many cities resulted in a corresponding neglect of the vast slum and twilight areas in other parts of these cities. It is time we redirected our efforts to these areas and upgraded their environment by combined selective rebuilding and rehabilitation operations.

If the foregoing approach is accepted as sensible and realistic, we shall end up with cities where more of the old urban fabric is kept and only modestly modified; the combination of such measures as noise and air-pollution abatement, environmental and traffic management, selective slum clearance and rehabilitation, conservation of historic areas and some redevelopment of worn-out areas will result in an urban environment which may not be radically different from the existing one but which will in many respects be a vast improvement on existing conditions.

Freed from many of the ills and dangers of present city life, city dwellers will be able to enjoy more fully the wealth of opportunities in jobs, housing, education and leisure activities within an urban environment rich with character and vitality. With these relatively modest and entirely realistic steps within our reach we could make city life at least acceptable but possibly positively attractive and desirable.

However, while there will be greater freedom in some respects, there will have to be restrictions in others, particularly with regard to the use of the private car. If the more modest approach outlined above is to be adopted, one of the main corollaries would be a necessary reduction in private-car trips, particularly the journey to work, since insufficient road space would be available for that purpose. This is, however, in any case only a question of degree, since at no time could any major city ever accommodate all private-car work trips. The question is simply whether 10 per cent, 20 per cent or perhaps 50 per cent (but certainly not 90 per cent or 100 per cent) of commuters will be able to drive in their cars to work. These necessary restrictions will be less irksome, indeed may not be seriously resented, if an efficient, cheap and modern public transport system, made up of a combination of several modes of transportation, were readily available. There will, indeed, be other necessary restrictions like the need to accept some relatively high densities, modest indoor and outdoor space standards. But millions of people will continue to accept these limitations as necessary and sensible in exchange for leading a fuller life.

Meaningful comprehensive redevelopment

In discussing a modified, more modest approach to urban renewal in the previous section, I have suggested that we should concentrate our comprehensive redevelopment activities where they would make the best contribution. In other words, in spite of a plea for a more careful and less sweeping approach to the renewal of our towns and cities, some comprehensive redevelopment will still be necessary. Since our resources are likely to be limited for a long time to come and comprehensive redevelopment makes a substantial call on them, it would seem common sense to adopt such policies whereby they can yield the best results from the point of view of the town or city as a whole.

I suggest therefore that the present policy or lack of policy with regard to comprehensive redevelopment, largely applied to vast housing areas and profitable central-area sites, should be reconsidered. A good deal of the housing could be redeveloped more modestly by a combination of rehabilitation and selective demolition and renewal, while we may wish to forgo some costly central-area comprehensive redevelopment schemes altogether at this stage. Instead, three major categories of areas should be defined for possible comprehensive redevelopment: the major interchange points, areas in depth on either side of the new urban motorways and really bad worn-out areas beyond repair.

Major interchanges

Since these are considered to be key elements and future growth points in our towns and cities because of their optimum accessibility, they should be developed in the best possible way. This is likely to mean a radical reorganization of substantial areas around these interchanges to accommodate fully integrated systems of different modes of travel (e.g. rail, bus, taxi, private car and pedestrians changing from one mode to another). And in order to exploit to the full this high degree of accessibility, a concentration of other activities such as shopping, offices, high-density housing and entertainment is both reasonable and desirable. However, in order to achieve all this, possibly in the form of multi-use multi-level building complexes, comprehensive redevelopment techniques will have to be applied. Some of these interchanges would be in the suburbs where they are likely to develop into new district centres, e.g. Vallingby in Stockholm (see page 88), while others may be in the central areas of our cities, e.g. Place Ville Marie in the centre of Montreal (see page 131). These recent examples prove that this kind of development can be not only very attractive and convenient to the users but also highly profitable.

Areas on either side of urban motorways

Since for social and visual reasons urban motorways, particularly when elevated, should not be inserted into the existing urban fabric leaving buildings standing on either side of them, the only civilized way of resolving this problem is to redevelop comprehensively in depth on either side of urban motorways. This, of course, presupposes that these are routed through the most worn-out areas, but this may not always be possible and some less derelict areas may also have to be included. However, the pay-off of such an approach would be very considerable. Not only would one avoid socially and visually unacceptable relationships between new motorways and existing buildings lining them, but one can recreate a new environment in scale and fully integrated with the motorways. Comprehensive redevelopment would make it possible to reorganize the local street pattern and build over, under and sideways to the motorway with structures specifically designed for that purpose. Thus could the tremendous impact of new urban motorways not only be absorbed but turned into a positive advantage opening up new and exciting design possibilities. A drive along new motorways imaginatively integrated with a remodelled urban fabric can also become an attractive visual experience for drivers and passengers.

Badly worn-out areas

Even when we have reconsidered our approach to the renewal of slum and worn-out areas and opted for a less sweeping approach entailing a combination of rehabilitation of existing housing and selective building of new housing and other allied facilities, it is likely that we shall find some areas too far gone for that approach. In such cases, comprehensive renewal is probably still the best and indeed the only answer. In other words, it is likely that present policies of wholesale clearance, while considerably restricted to fewer areas, will still be a valid method of dealing with the worst areas.

If the policies outlined above were adopted, we would make a more sensible and effective use of comprehensive redevelopment techniques and probably obtain as good if not better value for money and possibly higher social benefits than with our present somewhat haphazard and uncoordinated policies with regard to comprehensive redevelopment.

14 Making a Fresh Start

British new towns—problems and opportunities

Since this book is concerned with the planning of our urban environment, our considerations cannot be limited to the problems and opportunities of existing towns and cities, although the great majority of people live in them and will continue to do so. However, already over 1 million people live and work in new towns we have created in the course of this century in Britain and it is certain that an increasing number of people will be citizens of further new towns and cities during the next few decades. Since the population of Britain is likely to increase by the turn of the century by another 12 million people and since space must also be found in addition to this projected increase for hundreds of thousands of people for whom there is no room in existing towns and cities, we shall have to embark upon a massive programme of further new and expanded towns and cities. Similar programmes, albeit on a smaller scale, are now an essential tool of national planning policies in the Scandinavian countries, France, East European countries, as well as developing countries like Venezuela. In the USA, the Housing and Urban Development Act of 1970 establishes the framework for the creation of new communities.

At first sight, the problems with new towns should be fewer and easier to solve. Instead of having to demolish worn-out buildings, streets and services and rehousing the existing population and traders before any renewal work can proceed, we have largely green fields upon which we can plan and build. Instead of high land values and fragmented ownership in existing towns we have at our disposal cheap agricultural land which can be brought into public ownership by the New Town Corporations. Instead of having to insert slowly and often painfully piece by piece new structures and roads into an existing urban fabric, we can build large areas comprehensively with all the necessary roads, buildings and open spaces without any major physical, social or economic disruption.

Instead of different development committees responsible for housing, roads, education, social services and parks, a single Development Corporation is responsible for the total physical development even though educational buildings, for instance, remain the separate responsibility of County Education Authorities. These are but a few of the obvious advantages in planning and building new towns as opposed to rebuilding existing ones.

Yet there are many other problems which beset the planning and building of new towns. The very fact that one has to start new towns with only small communities in existence and that the growth of our new towns has been relatively slow (e.g. most Mark I new towns of the late 40s in Britain are reaching their planned populations of 50 000 to 80 000 only in 20 years or more) throw up a number of difficulties. There is bound to be at first an underprovision of major shopping, cultural and entertainment facilities until a population is reached which is large enough to support such provisions; the running of viable and efficient public transport services usually suffers from inadequate patronage; the population structure is likely to be unbalanced in that there will be a preponderance of young couples with small children, and as a result 20 to 25 years later, of middle-aged couples with a large number of youngsters looking for jobs. The same problems have arisen with regard to income groups, with a vast majority of skilled and semi-skilled workers and their families settling in the new towns during the first decades due to a preponderance of labour-intensive, manually operated industries. Indeed, one of the major difficulties has been that of attracting the right kinds of employment at the right time to provide employment consistent with a steady inflow of new population. These and similar problems are peculiar to new towns as compared with old towns with their existing facilities and services, a rich mix of household structures and of people of varying incomes and status.

The socio-economic problems experienced in British new towns have to some extent been aggravated by conceptual errors which were common to the first generation of post-war new towns which, however, have been gradually rectified in the more recent new town plans. For instance, the strongly centralized physical structure and the concentration of industries into a few large areas have been replaced by a more dispersed grid structure and a more even distribution of industries. The gross under-estimate of car ownership and usage on the one hand, and of the essential role of public transport on the other, has given way to a greater sense of realism and more sophisticated planning for both public and private transport. The quasi-self-sufficient neighbourhood has been abandoned in favour of smaller, inter-dependent service units which allow for a greater social overlap.

With regard to size, it might well have been a better socio-economic and physical investment if we had planned and built fewer but larger new cities instead of a multitude of small new towns. Since the provision of first-class shopping, higher educational, cultural and entertainment facilities requires a supporting population of several hundreds of thousands of people, only cities of about a quarter of a million population and over are really in a position to provide such facilities. Recent considerations in Lancashire, South Hampshire, on Humberside, and Severnside, and the designation of Milton Keynes in North Bucks as a city of a quarter of a million all point in this direction.

Concerning the function of new towns, this was seen somewhat narrowly as merely 'overspill' reception areas for population and industry for whom there was no room in existing cities. While one does not question this basic requirement, unique opportunities were lost to provide for other major functions as well, for instance the development of one of the new universities. We in Britain have since the war planned and are in the process of building 26 new universities and as many new towns, but not in a single instance has the location of a new university coincided with that of a new town. Yet possibly no other single major function would have helped as much to redress the imbalance of social class or family structure as a large new university could have done if it were part of a new town.

Surprisingly few new towns have experimented in any significant way with their educational, health or social services, or indeed in the physical environment, in spite of the potentially favourable conditions. While it is true that housing and working conditions are a considerable advance on existing towns—as they indeed should be considering the tremendous scope and freedom to develop compared with rebuilding parts of existing towns and cities —the quality of urban life as such is in some respects inferior to that existing towns can offer. The liveliness of streets in existing towns which is largely due to the concentration of people and a mixture of uses—though full of conflicts such as between pedestrians and fast through traffic—has tended to give way to an over-orderly arrangement of carefully separated activities, often resulting in a lack of vitality and a sense of isolation and loneliness. Visually, the exciting tensions between old and new buildings is lacking since large areas have been built together wholesale and are often stamped with economy rules in force at that time. Socially, because of a tendency towards a single-class community structure, opportunities of mixing between different income groups, between manual workers and professionals, have been diminished.

However, most important of all, the need to accommodate future growth and change has not yet been fully faced. Most new towns have been envisaged to grow up to a certain target population, and were expected somehow to stop developing when the target has been reached. It is true that several new towns are now being replanned to accommodate a larger population than was originally projected, but this is being done, more or less, as an afterthought. The problem that remains to be solved is how to plan a large new town or city with a firm investment commitment for each stage in such a way that growth is not inhibited and many yet unforeseen developments can be absorbed.

Thus the urban environment which has been created even in the best post-war new towns, while physically often attractive, has many other shortcomings and we shall have to review many of our socio-economic goals if we are to succeed fully in creating an urban organism and environment in new towns which is more than a limited advance on conditions in existing towns. In this we can go a long way by learning from past mistakes as well as successes and, above all, by exploiting more vigorously and imaginatively the unique opportunities which the planning and building of new towns or, better still, new large cities offer.

And these opportunities are great and exciting. A new pattern of urban living can be provided for a growing number of people who may not like restrictions on their space demands and use of their car or cars, as are inevitable in existing towns and cities. They will be able to live in new cities where there is ample space to meet their requirements. One of the best examples of such a new pattern of living in an attractive and well-functioning environment is the new town of Tapiola, Finland.

220

Tapiola New Town, near Helsinki. View of the town centre in the middle of the picture, with blocks of flats set amongst trees in the background. *Photo by courtesy of the Managing Director, Tapiola*

Land for housing and all other development can be provided at substantially lower cost than is available in metropolitan areas, and unique opportunities exist for the construction of houses in large quantities which result in higher efficiency and lower costs. New cities could be testing grounds of new technologies, construction methods, educational and health programmes and of social development. They could also make an important contribution to the housing and employment of the urban poor.

Many of the physical problems which mar town life at present can be tackled at source. Solutions can be worked out whereby good accessibility and a high standard of environment can be reconciled by a judicious location of the main traffic generators and the road network serving them. By contrast with existing towns, a high degree of private-car usage for all trips can be accommodated. Where an efficient public transport is a primary objective, the urban form can be organized to optimize such a service, and that part of the population which does not drive cars can be accommodated within walking distance of such public transport facilities. Alternatively, a more personal form of public transport like the minibus could serve uniformly these people wherever they may live. The separation of fast vehicular from pedestrian traffic is also a relatively easy matter and all major roads can be designed as single-purpose vehicular roads without footpaths or buildings lining them on either side, as is the case with roads in existing urban areas.

While experiment and innovation should be basic to the approach of new town development one may well find that some of the time-honoured urban elements, like the street and the square, can be re-used in a new and meaningful way. The street, particularly, no longer dominated by vehicular traffic, can once again form a pleasant and ever-changing sheltered space for the pedestrian on the move, while the square can continue to provide an attractive setting for houses grouped around it with shared communal facilities like play spaces set within its grass and trees.

221

Air pollution and noise interference can be minimized, since again the problems can be tackled at source. Work trips along imaginatively landscaped roads planned to take the peak loads may well be pleasure drives compared with the frustrating stops and go's on the streets of existing towns, and the factories and offices, all built to modern standards, can be set amongst trees and provided with ample car-parking facilities. New forms of light and easily manoeuvrable and possibly automated vehicles can provide public transport for the non-drivers and indeed that proportion of drivers who may prefer to use such a public transport system to driving their own cars, particularly to and from work. Thus good accessibility and maximum freedom to move about in comfort and safety are likely to be two of the greatest attractions of new towns and cities.

However, in order to take the fullest possible advantage of the new opportunities open to us when we plan and build new cities we shall have to set our sights a good deal higher than we have done in the past. Not only must we employ the most up-to-date methodology in the planning process, but even before we embark on any physical planning we shall have to be much clearer and more explicit about the socio-economic goals of the society for whom we are planning and building.

For example, the ideal new pattern of social development will have to make the most of the established towns within the area. The aim to attract overspill population might be in conflict with the ideal social mix for the new city. The ideal social structure for the city as a whole must be reconciled with the aim of fostering social integration at local level. The advantages of high density in residential areas, in maximizing social interconnection and facilitating public transport, must be reconciled with the convenience and accessibility for private motor cars, at future high levels of car ownership. The provision of maximum freedom for the town to change as it grows, and to accept changing requirements for land use, will be at odds with the need to make the most efficient distribution of land use in terms of what we know today. The provision of a road network giving maximum convenience to car users must not prevent the possibility of providing viable public transport.

These questions should be faced, debated, and resolved in the early phases of the planning operation.

Appendix 24

The Plan for Milton Keynes
Main consultants: Llewelyn-Davies, Weeks, Forestier Walker & Bor

Introduction

This book has so far attempted to deal with the whole range of urban planning aspects under various headings leading to a comprehensive overview in this Part. The reader may now wish to see how all these facets are brought together in practice in a single planning process. Since the greatest opportunities of planning for growth and change present themselves in the planning of a new city, I propose to refer in some detail to the Milton

Keynes Plan, amongst the latest and largest new city projects at present planned in Britain. It also represents, I believe, a live example of large-scale planning which attempts to respond to the challenges of our time and thus sums up the approach which permeates this book.

The Plan for the new city which was published in March 1970 was prepared by a multi-professional team of planners, architects, engineers, urban economists, sociologists, land-scape architects, agricultural experts and historians under the direction of Richard Llewelyn-Davies and myself.

The background

The new city of Milton Keynes is located about 50 miles to the north-west of London, halfway between the capital and Birmingham along the oldest and most important transport route in the country. The Romans built the Watling Street to the north-west (now the A5), in the 18th century the Grand Union Canal which runs through the area was built, in the 19th century the railway to Birmingham, Manchester, Liverpool and Glasgow, and in the 20th century the first British motorway—the M1—was constructed (see Figure 1).

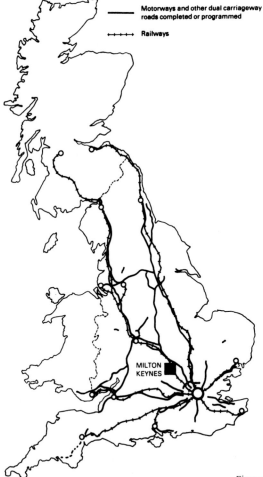

Figure 1. Milton Keynes in relation to national communication routes

223

A new city in North Buckinghamshire was first envisaged in 1962 by the Buckinghamshire County Council to provide homes and jobs for people in the south of the county, from London and the future population of the south-east as a whole. The Minister of Housing and Local Government in his South-East Study in 1964 confirmed the need for a new city for 250 000 people in the vicinity of Bletchley and in 1967 the South-East Economic Planning Council in its 'Strategy for the South East' incorporated the proposal for the new city of Milton Keynes in the north-west corridor of London's growth. 'The Strategic Plan for the South-East' prepared by the South-East Joint Planning Team and published in 1970 confirmed Milton Keynes together with Northampton as one of the five major growth areas in the South-East.

The new city needed to be planned to meet the needs and aspirations not only of urban society as it is in Britain today but as it is likely to be by the year 2000 when the city is fully developed. According to economic projections people's real incomes will at least double by then given a very modest growth rate of the national economy by only 2·5 per cent (see Figure 2). This means that people will be demanding more space in and around their

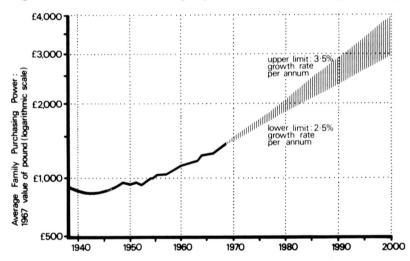

Figure 2. Growth of the national economy: annual output per head of persons employed: 1938–2000. This graph shows the trend in the growth of the national economy which will be reflected in family purchasing power

homes, owning more cars, spending more time and money on education and having more leisure time. People will be more aware and articulate, and will therefore wish to play a more active role in the shaping of their environment. At the same time, the new city needed to be open to the disadvantaged and poor and to provide them with homes and job opportunities which had been denied to them in new towns in the past, as well as to attract people in the highest income groups to play their part in the city's life rather than settle in outlying villages. The fact that the city is being planned for a quarter of a million people opens up exciting opportunities to provide a comprehensive range of jobs and of educational, health, shopping, cultural and entertainment facilities on a metropolitan scale.

The planning process

Before any physical proposals were developed the members of the Milton Keynes Board under the chairmanship of Lord Campbell, their officers and the consultants discussed and identified a series of goals which would guide the development of the new city. Amongst these were all-embracing ones like flexibility and keeping options open, particularly with regard to transport, and building a socially balanced city. In terms of subject matters, they included goals with regard to the urban society of the future, transportation and employment, housing and social development, health and education, leisure and agriculture, and special working parties concentrated their attention on these. After a three-month discussion period, altogether some 70 specific goals were identified and agreed upon which were then brought together under six main headings, as follows:

1. Opportunity and freedom of choice.

2. Easy movement and access.

3. Balance and variety.

4. An attractive city.

5. Public awareness and participation.

6. Efficient and imaginative use of resources.

1. A city of opportunities would provide a variety of choices for all its residents—and for those living outside it. Opportunities for a large variety of jobs and for changing jobs, for education and choice of education, for a wide range of housing and change of housing, for genuinely competitive shopping, for diversity of leisure opportunities.

2. Easy movement and access means that there must be a high degree of accessibility between all activities and places making up the city: homes, jobs, education, health, shopping, recreation. There should be freedom of choice between high-quality public and private methods of transport not only for those who need it but also for those who might choose it instead of private transport. Provision should be made for the use of the car unconstrained by congestion and for free and safe movement as a pedestrian or cyclist.

3. By balance is meant the concept of avoiding undue bias towards any one group by creating a wide range of jobs requiring different skills and levels of education. It also means ensuring the provision, simultaneously with housing and places of employment, of all the necessary services, educational, social, shopping, cultural and leisure facilities. Variety will be provided by creating a large number of different places within the city all with their own character and identity as well as building a wide range of housing to choose from in terms of types, design and tenure.

4. An attractive city would be lively socially and visually—it would offer variety and diversity, in terms of social provisions and the built environment, in short an attractive way of life. There would be a full recognition of the two different but complementary scales which will characterize future cities—the large scale of the fast-moving vehicle on generously landscaped main roads, of vast shopping halls, stadia, some high-rise buildings where they take advantage of favourable considerations and emphasize important features —and the small and intimate scale of the local environment, historic villages, and new housing groups, greens and paved spaces to experience at walking pace as distinct places with their own identity.

5. A city aware of its problems and able to deal with them would diminish the difficulties which have been experienced in earlier towns. It would be continually informed of its

own performance and ready to take action whenever appropriate. Its residents, business-men and interest groups would themselves be informed and thereby be enabled to partici-pate effectively in the conduct of the city.

6. A city that made efficient and imaginative use of the resources put into it would ensure the multiple use of these resources. It would ensure that the physical distribution of these resources allowed for their efficient operation. It would devise the appropriate management or administrative techniques to achieve high utilization of the resources. It would act as a catalyst to the use of private social resources—both to the benefit of the individual and of the community.

Having established these goals as guide lines for the development of the new city a number of possible urban forms were prepared to explore alternative ways in which the city elements could be arranged. Within these alternatives, several permutations were con-sidered of such factors as different types of public transport, patterns of movement, resi-dential and employment densities and hierarchies of services. Thus a number of 'packages' each containing a series of social, economic and physical relationships together with their resultant physical form were then tested against the goals and those which did not meet the goals were eliminated. Eventually, only two basic alternatives remained, that is a plan based on a fixed-track public transport system with bands of development on either side of it and a concentration of employment centres near the stations, and a dispersed pattern of transport and employment. The plan based on fixed-track transport was found to restrict choice of where to live, work and how to move about the city and was incidentally not viable since there could not be enough ridership for this type of public transport and it was very difficult to grow it in phase with the new city. The concept based on dispersal was selected since it met best the goals, particularly those of freedom of opportunities.

This concept was then developed into an Interim Report which was published in February 1969 in the form of a report and an exhibition which toured the existing towns and villages in the designated area. A synopsis of the Interim Report was delivered to every home within the boundaries of the new city and comments from the public were sought at 25 public meetings in the area. The public responded with many suggestions and some criticism (see Appendix 11), mainly of details rather than principles, which led to certain modifications in the plan.

The Interim Report enabled the preliminary ideas for the Plan to be discussed and con-sidered by the public and by the authorities concerned and formed the basis for further work in depth which culminated in the production of the Plan for Milton Keynes in March 1970. The Secretary of State for the Environment approved the Plan with two minor modi-fications in May 1971.

The physical proposals

The physical proposals stem from the goals and objectives for the new city, outlined above, and from the limits and opportunities given by the designated area as it is today. The existing towns will retain their individual characters and grow to form important centres within the new city. There are also 13 villages within the designated area, most of which are

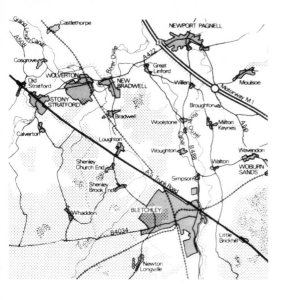

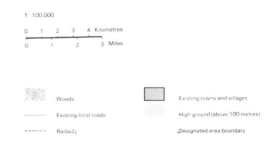

Figure 3. The designated area showing existing towns and villages

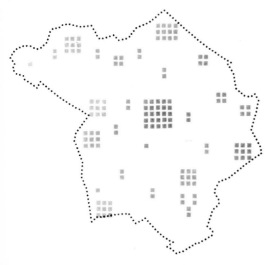

Figure 4. Preferred distribution of employment areas

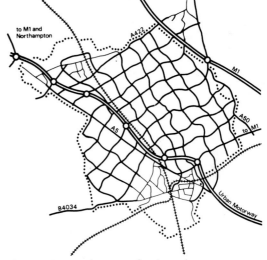

Figure 5. Proposed pattern of main roads

of considerable architectural and historic value. Their identity will be respected and their environment enhanced by careful conservation (see Figure 3).

Because of the distribution of the existing settlements and the disadvantages of concentration the Plan is based on a fairly high degree of dispersal (see Figure 4). The most suitable road network to accommodate this dispersed pattern of travel was found to be a grid. A network of ground-level dual two-lane carriageway roads approximately 1 km apart, with eight possible access points entering each kilometre square, was selected (see Figure 5). Most intersections will be at ground level. These could be controlled by linked traffic lights which would allow 'waves' of traffic to move in both directions with the minimum interruption.

227

A new urban motorway which bypasses the A5 at Fenny Stratford and Stony Stratford is proposed in the early stages to link the city's road network with the region while three inter-changes with the M1 with new links to Milton Keynes will provide connection to the national motorway system.

Most of the larger employment areas are sited near the edges of the designated area with the main exception of the new city centre in the middle of the area. This limited con-centration of traffic can be accommodated by providing three lanes in either direction in the vicinity of the centre and is justified because of the very substantial social and economic advantages of a main city centre for the people of Milton Keynes and the surrounding sub-region.

A major feature in the new city will be a linear park embracing the Grand Union Canal route and the River Ouzel, and traversing the city from north to south. Along the Ouzel a number of small lakes will be formed, which can be used for boating and other forms of recreation.

Education, health and leisure facilities have been planned as an integrated service. Thirty thousand people will be served by a group of three secondary schools and a health centre, and a scarce resources centre with specialized resources which are short in supply such as language or science laboratories, further educational classes, libraries and swimming pools. These facilities will be shared by school-children and the public at large. The Open Univer-sity has already established itself along the banks of the River Ouzel and a centre for higher education is located between Stony Stratford and Wolverton where both com-munities would benefit from this injection of new life and activity. The main health and hospital campus will be built on the edge of the Linear Park, not far from the main centre, with immediate access to the main regional route (Figure 6).

The primary road is crossed by major pedestrian routes at several points on each side, generally by underpasses located to serve main pedestrian movements as well as the more 'random' movements of a child to visit friends or to play. Schools, shops, clinics, local

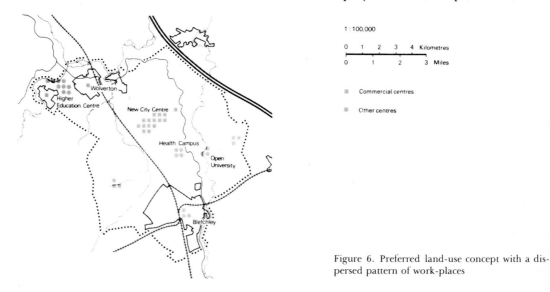

Figure 6. Preferred land-use concept with a dis-persed pattern of work-places

industries and other facilities, as well as bus stops, will be grouped at any or all of these crossing points called 'local activity centres' (see Appendix 6).

Residential areas within the primary road grid are therefore not seen as inward-looking neighbourhoods, but have been structured to encourage social interaction, movement and choice. They will house on average about 5000 people and will be small enough to have a distinctive local character and identity. Traffic on all roads within them will be below 300 vehicles per hour at peak hours and local roads will be circuitous to discourage vehicles to travel at high speed. These measures will help to ensure safety and to keep noise and air pollution within acceptable levels. A possible development of several residential areas with their local activity centres in an area of the new city adjoining the Linear Park shows the great variety in layouts possible within the framework of the Plan (Figure 7).

The new city centre has been conceived as a basically ground-level system of spaces, buildings and access routes designed to offer a range of locations and route opportunities to the individual user and to government and commercial decision makers and designers. The aim is to recreate some of the richness and variety, bustle and delight of existing city centres while avoiding their inconvenience and congestion. While a climate-controlled hall is envisaged for the main shopping core, this could with advantage be combined with traditional shopping streets and tree-planted squares. A possible form the city centre might take is illustrated in Figure 8.

Housing

Activity centres (variously comprising shops, local employment, first and middle schools)

Main roads (approximately one kilometre apart)

Local roads

Open space, trees and playing fields

Main pedestrian routes

Canal

1:10,000   0   100   200   300   400   500   Metres

Figure 7. An impression of a part of the city. The proposals for planning the local environment are illustrated on this sketch which shows how a typical part of the city might be developed

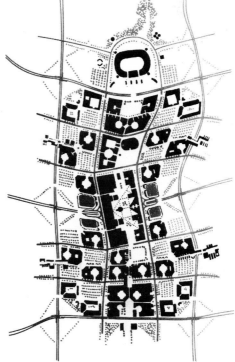

Figure 8. The environment of the new city centre. A possible layout is shown for roads, buildings, main pedestrian routes and main planted areas. In the centre is a climate-controlled shopping mall linked to public buildings, offices and housing

229

A public transport system is proposed using small buses which can be brought relatively close to every doorstep (average walking distances to bus stops will be two minutes) at a peak hour frequency of about three minutes. Careful routing of buses can enable most journeys to be made without change and nearly all journeys with not more than one change (see Figure 9). This public transport system could provide an attractive alternative to the private car and thereby encourage a percentage of car owners to use it, in addition to those who have to use it. The proposed system can be established immediately, can grow in easy stages and provides for the maximum flexibility to accommodate future growth. A recent technological development called 'dial-a-bus' (see Appendix 17) is being explored for introduction into existing and new areas of Milton Keynes.

In addition to the Linear Park already mentioned, the following recreational facilities are proposed: the retention and conservation of all existing woods, four golf courses and other outdoor sports facilities, indoor sports centres, including a major facility in the new city centre, and possibly a race course. Regional or national facilities include a major entertainment centre, a concert hall, theatre and arts centre, a sculpture park, a football stadium and a dry ski slope to cater for every taste and age group (see Figure 10).

Most of the designated area is at present farmed. Although in the long run farming is bound to cease, it is of great importance to plan so that farmland kept in use during the development period can be successfully farmed and efficiently managed. The proposals for the first 10-year development have been influenced by this consideration (see Figure 11). Other important factors in this connection are the need to link at an early stage the existing towns in the area with each other and with important transport routes, particularly

1 : 100,000

0   1   2   3   4 Kilometres

0   1   2   3 Miles

● Public transport interchanges

— Possible main public transport routes

Figure 9. Possible public transport routes in the first ten years

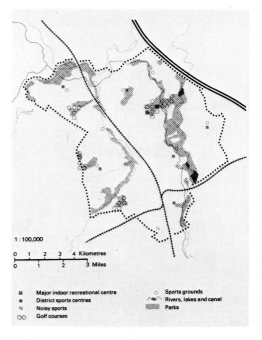

1 : 100,000

0   1   2   3   4 Kilometres

0   1   2   3 Miles

▨ Major indoor recreational centre   ○ Sports grounds
▨ District sports centres   ᔓ Rivers, lakes and canal
N Noisy sports   ▨▨ Parks
○○ Golf courses

Figure 10. Sport and physical recreation provision

230

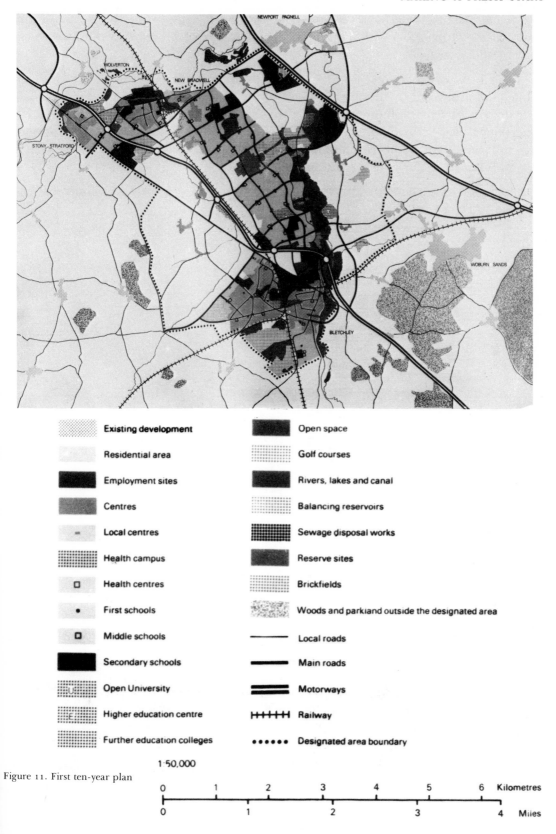

Existing development		Open space	
Residential area		Golf courses	
Employment sites		Rivers, lakes and canal	
Centres		Balancing reservoirs	
Local centres		Sewage disposal works	
Health campus		Reserve sites	
Health centres		Brickfields	
First schools		Woods and parkland outside the designated area	
Middle schools		Local roads	
Secondary schools		Main roads	
Open University		Motorways	
Higher education centre		Railway	
Further education colleges		Designated area boundary	

1:50,000

Figure 11. First ten-year plan

the M1 and the new A5 urban motorway, the need to take advantage of early provision of sewers in the Ouzel River Valley and the need to make an early start on the development of the new city centre.

The capital cost of building Milton Keynes will be shared by the Corporation, by local and public authorities and by the private sector. Total capital cost of the new city is broadly estimated to be £700 million at today's prices to be spent over 25 years and tentatively apportioned, without commitment, as follows: Milton Keynes Development Corporation £333 million; Local Authorities and other public bodies £169 million; private enterprise £198 million.

An impression of the new city of Milton Keynes as it may look from the air in the year 2000 is shown in Figure 12.

Figure 12. Impression of the new city of Milton Keynes as it may look from the air in the year 2000

Summary of main features of the Plan

The basic approach to the physical design is to provide a flexible framework of roads and services which could accommodate changes and growth, and this objective is best achieved by the non-directional road grid. This system can also grow in phase with the city's development and with it will grow the mini-bus service. This will avoid the construction of urban motorways which would be under-used for some time. Many of the grid roads will start as two-lane roads to which another two lanes will be added as and when required. Once there is a substantial build-up of traffic the computerized traffic lights can be installed. When technology has further advanced the mini-bus service can be converted to a dial-a-bus operation. The educational, health and social facilities will be plugged into the system as and when required. However, within this flexible concept, firm decisions with regard to the infrastructure for the first 10 years have been made so that the building of the new city can proceed with full speed and determination.

The ease with which people will be able to move about the new city is seen as the key to making the great variety of opportunities in homes and jobs, education and health, shopping and recreation available to everybody. The non-directional kilometre road grid together with a dispersed pattern of employment provides an equally good accessibility in all directions to all parts of the new city either by means of a frequent mini-bus service available within easy walking distance from every home or by personal transport unconstrained by congestion. There will be freedom of choice between public and private transport and the average door-to-door travel time for the journey to work will be 12-15 minutes by car and 20 minutes by mini-buses.

As the kilometre grid roads are mostly dual two-lane ground-level roads with computerized traffic signals at the crossing points, it will be possible to accommodate the use of the private car unconstrained by congestion in an environmentally acceptable way without recourse to costly and socially as well as visually disruptive urban motorways.

Since the basic philosophy of the plan is to provide a framework for options to be taken up it will be essential for people living in the new city and for those moving in to be fully informed of these opportunities. This will mean not only effective information services but frequent discussions with the public, who are expected to participate to the full in the planning process. A system of monitoring and evaluation will have to be devised whereby the decision makers are being kept continuously informed of the performance of what has been provided. This feed-back will enable them to keep their policies under constant review and revise them as necessary. Thus a genuine opportunity will exist for the inhabitants to influence decisions and to contribute with their ideas and efforts to make the new city what they want it to be within the planned framework and basic policies of the Plan.

The Plan also maximizes the opportunities for the many individual designers who will be engaged in the implementation of the Plan and who will be able to develop their ideas with fewer constraints and more freedom than has been possible in the past. This flexible and open-ended approach is particularly relevant to the planning of a new city for a quarter of a million people which will reach its maturity only in the year 2000.

New towns in the USA

In discussing new towns in the USA it is of interest to note that almost every American city has in fact been a new town founded within the last three and a half centuries. King Philip II of Spain's planning legislation 'Laws of the Indies' influenced the design of Los Angeles, while the plan for Williamsburg, Virginia, owes much to Christopher Wren's plan for the City of London. William Penn drew up the plans for the new city of Philadelphia in 1683. In the mid-18th century General Oglethorpe laid out Savannah, while the plan for New Orleans, which dates back to 1722, is French in origin. In the latter part of that century L'Enfant under Presidents Washington and Jefferson planned Washington, DC, as the capital of the new American nation. During the 19th century many company new towns were created, as well as utopian and religious new settlements, culminating in Salt Lake City. Yet others sprang up in connection with the new railway system which was being built across the continent. America's first garden city, inspired by its British predecessors, was Radburn in New Jersey (begun in 1928), planned by Clarence Stein and Henry Wright. The present-day equivalent take the form of resort or retirement towns, or as towns originally built for workers in large power and reclamation projects (Boulder City, Nevada, and Norris, Tennessee, 1932–35), or as atomic-energy towns towards the end of the Second World War (Los Alamos, New Mexico, and Oak Ridge, Tennessee).

However, these are exceptions to the general rule of undirected growth which poses problems as difficult as the deterioration of the central city areas. The population of the US is expected to increase by another 100 million by the turn of the century and growth will occur predominantly in and around existing urban concentrations of population. This growth has been taking the form of a low-density undifferentiated sprawl which is both costly and inefficient. Seven metropolitan regions—Los Angeles, New York, Chicago, San Francisco, Detroit, Miami and Washington—will have to find room for as much as one-third of the net population increase. And with the growth it will become increasingly difficult to keep in check the growing pollution of air, water and land.

In the American context, new towns could be an important and attractive alternative to this undirected sprawl which is overwhelming the metropolitan regions. They could provide a logical framework for private development. The nation's inevitable growth can be channelled into new urban forms, with a proper balance among homes, jobs, services and the high standards of design. A new town programme could revitalize rural communities and make available to them the basic advantages of contemporary urban life. New towns could provide positive alternatives to the out-migration of the poor and the black that continues to increase the social and financial problems of the large cities.

These were no doubt some of the considerations which led to the enactment of the New Communities Act of 1968, to guarantee the financing of new cities. The New Communities Act is specifically designed to harness the resources of private enterprise. It provides a promising new and effective method for improving the quality of life for many millions of Americans. Several of the highest officials of the Administration have expressed support for a new towns programme. President Nixon indicated in general terms a commitment to satellite cities, and Vice-President Agnew even wrote the preface to a document produced

234

by Urban America Inc making a bold call for 100 new cities (see *The New City*, a National Committee report on urban growth policy, published for Urban America Inc, by Frederick Praeger). All this recent interest in the creation of new communities has now culminated in the 1970 Housing and Urban Development Act which provides, for the first time, a national framework reinforced by appropriate financial provision for, amongst other things, the planning and building of new towns in the US.

It is true, of course, that there are many obstacles to new community development in the United States. The scale of new communities requires a vast amount of capital to acquire the land and to install the basic facilities. A new community requires a long development period before a positive cash flow is generated whereas the ordinary sub-division builders operating on the periphery of existing developments can affix themselves to an existing infrastructure at little cost. These services must be provided first in new towns before builders can develop. There is need for helpful, strong leadership on the part of the Federal Government to encourage, monitor, cooperate.

One of the most difficult problems associated with new community development is that of land assembly. Experience of the new town of Columbia shows that the land market (even in the fastest growing metropolitan area of the USA) permits the assembly of a contiguous 15 000 acre site at a reasonable cost. Congress, however, had been unresponsive on several recent occasions to proposals for Federal aids for State and local assembly of land for New Community Objectives. Stronger Federal support, as now envisaged in the 1970 Act, will be necessary in order to ensure that a proper portion of the different Federal grant and aid programmes is allocated to new communities.

James Rouse, the founder of Columbia, sees a way to overcome some of these difficulties:

"It seems apparent to me that there are two distinct processes involved in urban development that are not always sufficiently distinguished. One is land development and the other is the development of buildings on the land. The development of the land is, I think, essentially a public action and I believe that most of the things that we are doing in this respect in Columbia could be done by a local community corporation. In our own book-keeping and in our own management, we keep entirely separate the functions of land development and disposition and the development of buildings above ground. The latter activity has to buy land from the land development company and pay an economic price for it. Looked at in this way, it is possible to envisage some form of community development corporation assembling land, using compulsory purchase powers denied to private developers, which enable it to overcome specific points of resistance where necessary, extending the main water and sewage utilities, putting in the roads and providing for open spaces, building the amenities, and incorporating all these amenities in the basic land price. It then markets the land, specifically using private enterprise to subsidize the uneconomic aspects by obtaining a higher price for the land enhanced by these amenities. They are thus built into the whole economic model."

(From James Rouse's contribution to 'Private Capital for New Towns', occasional paper 28, published by the Institute of Economic Affairs, 1969.)

Columbia New Town in Maryland is a living example of how these problems can at least partly be resolved. It is true that in this instance some parcels of land could not be acquired and the planners had to plan around them as best as they could, and that the new town has so far not been able to make a significant contribution to the alleviation of the problem of the urban poor. However, what has been achieved in practice in the face of the formidable obstacles which had to be overcome is certainly remarkable (see Appendix 24).

A similarly bold experiment in American new town development is Reston, Virginia, planned in the form of villages for a population of 75 000. Conceived by Robert E. Simon Jr, who headed Simon Enterprises, 6750 acres of land were purchased in 1961. Simon wanted Reston to be a unique, private real-estate venture which would integrate residences, industry, commerce, schools, churches, cultural institutions, social and recreational facilities in an essentially independent community structure which would be economically viable and socially desirable. Of the seven main goals which were set for the new town, perhaps the one which aimed at fostering beauty—structural and natural—as a necessity of the good life has already been achieved in much of the development as the photographs show. But the goal that Reston be a financial success was threatened when it ran into financial difficulties. With regard to the other goals, it is too early to judge whether they will be met, but Reston is up against similar difficulties as Columbia in attracting a full range of income groups, particularly the urban poor. Nevertheless, Reston has succeeded in its development so far in creating a very attractive environment for those who can afford it, an environment which in many ways is an advance on British new towns.

There is, however, one very strange aspect which illustrates the competing forces at work—those who plan new towns and those who plan highways. Reston was conceived as a new town within commuting distance from Washington, DC. Indeed, the Dulles Airport expressway skirts Reston but runs past it without any connection to the new town, and if you want to get from Washington to Reston you have to use the tortuous local roads.

Reston New Town, Virginia. Lake Anne Village. *Photo: Ollfe Atkins*

Reston New Town, Virginia.
Lake Anne Village centre.
Photo: William A. Graham

Appendix 25

Columbia New Town, Maryland, USA

This new town venture by the Columbia Association is a major achievement, particularly in Maryland, which requires a 90 per cent majority to create an 'incorporated city' and where the counties carry out most local government functions.

The mainspring of this new town development is the Columbia Association, which is a non-profit organization controlled by James W. Rouse, President of Rouse Inc., and set up to provide and maintain open spaces, recreation areas, social community facilities and so forth. The land has been given by Rouse, but essentially all the development, which is paid for by a town tax, is carried out by the Association. This is legalized by writing an agreement into all land sales which makes purchasers shareholders in the Association but liable to local taxation. Each village and neighbourhood also has its council which sends representatives to the main Columbia Council, which at present has a non-voting representative on the Association Board.

237

Connecticut General provided all the 'front' money—$23·5 million for 13 670 acres. Rouse is the developing agent but has set up subsidiary companies for land, industry, commerce, housing, etc. He bought and strictly controls all the land through the extensive use of restrictive covenants. Except for the State highways, he has built all roads. These roads have to be built to county specification. After a year the county takes them over and maintains them thereafter. He spent $6 million on sewer and water systems which he has handed over to the county, which is paying him back in instalments as development proceeds and people are added to the tax roll.

The county have provided all education services on an elementary, middle and high school basis with no grading and no classrooms. Learning pods of 200 children mill about listening to whom they choose and learning whatever they want to. The staff (teaching and administration) to student ratio is 1 : 18.

Rouse provided in advance of need a representative neighbourhood and village centre. Shops were subsidized on a graded rent scheme. Community facilities in these centres (see Figure 1) were built by him and then sold at cost to the Columbia Association or County. He also put in a golf course and some of the lakes as initial leisure facilities.

Figure 1. Columbia New Town, Maryland, USA, Wild Lake Village Green. *Photo: Winants Bros. Inc.*

Above Figure 2. Columbia New Town, Typical private enterprise housing near a lake landing stage. *Photo : Tadder, Baltimore*
Right Figure 3. Mini-bus running on 'reserved track'

A comprehensive medical plan financing all facilities at a cost of about $46 per month per family has been developed and about 60 per cent of the residents have taken it up so far. The Columbia Association has also built a fire station which it rents to the county.

Eleven major house-building firms are involved (including Levitt) (see Figure 2). They are all mixed up in each village but have tried to build their show houses in one place so that serious house hunters can compare styles and prices easily. An inter-faith Housing Corporation is building some housing which will be managed by the American Baptist Corporation. There are several other non-profit corporations interested in building moderate rather than low income housing. The Columbia Association has an architectural review committee that vets designs, which, judging by the variety of styles, interprets its functions very liberally. The Columbia Association is also running a special mini-bus service with buses travelling on reserved tracks (see Figure 3).

239

Appendix 26

New town at Amherst, near Buffalo, USA
Planning Consultants: Llewelyn-Davies Associates, New York

The New York State Urban Development Corporation (UDC, see Appendix 8) was created by the State Legislature of New York in 1968. The new Corporation, headed by Edward J. Logue, was given exceptionally wide powers as a planning and development agency including the powers to issue bonds to a total value of $1 billion, to acquire land by eminent domain, and to override where necessary local ordinances, zoning and building codes.

Although the UDC's programmes were initially aimed at resolving redevelopment problems in inner areas, the organization soon became concerned with the development of balanced new communities in suburban and semi-rural areas. In broad principle this was seen as the second aim of a general strategy for renewing the inner city areas of the State, whereby renewal efforts were to be directed simultaneously by the UDC, at the inner city area and at the metropolitan periphery.

An early opportunity for the development of a major new community came when the University Construction Fund of New York State announced plans for the construction of a new campus for the University of Buffalo in the township of Amherst on the north-eastern edge of the Buffalo metropolitan area. The programme called for the construction of facilities to support 40 000 students and 10 000 faculty and staff by 1975. In 1968, the State Office of Planning Coordination published the findings of a study of the impact of the new faculty on the Buffalo region. These showed that the new campus could be expected to generate between 10 000 and 15 000 off-campus jobs in the service and light industrial categories by 1985, and that, taking into account the needs of students not accommodated in State dormitory programmes, a demand for some 40 000 units of accommodation would accrue in the Amherst sub-region between 1970 and 1985.

At the request of Governor Rockefeller, the UDC agreed to prepare a development programme which would respond to the demand for accommodation and services, while at the same time serving the best interests of existing residents of the Amherst area. Accordingly, in the spring of 1969, Llewelyn-Davies Associates were asked by the UDC to undertake studies and prepare recommendations for a new community in Amherst. The size of the new community was unspecified, but it was agreed that social and fiscal balance were of paramount importance.

In June 1969 Llewelyn-Davies Associates opened an office in Amherst and began work on a three-phase programme which would provide interim recommendations to the UDC by Christmas 1969 and a final report in March of the following year. This was to be followed by a three-month period of public discussion and finalization.

In the first stage of their programme, LDA tackled three main areas of study:

1. Studies of the nature and rate of the growth likely to result from the development of the new campus. Much of the groundwork in this field had already been carried out by consultants to the State Office of Planning Coordination.

2. Studies of alternative strategic planning concepts and possible sites for the UDC Development.

3. Studies of the financing of the development and in particular the effects of the operation on the existing fiscal structure of Amherst and the surrounding area.

After comparing and testing several alternative development procedures, LDA made their interim recommendations available to the UDC in June 1970. These called for the development by the UDC of a new community which would achieve a population of 25 000 by 1985; the 2400 acres of land needed for the development were on the north side of the site for the new campus, between the two existing arterial highways. The proposed programme called for the construction of some 8400 new homes at an average net density of 11·9 dwellings per acre. In addition, land was provided for new schools, two major regional shopping centres as well as a number of smaller centres, and 18 acres of land per thousand population for recreation, open space and public facilities.

Primary highways needed to provide access to the new community had already been proposed by the State Department of Transportation to serve the new campus. LDA proposed a new arterial highway to link the new campus with the new community. In addition, plans were made to incorporate into the new community a proposed rapid-transit line which would link the campus and the community with downtown Buffalo.

15 Conclusions

"What is needed now is an unleashing of the national imagination on a scale that compares with the effort and expenditure undertaken in national defence or the competition of the space race. Only then will citizens of developed societies be ready to dedicate to urban development the devices of modern technology, the public programming and the public and private cooperation in the investments which have emerged over the last decade as indispensable instruments for tasks of high national importance."

Delos Five, *Ekistics*, October 1967

We are witnessing a new renaissance in town planning in Britain. After the over-optimistic enthusiasm of the 40s and the disillusionment of the 50s we have come to realize that in our small island planning is an indispensable necessity for the increasing complexities of life of an expanding population. Since 1960 there has been, in the United States, a strong resurgence of interest in urban affairs, orderly growth, decent housing for everybody and a civilized urban environment, and these issues are now high on the national agenda.

In urban planning we are moving in Britain from the rather static statutory and largely restrictive kind of planning into a new field of positive planning at two levels: at the strategic policy level we are concerned with flexible long-range integrated land-use/transport plans, at the local level we shall concentrate on the three-dimensional implementation within the framework of the strategic planning policies. In the USA there is a move towards more positive action-orientated planning both in terms of urban renewal and the planning and building of new cities, though there is still no national planning legislation of a comprehensive nature comparable with that of Britain.

In our major towns and cities the vital role public transport will have to play in the future is being increasingly recognized, particularly in US cities which had allowed their public transport facilities to run down and had hoped that extensive freeway construction would solve their traffic problems. Many American cities are now making a concerted effort to rebuild their rapid-transit systems. European cities would be foolish to ignore this US experience.

We are moving towards a more affluent society. In such a situation clearly the element of choice which can be exercised by people regarding their homes and jobs, their recreation and their transportation will correspondingly increase. It is therefore imperative that we are much more aware of people's preferences than we have been in the past and that we follow up people's satisfaction or discontent with what has been provided for them. This in turn means a shifting of emphasis from input to output. Professor Mel Webber of Berkley, California, is right in criticizing official planning as having been over-concerned with inputs, such as the number of housing units or school places provided, certain densities 'achieved', the miles of roads built. Very little, if any, interest is then shown in the performance of these provisions once they have been made. Too seldom do we ask ourselves the question: 'Does it work when you try it?' In other words, we must go back and evaluate what happens, we must measure output so that we correct further inputs in the light of people's experience. And this brings us to the need for a sensitive monitoring system to inform the planners of the performance of the service they have provided. It also calls for a much greater degree of citizen participation in the planning process so that people's preferences are taken into account during the formulation of planning policies and objectives, as well as during their implementations.

There is a great broadening in approach and scope with regard to urban planning in the USA and Britain, aided by new and sophisticated planning techniques using computers, and the construction of alternative physical and mathematical models. With this more scientific approach an increasing number of different specialists are being brought into the planning process to make their contribution within multi-disciplinary planning teams. Thus a new kind of planning is emerging based on objective analysis in depth and providing an increasing variety of different solutions from which people will be able to choose.

These new planning ideas and techniques will have to be matched with radically improved management techniques and a reformed planning machine. In both countries people will be participating in the planning process to an unprecedented extent. While in Britain a special Government Committee has reported on ways and means of increasing public participation in planning, in the USA the Federal Government is placing increasing importance in genuine participation of the local community. Planning is at last seen as what it should be—an integral part of daily life affecting everybody and therefore of active interest to the community.

Our urban planning problems are immense, but so are our opportunities to reshape the existing urban environment and create new towns and cities. We shall do more building between now and the turn of the century than in the whole of the previous history of Britain. If our planning policies are wise, farsighted and, above all, humane, and if their implementation is carried out skilfully, imaginatively and with the genuine participation of the people, it could be the making of our cities.

Bibliography

Chapter 1

Town and Country Planning Act, 1968, HMSO, 1968

'North-West Economic Planning Study', North-West Economic Council, HMSO, 1965

Chapter 2

'Our Older Homes—a Call for Action', Report of the Sub-Committee on Standards of Housing Fitness, Ministry of Housing and Local Government, Welsh Office, HMSO, 1966

'The Deeplish Study—improvement possibilities in a district of Rochdale', Ministry of Housing and Local Government, HMSO, 1966

'Homes for Today and Tomorrow', Parker Morris Report, Ministry of Housing and Local Government Advisory Group, HMSO, 1961

'Elmwood's People Rebuild—Elmwood Park 2', Llewelyn-Davies Weeks Forestier-Walker & Bor, September 1968

Family and Kinship in East London, Wilmot and Young, Penguin, 1962

Chapter 3

'The Future of Development Plans', Report of the Planning Advisory Group, Ministry of Housing and Local Government, HMSO, 1966

Commission on the Third London Airport: Papers and Proceedings, Vol. VIII, Part I—'Airport City Urbanisation Studies', HMSO, November 1969

'Grangemouth/Falkirk Regional Survey and Plan', Scottish Development Department, HMSO, 1968

'Cost-Benefit Analysis in Town Planning—a case study of Cambridge 1966', N. Lichfield, Cambridgeshire and Isle of Ely Council, 1966

Liverpool Interim Planning Policy. Statement and Maps, Walter Bor, Liverpool City Planning Officer, 1965

'Washington New Town', Llewelyn-Davies Weeks & Partners, December 1966

'The City is not a Tree', Christopher Alexander, *Design*, February 1966

'Cost-Benefit Analysis in City Planning', N. Lichfield, *Journal of American Institute of Planners*, November 1960

'A Research Programme for a Scientific Method of Planning', Yona Friedman, *Architectural Design*, August 1967

'National Resources', P. A. Stone, *Architectural Review*, November 1967

'A Goals Achievement Matrix for evaluating Alternative Plans', M. Hill, *Journal of American Planners*, January 1968

The Life and Death of Great American Cities, Jane Jacobs, Jonathan Cape, 1961

Chapter 4

'Management in Local Government', Maud Report, Ministry of Housing and Local Government, HMSO, 1967

Report of Royal Commission on Local Government in England, Chairman: Lord Redcliffe-Maud, Ministry of Housing and Local Government, HMSO, 1969

Report of the Committee on Local Authority and Allied Personal Social Services, Chairman: F. Seebohm, Ministry of Housing and Local Government, HMSO, 1968

New York State Urban Development Act, 1968

'The Future of Big Cities', Donald C. Stone, Ditchley Foundation, 1968

Chapter 5

'People and Planning'—report of the Committee on Public Participation in Planning, Chairman: A. M. Skeffington, Ministry of Housing and Local Government, HMSO, 1969

The Plan for Milton Keynes, Technical Supplement No. 2: The Presentation of the Interim Proposals, Llewelyn-Davies Weeks Forestier-Walker & Bor, 1968

'Planning Workbook for the Community', John Morris Dixon, *Forum*, December 1969

Chapter 7

'The First 100 Families', Central Housing Advisory Committee, HMSO, 1964

'The Needs of New Communities—a report on social provision in new and expanding communities', Ministry of Housing and Local Government, Welsh Office, HMSO, 1967

The Levittowners, Herbert Gans, Penguin, 1967

Rebuilding Cities, Percy Johnson-Marshall, Edinburgh University Press, 1966

Chapter 8

'The Milton Keynes Development Plan', Milton Keynes Development Corporation, 1970

'Liverpool City Centre Plan', Walter Bor & Graeme Shankland, 1966

'Strategy for Human Settlements', Delos Five, *Ekistics*, 1967

'The Soft Revolution', Sumner Myers, *Architectural Forum*, Jan/Feb 1968

'Minisystems in the City', Brian Richards, *Architectural Forum*, Jan/Feb 1968

Modern Railways, Vol. 22, pp. 18–22, 1968

Railway Gazette, April 1965

'United States Mass Transportation Demonstration Projects', Thomas J. Lambie, *Traffic Engineering and Control*, September 1965

'The Airborne Stampede', John Morris Dixon, *Architectural Forum,* Jan/Feb 1968
Town Traffic in the Motor Age, P. H. Bensten, p. 138, Danish Technical Press, 1961

Chapter 9

Civic Amenities Act 1967, HMSO, 1967
'Traffic in Towns', Buchanan Report, Ministry of Transport, HMSO, 1963
'Fitzroy/Burleigh, Cambridge', Llewelyn-Davies Weeks Forestier-Walker & Bor, 1969
'Toledo—Renewal of the Core', Llewelyn-Davies Weeks Forestier-Walker & Bor, 1968
'Motorways in the Urban Environment', British Road Federation Report by Llewelyn-Davies Weeks Forestier-Walker & Bor and Ove Arup & Partners, 1971
'Complexity and Ambiguity in Environmental Design', Amos Rapoport and Robert Kantor, *Journal of American Institute of Planners*, July 1967
Town Scape, Gordon Cullen, Architectural Press, 1961

Chapter 10

'High Buildings—a blessing or a curse?', Walter Bor, *Architectural Design*, September 1964
'Office Design: a study of the environment', ed. Peter Manning, Pilkington Research Unit, 1965
'Windowless Buildings', R. G. Hopkinson, *New Society*, June 6, 1968

Chapter 14

'Private Capital for New Towns'—Occasional Paper 28, Institute of Economic Affairs, 1969
'The New City', a National Committee report on urban growth policy, Urban America Inc., Frederick Praeger, 1969
Plan for Milton Keynes, Vols. I and II, Milton Keynes Development Corporation, March 1970
'Strategy for the South-East', South-East Economic Planning Council, HMSO, 1967
'Strategic Plan for the South-East', South-East Joint Planning Team, HMSO, 1970

Additional Reading

'Tomorrow's Transport', US Department of Housing and Urban Development, 1968
'Design of Roads in Urban Areas', Ministry of Transport, HMSO, 1967
'Traffic and Transport Plans', Roads Circular 1/68, Ministry of Transport, HMSO, 1968
'Town Design', Richard Llewelyn-Davies, *Town Planning Review*, Vol. 37, October 3, 1966
'Traffic in Cities', *Architectural Forum*, Jan/Feb 1968
The Image of the City, Kevin Lynch, MIT Press, 1960
A View from the Road, Donald Appleyard, Kevin Lynch, John R Myer, MIT Press, 1965
New Movement in Cities, Brian Richards, Studio Vista/Reinhold, 1966
The Architecture of Towns and Cities, Paul Speiregen, McGraw-Hill Book Company, 1965
Town Design, Frederick Gibberd, Architectural Press, 1967
Cities of Destiny, Arnold Toynbee, Thames and Hudson, London 1967
Design of Cities, Edmund Bacon, Thames and Hudson, 1967
Town Planning in its Social Context, Gordon Cherry, Leonard Hill Books, 1970
The New Towns, 2nd edition, Frederick Osborn and Arnold Whittick, Leonard Hill Books, 1969

Index